FULL CIRCLE

FULL CIRCLE

THE STORY OF AIR FIGHTING

AIR VICE-MARSHAL
J. E. JOHNSON CBE DSO DFC

Illustrated by
David Shepherd

CASSELL

Cassell Military Paperbacks

Cassell & Co.
Wellington House, 125 Strand
London WC2R 0BB

First published by Chatto and Windus 1964
This Cassell Military Paperbacks edition 2001

British Library Cataloguing-in-Publication Data
A catalogue record for this book is available from the
British Library

Printed and bound in Great Britain by
Cox & Wyman Ltd., Reading, Berks.

CONTENTS

Acknowledgements   Page ix

 1 OVER THE HILL   1

 2 THE FLYING GUN   11

 3 SCOUT SQUADRONS   21

 4 THE TEAM   33

 5 THE HUNTING PACK   42

 6 'REMEMBER BALL'   53

 7 THE CIRCUS   66

 8 'A RED EAGLE—FALLING'   78

 9 THE LUFTWAFFE   89

10 FIGHTER COMMAND   99

11 *BLITZKRIEG*   111

12 'THE SENIOR OFFICER PRESENT'   126

13 *'BOMBEN AUF EN-GE-LAND'*   136

14 'THE HOLE'   149

15 FALLING LEAVES   158

16 FIGHTING TALK   169

17 IN THE DARK   179

18 FORTRESS MALTA   190

19 THE DESERT   201

20 COVER OF DARKNESS   215

21 SEVEN LEAGUE BOOTS   226

CONTENTS

22 THE EASTERN FRONT   240

23 DECLINE AND FALL   248

24 OVER THE YALU   261

25 HINDSIGHT   273

   INDEX   287

ILLUSTRATIONS IN TEXT

1	Henri Farman biplane with observer firing rifle	7
2	A two-seater gliding in to land	10
3	A gunner in a tractor firing over the top mainplane	12
4	A Fokker monoplane	17
5	A Fokker in an Immelmann turn	19
6	Nieuport Scouts in line abreast	28
7	Nieuport Scouts in line astern	29
8	Nieuport Scouts in echelon	29
9	Three Fokker monoplanes in vic formation	35
10	Guns and sights on S.E.5	55
11	Morice, with observer standing up	61
12	Albatros in the ring sight	62
13	Camels strafing	66
14	Fokker Triplane in the ring sight	72
15	McCudden attacking a two-seater	76
16	Crashed Fokker Triplane	82
17	Dispersed Scouts	87
18	Four Messerschmitts turning in line abreast	95
19	Spitfire I	104
20	Two vics of Hurricanes, sections line astern	106
21	Stuka in a steep dive	109
22	Crashed Hurricane on Dunkirk beach	125
23	Four Spitfires in line astern	128
24	Messerschmitt 109E in the reflector sight	129
25	Radar masts on the coast	134

26	Crashed Messerschmitt	178
27	Two Spitfires dive-bombing	203
28	A 'clipped' Spitfire 5	212
29	A Stuka, nosed-in	214
30	A Lancaster in a corkscrew manoeuvre	223
31	Four Mustangs	232
32	Focke-Wulf 190 in the gyroscopic sight (i)	249
33	Messerschmitt 262	254
34	Messerschmitt 163	255
35	Focke-Wulf 190 in the gyroscopic sight (ii)	260
36	Four Sabres, crossing over	269
37	Mig-15 in the radar sight	271

ACKNOWLEDGEMENTS

Much of my service in the Royal Air Force has been with fighter squadrons, and I have always been interested in fighter tactics which, within my lifetime, have come full circle. Thus I considered it a unique opportunity to record this story of air fighting, and my thanks are due, in the first place, to many friends in the Royal Air Force who have helped me with information, advice and hospitality. They are too many for me to mention all of them by name, but they include, in particular, Group Captain J. Miller, Air Commodore D. Crowley-Milling, Group Captain D. A. Green, Group Captain 'Tim' Morice, Air Chief Marshal Sir Harry Broadhurst, the late Wing Commander Gerald Maxwell, Air Commodore Deacon Elliott, and Air Commodore M. LeBas, who was largely responsible for the two chapters *Fortress Malta* and *The Desert*.

I have had full access to the records of the Air Historical Branch of the Air Ministry, and I would like to record my grateful thanks to the Head of that organisation, Mr. L. Jacketts, and also to his predecessor Mr. John Nerney, for, in his own words, 'adding a touch here and there'. I thank Dr. Simpson, of the United States Air Force Air University, for access to papers concerning Luftwaffe experiences in Russia.

I am grateful to Major Oliver Stewart for reading that part of the manuscript dealing with the First War, and for his invaluable criticisms and suggestions.

I am deeply indebted to Professor R. A. McCance, of Cambridge University, who, during the past four years, has offered the most lively comment and suggestion, and who has guided this book all the way.

Finally, I would like to thank my friend David Shepherd for his many illustrations, some of which took a considerable amount of his time.

Aden, 1964   J. E. J.

Chapter 1

OVER THE HILL

At the beginning of the First War four squadrons of the Royal Flying Corps flew to France and scouted for the British Expeditionary Force. The pilots found that they had to fight for their information and there began a crude form of duelling in the air. These early air fighters flew and fought alone, but they soon discovered that a lone pilot could not guard his own tail and they began to hunt in pairs. Pairs grew into sections of four or five machines, sections into squadrons, and squadrons into wings of sometimes fifty machines. So team fighting was developed, and great daylight air battles took place. Scouts were also used for night fighting, and for bombing and strafing.

During the Second War the fighter was used for defensive and offensive day fighting, for night fighting, for reconnaissance, and for bombing and strafing. In the Battle of Britain fighter pilots fought in much the same fashion as their forebears, but as more powerful engines gave greater speeds and heights, the manoeuvrability of fighting aeroplanes so decreased that in combat it was not possible to hold together more than a dozen fighters. This trend of diminishing numbers continued and in the Korean War jets fought in sections of four. Today, both the supersonic fighter-interceptor and the supersonic strike-fighter fly alone, like the first scout, and within the last fifty years the tactics of air fighting have come full circle.

At the turn of this century the pioneers were building their aeroplanes and on 17th December, 1903, Wilbur and Orville Wright, at Kitty Hawk in North Carolina, were the first to get into the air in a powered machine. Other countries were not far behind, and in 1909 the Frenchman, Louis Blériot, inspired everyone by crossing the English Channel. In Britain a few Army officers had taken to the air and thought of flying as another exciting sport, like a high-speed slalom or a fast bobsleigh run, except that there was more danger, which made those who came to watch the fun lie flat on the ground to make sure the flying machines had left it; but if Blériot could cross the Channel, surely, thought these officers, an aeroplane could scout well ahead of troops and its pilot could see what lay on the other side of the hill?

In war there is always a demand for reconnaissance, for the soldier can only see as far as the hedge or hilltop in front of him, and yet his commander must know what lies over the hill. Has the enemy got troops, guns, and transports? And where are his reserves and depots? The soldier knew about the fringe of enemy activity and sometimes tried to get through this fringe with cavalry patrols, whose vision was also restricted. The young officers pressed for scouting aeroplanes to fly over the fringe, but they were up against some of their masters, who thumped the table and declared that it would be quite impossible to see anything on the ground when flying at forty miles an hour!

During the Army exercises of 1910 a keen ex-officer, who was determined to see the aeroplane developed, caused a stir when he reported for duty in, or rather 'on', a Bristol biplane. The pilot had some difficulty in persuading the military to make use of his services for the cavalry thought the engine noise would frighten their horses. Eventually a reconnaissance flight was arranged, but the supporters of military aviation suffered a severe rebuff when the mission was cancelled because of a high and gusty wind.

However, in the following year they were rewarded with an Army Order forming the Air Battalion of the Royal Engineers 'to which will be entrusted the duty of creating a body of expert airmen . . . the training and instruction of men in handling kites, balloons, and aeroplanes'. The Air Battalion was soon organized and pupils were selected to be trained as pilots; less than half of one per cent failed to qualify, and the best pupils were either sailors or horsemen. They were taught to fly at Larkhill, on Salisbury Plain, in a machine which cruised at fifty miles an hour some thirty feet above the ground. The pupil sat behind his instructor and gripped him with his knees while his feet dangled in free air. Both men could reach the control column, but only the instructor could operate the rudder bar. After some dual tuition pupil and mentor changed places, and soon the great day arrived when the pupil was ready to make his first solo flight.

During the summer of 1911 the annual military manoeuvres were held in Cambridgeshire, and the Air Battalion was ordered to participate. Two aeroplanes, representing the air power of Great Britain, succeeded in getting to the venue. One pilot flew into a thunderstorm and his machine was so tossed about by the great pressure that he lost control and fell into a pendulum-like motion. Fortunately the pilot kept his head and jumped when he was about ten feet above the ground. The crash attracted a large crowd, among whom were two men who had been bathing near by; owing to the excitement, some time passed before it was noticed that the bathers were still stark naked.

The records of the early days of Service flying reveal a story of divided opinions, of interrupted experiments, of the boldness of the handful of designers, of the deep conviction of the fanatics and the usual cautious approach of the Government to a new and costly venture. But the shadow of a militant Germany lay across the peace of Europe, and although she was primarily interested in airships she was also building military aeroplanes. France, our friend and neighbour, possessed more than two hundred combat machines and our observers reported that French pilots were well trained in reconnaissance and the control of artillery fire from the air. Meanwhile the Air Battalion possessed nineteen qualified pilots. Clearly it was a time for action. A committee was appointed to consider the future of military aviation, and in 1912 the Royal Flying Corps was formed and absorbed the Air Battalion.

The architects of the Royal Flying Corps deliberated long over the size and shape of the tactical unit that would be the fighting element of the new arm. Previously, in our long history of war, all ranks of a combat unit, from colonel to private and from sea-going admiral to rating, had fought together, and the all-important problems of command, leadership, discipline and morale were easy to define. In these new air formations only a small proportion of their members, the aircrew, would come to grips with the enemy—and these few as individuals, not as a team. The new units must contain sufficient technicians and ground staff to put a number of machines into the air. Yet they must not be too cumbersome, otherwise the unit commander could not maintain enthusiasm and drive on the ground and supervise the training of his aircrew. In France the fighting formation was the *escadrille*, consisting of six aeroplanes together with the necessary pilots and maintenance personnel; we thought this too small a unit, and it was decided that the tactical element of the R.F.C. should be called the squadron, and that each squadron should consist of three flights of aeroplanes with four machines to a flight.

To understand the early air fighting we must study the training of the squadrons immediately before the First War. The prewar squadrons were designed to provide an expeditionary force with eyes. The crews were trained to reconnoitre ground, to mark the positions of enemy troops, guns, trenches, and fortifications on their maps. Officers bought their own cameras and began to experiment in air photography. They thought that if they flew at 3,000 feet they would be immune from rifle fire and that another thousand feet would make them relatively safe from the anti-aircraft batteries the Germans were known to possess; at the same time these low heights would give the observer a detailed view of the ground below. Thus the speed of their aeroplanes was not of great importance. They wanted a stable observing platform with a moderate cruising speed of about fifty miles an hour. It was just as well that we considered speed unimportant, for the only small engines available were the 70-h.p. Renault and the 80-h.p. Gnome, both made in France, while the Germans were building engines of 200 h.p.; it would be two years before we were independent of French factories for the supply of aeroplane engines.

The question then arose whether or not the scouting aeroplanes should carry machine guns. Some people thought that machine guns would prove too heavy for these frail aircraft and that airships would provide better gun platforms. Others argued that the reconnaissance pilot should avoid, rather than seek, combat, and that even if guns were available they should not be carried. Fortunately some of those in authority realised that sooner or later fighting in the air would be inevitable, and the Lewis machine gun was selected to be carried on some machines. The aeroplanes available were mostly two-seaters and were either pushers or tractors; pushers had the engine at the rear end of the nacelle and were slower and less manoeuvrable than the tractors, whose engine was at the front. It was decided that the Lewis gun should be carried in the pushers so that the observer who sat in front of his pilot would have a large cone of fire, upwards, downwards, and to either side: obviously he could not fire backwards because of the position of his pilot and the engine. Little consideration was given to the problem of mounting the machine gun on the aeroplane, and in the beginning the mounting was usually improvised by the observer to suit himself.

When the First War began, in 1914, four squadrons of the R.F.C. were sent to France. They possessed an assortment of different aeroplanes, including Henri Farmans, Blériots, B.E.2s, B.E.8s (known as 'bloaters'), and Avros. All were two-seaters, and the B.E.s, with their speed of about sixty miles an hour at their ceiling of some 3,000 feet, were judged the best, for they were very stable and gave the observer an excellent view of the ground. Back in England research continued on the Lewis gun, but the four squadrons flew to France as a reconnaissance force and the only weapons available to them, and to the Germans, were pistols and rifles.

The squadrons established themselves in the war zone, where they were received with the greatest enthusiasm by the French. The British Expeditionary Force began the four years of fighting with the long and difficult retreat from Mons, and the squadrons fell back with the troops and learned how to move at a moment's notice. They found that in this fluid battle their road transport was one of their most precious possessions, and if their aeroplanes were somewhat assorted, their vehicles were even more so. One squadron operated some furniture vans and a lorry designed for holding refuse. The ammunition lorry of another unit had belonged to the proprietors of a famous sauce and was painted a vivid scarlet with the words *The World's Appetizer* in gold letters on the side. This colour scheme was of great assistance during the retreat from Mons, for the pilots could easily spot it from the air and at once knew the position of their ground parties.

Like the fighter pilots of a later generation, they rarely came face to face with the horrors of the ground fighting. During the fateful weeks of that splendid autumn they lived like nomads, leap-frogging from airfield to meadow, from meadow to parkland or pasture, in fact anywhere they could find a few hundred yards of level ground. One night they would sleep in a barn on the edge of the airfield; the following evening would find them bedding down in a deserted chateau, and their next abode might be a comfortable hotel. Some of their machines barely escaped capture on the ground by the advancing Germans. Hurried plans were made to arm the ground personnel, and at night the aeroplanes were sometimes grouped together inside a lager formed by lorries and cars; the headlights would illuminate the defenders' field of fire and would probably stampede the enemy cavalry.

They found that the prevailing westerly wind could be their greatest enemy, certainly more formidable than the German anti-aircraft fire, which they dubbed 'Archie' after a popular music-hall refrain of the times. Their flights were usually in an easterly direction, and if they flew at fifty miles an hour and the wind blew at forty their speed over the ground was ninety miles an hour. But on the return journey, perhaps tired and harried by Archie, steering into the teeth of the wind, their small engines carried them over the ground at only ten miles an hour, and there was the danger of a forced landing, perhaps in enemy territory, through lack of petrol. They found that the way home always lay 'uphill'.

On their patrols they often saw enemy targets such as troops and transports, which they regretted could not be immediately attacked. Frustrated by this state of affairs, they began to carry hand grenades which were stowed in their pockets and hurled at opportunity targets. Larger bombs were slung over their shoulders on a length of stout cord, while fire bombs, consisting of a gallon of petrol contained in a streamlined canister, ignited when they struck the ground and were quite effective. 'Fletchettes' (steel darts) were dropped, and these first few weeks of the war saw the birth of ground attack from the air.

During the first month of the war a German aeroplane appeared over one of our airfields at about 4,000 feet. The R.F.C.

pilots raced to their available machines, and some six machines took-off in pursuit. The British pilots were not quite sure how they would deal with the intruder; obviously their immediate task was to get near enough to the Hun to have a shot at him. Some pilots carried pistols, and their observers were armed with rifles, while others stuffed hand grenades into their pockets with the intention of dropping these on the enemy machines. One pusher carried a machine gun and was referred to as the 'gun machine'. However, despite such an enthusiastic defence, the German escaped unscathed because the leading defender failed to gain the necessary height. Half an hour after the enemy's departure the gun machine was still plodding along at a much lower altitude. As a result of this encounter orders were given to discard the machine gun because of its weight and instead the observer would carry a rifle.

During the following five weeks five German aeroplanes were brought down. Having sighted his opponent, the pilot had to manoeuvre his machine into a position usually alongside the German, where the observer would have an opportunity to aim his rifle, and the firing range was sometimes only a few yards. The observer would force the upper part of his body into a slipstream of sixty or seventy miles an hour to swing and aim his rifle. Meanwhile the pilot produced his pistol and, with one hand on the stick, fired a few rounds for good measure.

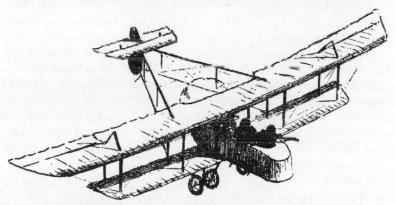

So they began to fight a few thousand feet above the ground. They learned the importance of having a height advantage, because it enabled them to surprise their foes and because once combat was joined their lightly powered scouts drifted earthwards as they twisted and turned for an opening. Sometimes they were so close to their enemies that they could distinguish their features and see the horrified surprise on their faces when they suddenly appeared. Sometimes the combatants jockeyed and cavorted about each other for thirty or forty minutes, especially when the two aeroplanes were of equal performance. Sometimes, after both adversaries had fired all their ammunition, they circled each other, saluted, and went their various ways because there was nothing more to be done.

'The first time I ever encountered a German machine' [relates W. Sholto Douglas], 'both the pilot and myself were completely unarmed. . . . I was considered somewhat heavy for an observer. . . . I therefore left behind my carbine and ammunition. We were taking photographs when I suddenly espied a German two-seater about one hundred yards away and just below us. The German observer did not appear to be shooting at us. There was nothing to be done. We waved a hand to the enemy and proceeded with the task. The enemy did likewise. At the time this did not appear to me in any way ridiculous—there is a bond of sympathy between all who fly, even between enemies'.*

Some pilots, both British and German, continued their aggressive tactics after they were out of ammunition, diving upon and circling their opponents like a hawk harrying a sparrow. Occasionally the pilot of the slower, less manoeuvrable machine would lose his nerve and land his aeroplane on a suitable stretch of ground, when the occupants would clamber out and race for the nearest cover, hotly chased by their opponents, who had landed near by. Sometimes the fight was continued on the ground with pistols, and prisoners were taken. But more often than not the victors were content to burn their opponents' aeroplane before taking-off again.

Contrary to orders, one R.F.C. team of pilot and observer mounted a Lewis gun on their aeroplane with a rope tackle of their own design. Soon afterwards they spotted a German two-

* *The War in the Air*, Vol. II, p. 137.

seater Albatros which, they discovered later, was flown by a non-commissioned officer with a commissioned officer acting as observer. The British pilot had a height advantage, so he dived below his opponent and then turned to fly in the same direction: from this ideal position the R.F.C. observer was able to pour two drums of ammunition into the belly of the Albatros while both machines made two complete turns. The Albatros was hit twenty times, and the German pilot decided to land. The British alighted alongside to claim their prisoners, and were astonished to see that the German officer had dragged his brother airman from the cockpit and was administering a sound thrashing.

As this year of 1914 drew to its end the fogs and rains obscured the Flanders plain and the R.F.C. had time to take stock. The previous months had seen the beginnings of a crude form of air fighting that was the prelude to the tremendous clashes of a later year. Aviators had learned that sometimes they must fight for their reconnaissance information and that the R.F.C. must possess suitable aeroplanes with machine guns to put out the eyes of the German Army. Because of their small engines the two-seaters were too slow and clumsy for fighting, and the R.F.C. wanted fast single-seaters, called scouts, armed with machine guns, to scout and fight. Soon Bristol Scouts, tractor-biplanes having a speed of 90 m.p.h. and a ceiling of 10,000 feet, arrived in France. Their crude armament consisted of two rifles, one on either side of the fuselage, which fired at an angle of some forty-five degrees to the line of flight so as to miss the propeller; accordingly, the unfortunate pilot had to manoeuvre in one direction and fire in another—like swinging at high pheasants with a bent sporting gun!

The squadrons were based a few miles behind the front lines and advanced or retreated with the land battle. So far, they had taken part in a war of movement from Mons to the gates of Paris, where the Germans were halted and driven back to the Aisne. But the pattern would change as the machine gun forced the troops underground, as the barbed wire became thicker, and as room for manoeuvre on the ground was lost. Trench warfare, a grim and bloody affair, would replace these early fluid battles.

The men who fought in the air were young volunteers, their average age not more than twenty-five, and were hand picked from some of the best material in the Army. Despite the squalor of war they liked to fly and were aware of belonging to a fairly exclusive society. They were light-hearted and perhaps the gayest company who had so far fought together.

Chapter 2

THE FLYING GUN

As the squadrons of the R.F.C. fell back from airfield to airfield during the retreat from Mons, so the combat units of the German Air Service followed hard behind their advancing armies. One of their pilots, Oswald Boelcke, was a keen, determined officer who proved himself a splendid fighter pilot, an outstanding leader, and a tactician of rare quality; his teachings were followed by his countrymen long after his death and his foes held him in high regard. Boelcke was one of the first 'aces' to emerge from the air clashes over Flanders, and his fighting career forms the early part of my story.

Soon after the war began Boelcke, aged twenty-three, gained his pilot's certificate and flew a replacement machine to France, strangely enough to the same unit, the 13th Section, in which his brother Wilhelm already served as an observer. They flew unarmed two-seaters, and their duties were to scout for the German Army, to pin-point the positions of Allied artillery, and to direct the fire of their own guns by a system of coloured lights fired from the air. At the end of the year Boelcke had made forty-two operational flights, and although both he and his observer carried pistols and rifles, they had not been involved in an air fight, but they had heard graphic accounts of the early clashes and knew that Germany was striving to produce an efficient scout.

As a weapon for their future scouts the British pinned their hopes to the Lewis gun, which was of simple design and had a useful rate of fire: the ammunition was fed to the gun from a rotating drum which could be changed in the air and held forty-seven rounds of .303 inch calibre bullets; later the double drum held ninety-seven rounds. The problem was where to mount the gun so that it could be used to good purpose in the air. On pushers the gun could be carried in front of the observer. But on tractors, which were the better fighting machines, because they were more manoeuvrable, the gun could not be mounted to fire along the line of flight, for the bullets would strike the blades of the propeller. Consequently on two-seater tractors the Lewis gun was sometimes carried on the top mainplane, sufficiently high to clear the blades, and aimed with a simple sight. The gunner had to stand to aim and fire, or to clear one of the frequent stoppages in the mechanism, not a simple matter in a gale of fifty or sixty miles an hour.

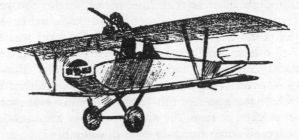

Early in 1915 the French took a big step forward with a scout carrying a device which made it possible for the machine gun to fire through the propeller. Shooting was greatly simplified because the pilot aimed his gun by flying his machine, and these *avions de chasse* were soon taking toll of their German opponents. Thus the struggle in the air swung in favour of the French. The Germans, in their slow, unarmed two-seaters, were unable to get on with their reconnaissance flights and made great efforts to provide improved machines. The result was another two-seater, called the C-type machine, in which the pilot sat in the front cockpit and his gunner was accommodated behind; a machine gun was mounted on the coaming of the gunner's cockpit and could be aimed backwards, upwards, or sideways. While not in the same class as the French scouts, it could at least offer some resistance, and it was not surprising that the adventurous Boelcke asked to be transferred to 62 Section, which was equipped with the new two-seaters. He soon found that even this crude form of fighting in the air was far more exciting and satisfying than the mundane tasks of reconnaissance and grenade dropping, and for all that his early fights were inconclusive, his letters to his parents expressed his delight at having what he called a 'whack' at Allied machines. His gunner, Lieutenant von Wühlisch, was a dapper little officer who had volunteered for this duty from a cavalry regiment, and underneath his flying overalls wore his red hussar's uniform.

The 6th July, 1915, fell on a Sunday and was a radiant day of high summer. Boelcke and Wühlisch were detailed to escort a German reconnaissance machine and protect it from attack by Allied scouts. They had been airborne only a short time when Boelcke's keen eyes spotted a French two-seater aeroplane approaching them from a greater height. In air combat the lower aeroplane is always at a disadvantage, so Boelcke slid out of the path of the oncoming enemy and with the hunter's instinct tried to hide his two-seater against the backcloth of the chequered countryside. This ruse succeeded, and the Frenchmen passed serenely overhead on their flight inside the German lines. Boelcke swung after him, and at full power began a long tail chase. After a cunning stalk of thirty minutes he came within firing distance and had gained a slight height advantage over his opponent.

Boelcke carefully positioned himself on the Frenchman's tail but slightly to one side, so that Wühlisch, seated behind his pilot, could bring his gun to bear. The French pilot, unaware that he was about to be attacked, continued to fly straight and level while his observer, flying over some of his own land, was lost in a reverie of happier days. Wühlisch opened fire from forty yards, and when the Frenchman realised his danger he put his monoplane into a spiral dive. Boelcke sat on the neck of the Frenchman, nursed his precious height advantage, and followed his opponent's every move. In the steep dives their speeds increased to more than eighty miles an hour and fell off in the shuddering tight turns to a near stalling speed of less than forty miles an hour. Sometimes Boelcke failed to hear the chatter of Wühlisch's gun, and when he looked round he saw the little hussar frantically clawing away at a stoppage in the mechanism. Then Boelcke dismissed the aiming problem from his tactics and concentrated on drawing closer to his adversary. When Wühlisch slapped him on the shoulder he kicked on coarse rudder, skidded to one side and the hussar fired again. Sometimes the French observer returned their fire, but his aim was erratic and the Germans were not hit.

They fought for twenty minutes and their aerobatics brought

them down to a height of 2,000 feet. On the ground, people clad in stiff black suits and dresses were making their way to church. They were astonished to hear machine guns thirty kilometres behind the front lines, and looking up, they saw the two opponents in a long, slanting dive. The leading plane carried the tricolour of France and that astern the black cross of Germany. They saw the rear machine draw to one side and fire short bursts. They watched the Parasol fall into a vertical dive and spin twice before it crashed into a wood.

The Germans saw the end of their opponents, and Boelcke landed his undamaged aeroplane in a suitable field near the wood. A number of German soldiers and French civilians were already making their way to the crash, and the two flyers were given a lift in a passing staff car. Arrived at the wreckage, they found both occupants dead: the French pilot had seven wounds, his observer five, and Boelcke thought they had died in the air. By one of those strange twists of fate the dead observer, one Comte Beauvicourt, was the owner of the wood into which he crashed. The victors were soon joined by other officers of their unit and all were entertained to lunch by the local German military. Congratulations poured in; Boelcke, already the holder of the Iron Cross, was commended by his superiors, and Wühlisch was decorated for his part in the fight.

This fight was important because it provides the first detailed account of an air engagement sought and waged according to plan. Boelcke's keen eyesight, his skill in luring the French pilot into a poor tactical position, and his patience in the long stalk had made the combat possible. In the ensuing fight, despite the awkward flying qualities of his Albatros, he always maintained the upper hand, manoeuvring with consummate skill to hold his opponent within his gunner's field of fire, keeping a sharp look out for other Allied aeroplanes and pressing home his attacks until his enemy was vanquished. The victory was due to Boelcke's airmanship and the skill of his gunner: it was his first confirmed success, and it was also his last in a two-seater.

Unfortunately for the Allies, a French scout fitted with the new device for firing through the propeller made a forced landing in the German lines and was captured before the pilot, Roland Garros, an aviator of pre-war fame, could carry out his orders and destroy his machine. The Germans soon reacted, and the machine was taken to Berlin, where it was given to a brilliant Dutch aeroplane designer, Anthony Fokker, whose instructions were to adapt the French idea to the German Parabellum machine gun. Fokker, who was twenty-four, had designed, built, and flown his own sporting planes and had already secured a contract both to build planes for the Germans and to train some of their pilots. His talent can be judged from the fact that the French invention and the Parabellum gun were given to him on a Tuesday evening; on the following Friday he returned to Berlin with the first interrupter gear fitted to an aeroplane.

Fokker found that the captured scout had no interrupter gear to prevent bullets hitting the propeller, but that each blade was simply fitted with a triangular steel plate to deflect striking bullets. The Dutchman thought this a dangerous gadget, because the deflectors reduced the efficiency of the wooden blades, which could still be sheared by bullets; and there was some risk from ricochets. He determined to improve on what he considered to be a dangerous and crude device. In simple terms the technical problem was to shoot between the two blades of the propeller, which spun at slightly more than one thousand revolutions per minute; Fokker likened his problem to that of a child who tries to throw stones through the revolving blades of a windmill.

Fokker completed his work, installed the gun and its interrupter gear on one of his monoplanes, lashed the tail of the aeroplane to his touring car, and drove through the night to a military airfield at Berlin. He demonstrated his gun, which, unlike the Lewis gun, was belt-fed, to a group of staff officers, who doubted whether it would work in the air because the propeller did not have steel wedges like the captured French machine. The Dutchman agreed to fire at a ground target from the air. The staff officers gathered round and scattered in all directions when the stream of bullets ricocheted from the hard ground. Although the target was riddled with holes, they were still not fully convinced and said that the gun ought to be tested in actual combat. So the Dutch designer, a civilian and a foreigner in Germany, was bundled off to the front in his aeroplane with orders to demonstrate his gun by the simple expedient of killing an Allied aviator.

The Flying Dutchman, masquerading in German field grey uniform as Lieutenant Anthony Fokker, flew to Boelcke's airfield at Douai with his Fokker EI monoplane, fitted with the machine gun that was to revolutionise air warfare. After a few uneventful patrols he came across a sitting duck in the form of an Allied two-seater cruising below him. Fokker began his attack in a long dive, but when the Allied plane was filling his sights and completely at his mercy he was nauseated with the whole affair and never fired a shot. He flew back to Douai, where he declared he was finished with fighting and was returning to his factory.

The question now arose as to which pilot should assess the new gun in combat. To some extent the problem was resolved by Boelcke, who, impressed by the radical, clean lines of the monoplane, flew it without permission; fortunately for him, the commanding officer at Douai was not too displeased by this breach of flying discipline, and Oswald Boelcke was selected to appraise both machine and gun. Before leaving the hazards of the combat zone Fokker found time to explain both his aeroplane and the mechanism of the gun to Boelcke.

Boelcke was delighted with the Fokker, whose 80-h.p. rotary engine gave it a speed of about 80 m.p.h. at 5,000 feet: compared with the clumsy two-seater Albatros, it was like riding a thoroughbred after a hack. He soon found that the single-seater gave him far more initiative and freedom of action than the Albatros, because in the former he combined the roles of pilot, navigator, and gunner, whereas in the latter he was simply the driver. His only regret was having to part company with Wühlisch, for they had found the indefinable affinity of those who fly and fight together.

He found that the best tactics for his speedy Fokker, with its high rate of climb and good manoeuvrability, was to prowl on the German side of the front lines, taking full advantage of any concealment offered by the glare of the sun, clouds, and their shadows cast on the earth. He carefully studied captured Allied aeroplanes so that he knew the type of gun they carried and its field of fire: thus he found the blind spots of British and French machines and fashioned his attacks accordingly. He could climb his Fokker to 5,000 feet, and at this height he found that most Allied aeroplanes flew below his. Unless there was plenty of cloud cover it was against orders to cross the front lines, and he usually hunted on the German side of the lines, where lay the advantage of the prevailing wind; and in the event of a forced landing he was on friendly territory, whereas Allied aircrews in the same predicament were almost invariably captured.

Having seen an opponent, Boelcke had the patience to hide and stalk in the correct up-sun position before attacking. Then his tactics were fashioned on the stoop of a hawk: he fastened on his victim from a long slanting dive, closing to short range and firing accurate, short bursts from his gun, which he aimed with a simple ring and bead sight. Having dispatched his opponent from a final range of a few yards, he climbed back to his cruising height and resumed his quest.

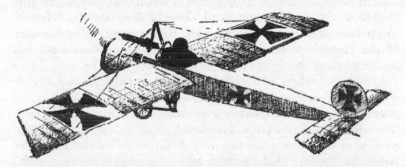

Aiming from astern was easy and seemed natural, because the Fokker monoplane was simply a flying gun which he flew at an opponent. The secret lay in closing to a good killing range, aiming, and then holding the gun platform steady when firing. After the intricate manoeuvres required in the Albatros so that Wühlisch could bring his gun to bear, fighting in the Fokker seemed simple and straightforward, and enemy machines could be shot down much quicker than before. The flying gun changed the conception of air fighting.

The German anti-aircraft gunners knew about the solitary Fokker pilot and recognised his machine. When they thought he was in danger of being attacked they fired a few warning rounds ahead of his monoplane, and they also provided covering fire when he evaded an opponent by diving towards the ground.

It was another pilot of 62 Section who found out how a Fokker could easily regain its height after a diving attack. This was Max Immelmann, a serious youth with a short, athletic body, whose only claim to fame, prior to his Fokker days, lay in the considerable number of aeroplanes he had crashed when trying to land; indeed, Boelcke heaved a sigh of relief when Immelmann, on his first solo in the new monoplane, got it down in one piece. But the following day, while getting more experience on the Fokker, he shot down a British biplane whose pilot was bombing the Douai airfield; this first victory of Immelmann's was a somewhat mild affair, since the R.F.C. pilot was flying without his gunner because his machine could not carry both gunner and bombs.

The German pilot's manoeuvre, known for long afterwards as 'the Immelmann turn', began with a dive upon his enemy. After building up his speed in the dive he pulled the Fokker into a climb and opened fire from behind and below to gain surprise. After firing he continued climbing, as if he were going to loop, but when his Fokker reached a vertical position he kicked on hard rudder, turned sideways and dived on his opponent from the opposite direction. The German dived, fired, 'Immelmanned', and attacked again, and the tactic was sound so long as the Fokker was superior to all other machines on the Western Front. The Immelmann turn was very successful because the aggressor quickly regained his height and could attack again and again. But later, when more powerful engines became available, it was a dangerous move, for the lower pilot could climb after the Fokker and attack when it hung almost motionless in the vertical position, not under full control, and presenting an easy shot.

Boelcke's victories mounted slowly, for owing to the 'Fokker scare' the French adopted a defensive policy, confining their *escadrilles* to short-range spotting and reconnaissance duties,

while the R.F.C. were forced to escort bombing and reconnaissance aeroplanes with the new Vickers Fighter, a two-
seater pusher with a speed of some 80 m.p.h. and a ceiling of

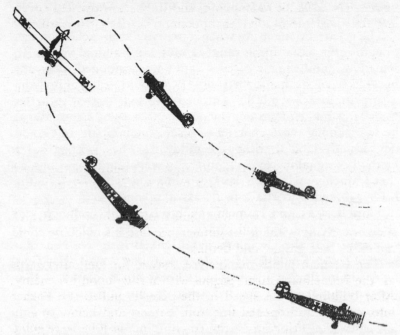

10,000 feet. Irked by the lack of combat, Boelcke began to leave
the sanctuary of the German lines and extend his patrols over
Allied territory. Like countless other scout pilots, he found the
sky's infinite horizons too vast for one man to search and cover
the whole time. He would spot an Allied aeroplane three or
four miles away, and most of his concentration would be upon
the stalk and the gaining of an up-sun position for his attack.
But he found that other hostile aeroplanes had a disconcert-
ing habit of appearing within a hundred yards, and this could
only have one ending.

He reasoned that in order to fly his Fokker, navigate to his
patrol line, quarter the big sky for hostile machines, dodge anti-
aircraft shells, and guard himself from surprise attack he
required another pair of eyes. Especially did he want this assistance when he focused his eyes on a particular segment of the

sky, because although at first he saw nothing, he often picked out an aeroplane after searching for twenty or thirty seconds. But, Boelcke asked himself, could not some Allied fighter creep up on him from the opposite direction and attack him within those thirty seconds?

The greatest danger lay when an enemy approached unseen to within the lethal firing range, about two hundred yards. If, somehow, another pair of eyes could be positioned alongside his Fokker, on his flank, then those eyes could protect him from a surprise attack while he searched and led. And who better than Max Immelmann to provide the other eyes? Especially as he was gaining more experience on the monoplane and could now usually land it without bending it! They worked out a method of signalling to each other, by waggling their wings, so that Immelmann, on the flank, would know when Boelcke, the leader, intended to attack or break-off a combat.

Thus Boelcke and Immelmann began to fly and fight together. They guarded and protected each other. They were so successful that the Germans, if not the British, realised that pairs of scouts would fare far better than lone scouts. The Germans lost no time in ordering more Fokker monoplanes, so that they could make their first bid for command of the air.

Chapter 3

SCOUT SQUADRONS

GREAT pilots are made not born, and young Albert Ball, from Nottingham, was no exception to the rule. A man may possess good eyesight, sensitive hands, and perfect co-ordination, but the end product is only fashioned by steady coaching, much practice, and experience. Not every outstanding pilot began well, and some well-known aviators have bent more aeroplanes than they have shot down. Ball does not fall into this latter category, but he suffered two crashes during his early training, and after one particularly heavy landing his irate instructor shouted that he was finished with flying unless he could find a flying school for girls. His artless, schoolboy nature is well illustrated in a letter he wrote to his sister, in which he described the gruesome death of a fellow pilot. Would you, he concluded, like a flight? It could easily be arranged!

After passing through the Central Flying School at Up-avon, Ball was awarded his wings and early in 1916 was posted to 13 Squadron in France. He was to fly a B.E.2c aeroplane with two seats and a Lewis gun operated by his observer: his duties consisted of photographing the German trenches and strong points, spotting for our own batteries, and reporting the fall of shells direct to the artillery by wireless, some long-range reconnaissances well behind the German lines, and sometimes a little bombing.

It was not an easy time for the new pilot and his observer. Over the enemy lines they had to fly straight and level to take photographs, and their slow B.E. was an easy target for Archie's black, angry bursts. If they flew low, below Archie's usual height, they were fired at by countless machine guns, and whether they flew high or low small sections of two, three, or four Fokkers barred their way and took a heavy toll; for the latest Fokker E III, despite its identical appearance to the E I, had a bigger engine, which gave it a speed of 90 m.p.h. Ball and his contemporaries pressed on and often flew twice and occasionally three times in a day, every day, until they were shot down, cracked under the strain, or were sent home for a rest. During this critical period, when the German Air Service made its first determined bid for air supremacy, the average R.F.C. pilot lasted for only a few weeks, and the more despondent referred to themselves as 'Fokker fodder'.

R.F.C. pilots and observers were told that if they were un-lucky enough to be brought down behind the Boche lines they should always try to burn their machines. One young pilot who was forced down by a Fokker was captured before he could set fire to his aeroplane, and his captor, a German aviator, noticing that the Englishman looked very anxious, said: 'I'll drive you to our mess for lunch. Don't worry about your machine. We already have lots of these old B.E.s, and I'll come back and burn it for you after lunch.'

The R.F.C. possessed little technical information about the German scout, and were anxious to obtain a photograph so that experts could tell whether it had a rotary or a fixed engine. The word was passed to the squadrons, and one gallant pilot, when about to be attacked by a Fokker, took no evasive action and deliberately allowed the enemy fighter to come within firing range. Our pilot then produced his camera and photo-graphed his attacker. He lived to tell the tale, and the experts anxiously awaited the picture for which he had hazarded his life. Unfortunately the print proved to be out of focus.

Despite the inferiority of his B.E. and the fact that he was a reconnaissance and not a scout pilot, Ball always had a crack at German aeroplanes whenever he had an opportunity. He learned of a decoy ruse for unsuspecting pilots when he spotted what he thought was a sitting duck some 3,000 feet below. Ball immediately dived to attack and jockeyed his aeroplane so that his observer was able to open fire. Then they heard the clatter of another machine gun and, looking round, saw a second Ger-man aeroplane on their tail. They were lucky, for they escaped with only slight damage; but the vital importance of always keeping a sharp look-out was not lost on him.

The commander of the R.F.C. was worried about the Fokker sections who constantly harried his aeroplanes, for he realised that their formation flying and team fighting had given the enemy a great advantage in this first struggle for control of the air. The German Air Service did not introduce formation flying for exhibition purposes but because it afforded mutual protection and strength in attack. Consequently, at the beginning of 1916 R.F.C. squadrons were instructed that reconnaissance aeroplanes must be escorted by at least three other machines and that the flight should be abandoned if any of the section became detached. Obviously the best escort to a B.E. was three scouts who, because of their superior speed and manoeuvrability, could give a reasonable degree of protection to the slower machine. But Ball's squadron only possessed one Bristol Scout and often they had to escort the B.E. with similar aeroplanes.

Today formation flying may seem fairly easy, when for years one has grown accustomed to watching hundreds of aeroplanes winging over a review point in immaculate formation and timed to a second, or when one watches the perfect evolutions of an aerobatic team of jet fighters. But in Ball's day, to begin flying in formation presented grave problems. There was no radio communication between pilots, so how was the team, once it had assembled over the airfield, to change direction, to turn, to climb, and to dive together? Today the leader of a jet fighter formation adjusts his throttle so that his team have ample power available to keep their positions, but in those days of small engines the performance margins were narrow, and once a man lagged behind he did not always have the power to catch up. Boelcke and Immelmann had shown that two scouts could fight together, but the difficulties were multiplied with larger formations.

To start with, the leader's aeroplane would have to be made conspicuous with bright paint or streamers which would form a rallying mark for all to see. Some system of signalling by hand or by firing coloured flares would have to be devised, so that orders could be given and received. But what if the leader's signal was misinterpreted by a pilot some distance away and he turned to the right instead of the left? R.F.C. pilots had been seconded from the Army and thought of the new air evolutions in terms of drill on the ground. But on the ground, if you turned to the right instead of the left you were confronted with a close-up of your neighbour's chin and the parade ground echoed to the bellowing wrath of the instructor; the same mistake in the air might have more unpleasant consequences. The difference between individual and team flying was the same as that between sticking to a horse and riding him.

They began their formation drill by practising simple turns and manoeuvres in pairs, and from pairs they progressed to a section of four led by the flight commander or his deputy. They practised two types of formation, a close wing-tip to wing-tip pattern for bad weather flying and a more widely spaced battle style for combat. As in other forms of warfare on land or sea, they learned that the basic human requirements are self-control, strict discipline, and perfect mastery of their machines. They learned to keep their heads, to act quickly in an emergency, how to vary their pace, to judge and hold their distance from each other, and to fly their aeroplanes with three-quarters of their attention focused on their leader. They studied the problems of communication and control in the air, and resolved that their aim should be to operate a squadron of twelve aeroplanes together. They thought that a formation of twelve, in three sections of four aeroplanes, would be the maximum number to fly together and that it would take months of training before this could be done.

For their combat formation they began with a simple diamond pattern as illustrated on page 35. The leader flew the reconnaissance aeroplane and, depending on cloud conditions and visibility, crossed the enemy guns as high as possible. The three escorting aeroplanes took up their stations 500 feet higher on each quarter and the rearguard flew 1,000 feet higher than his leader. Sometimes the escort was increased to six, deployed in three pairs. When his squadron flew in this fashion Ball noticed that the Fokkers were inclined to shadow and wait for an opening rather than attack immediately. Sometimes on a long flight of twenty miles a brace of Fokkers would take up a shadowing position higher and a mile or two from the British formation. Other German aeroplanes, attracted by the unusual sight of eight or nine aeroplanes near each other, would arrive on the scene until sometimes a dozen enemy machines followed the British formation. Then the vital task for Ball and his comrades was to hold their spacings so that the cross-fire from their Lewis guns gave mutual protection. Sometimes the Fokkers climbed into the sun and dived to attack. And if in the ensuing mêlée the B.E.s were separated from each other their losses were heavy.

No doubt the reader will be wondering why Ball and his contemporaries sallied forth in their vulnerable aeroplanes sometimes two or three times a day, day after day, and always on the offensive. During the autumn of 1915 and the following spring the Fokkers undoubtedly had the upper hand. Yet they were content to wait for customers on their own side of the lines, for the Germans were on the defensive, and few Fokkers, or other enemy machines, crossed the front. This was an odd state of affairs and showed that the leaders of the German Air Service did not understand the air weapon; but Trenchard knew how to get the best results.

Brigadier H. M. Trenchard took command of the R.F.C. in France during the late summer of 1915, and this great leader knew at once that his job of supporting the Army could only be done by fighting over enemy territory. Throughout the hours of daylight, day after day, the Army wanted two-seaters above and beyond the front lines to bomb, photograph, reconnoitre, and report the fall of artillery shells, and these could not survive unless the scouts went farther afield to try to hold the Fokkers. Even during the 'Fokker scourge' the work for the Army went on, R.F.C. casualties were far heavier than the Germans, questions were asked in Parliament, and much pressure was brought upon Trenchard to follow a more defensive line.

If Trenchard had the slightest misgivings about his views they vanished when, in the spring of 1916, he talked with Commandant du Peuty, of the French Air Service, and thrashed out future Allied air strategy. For at the beginning of the Battle of Verdun, when the Germans tried to take the great fortress, the French airmen kept up a vigorous and successful offensive, but when the ground fighting stiffened and the Fokkers began to fly in larger numbers there was a clamour for defensive patrols and the tables were turned. Both leaders understood this clamour, for when troops are attacked from the air thousands of eyes see the hostile aeroplanes and the effect on morale is often worse than the material damage; both realised, too, that they could never control the air by, as Trenchard put it, following the tactics of a policeman on his beat, because they had too big a beat to patrol. They both knew that an air umbrella over the troops is apt to leak, and when the French airmen resumed their offensive the colossal German effort was soon defeated. Hugh Trenchard never forgot the French experiences at Verdun, his faith in offensive action was justified, and this sustained him on future occasions when the enemy was master in the sky.

Trenchard, who thought only of his country, was loved by all his men, who, behind his back, knew him as 'Boom', for his loud, penetrating, booming voice could be heard from afar. One lovely summer day he sat in his office, with all the windows open, discussing with his chief of staff the future moves of certain squadrons to three new airfields. The two talked about his plans for some minutes, the chief of staff left and Trenchard rang the bell for his equipment officer, who entered briskly, saluted and said:

'The stores are already on their way to the three new airfields, sir.'

'How the devil did you know,' shouted Trenchard, 'I've only just told the chief of staff!'

'Sir, I was walking from the village and heard you as I was coming up the drive!'

Almost as legendary as Trenchard was his talented aide, Maurice Baring, who knew how to handle his master. One day, after a visit when things had gone amiss, they were returning by car to their chateau when Baring heard an aeroplane. He peered through the windscreen, through the side screens, and finally through the rear window to see the machine, when Trenchard shouted:

'What machine is it? Where's it from? Where's it going? And why is it so far behind the lines?'

He will ask me the name of the pilot next, thought Baring, but he replied quietly:

'I wasn't looking for the machine, sir. I was just trying to see if it was raining!'

Before the diamond and other crude formations could be

developed it was apparent that aeroplanes could only operate together provided they were of the same type and so had a similar performance in the air. Thus Trenchard's next important step in the story of air fighting was to follow the German example at Verdun, break up the heterogeneous collection of aeroplanes in each unit, provide the units with one type of machine, and organise the squadrons for specialised roles. The early months of 1916 saw a steady flow of new aeroplanes arriving in France, and the de Havilland Scout, a pusher-biplane having a speed of 90 m.p.h., could climb to 10,000 feet in twenty-four minutes, and was reported by the pilots to be superior in some respects to the latest Fokker. At least the tide was beginning to turn; but it would take some time to complete the re-equipment programme.

It was the French, however, who produced the outstanding scout of the period; this was the Nieuport Scout, a tractor-biplane with a Lewis gun mounted over the top plane. Sometimes called the 'Silver Hawk' because of its colour, its speed of 107 m.p.h. made it faster than any R.F.C. fighter, and it could climb to 10,000 feet in nine minutes. The Nieuport Scout was ordered for the R.F.C. and this was significant for two reasons: it was the first Allied aeroplane to exceed 100 m.p.h. in level flight, and it marked the end of the design struggle between pusher and tractor scouts. For by this time sufficient experience had been gained from the fighting in the air to determine the ideal requirements of the fighting aeroplane. These were a reasonable turn of speed to bring the enemy to combat, or to escape; a good rate of climb to intercept higher targets; a high ceiling to bestow the great advantages of surprise and time to select the method of attack and so control the air battle; manoeuvrability to live in the dog-fight; and adequate fire power, without which the other qualities would have little value. These demands could best be met, and developed for the future, by a clean, compact single-seater with the engine at the front. The introduction of faster and more powerful machines meant that the prevailing westerly wind, although still to be reckoned with, was no longer such a menace to Allied pilots.

While R.F.C. scout pilots practised on their new aeroplanes

their squadron commanders thought about the best type of
squadron formation for combat. Three patterns—line abreast,
line astern, and echelon—were considered, and since they
formed the basis of team flying and, to some extent, are still
flown today, they are worthy of detailed study.

In the line abreast style the pilots flew well up on their
leader. When they held their correct combat spacing between
each other, about fifty yards, they found that they could hold
their formation and watch for hostile aeroplanes. The leader
led from the flank so that with single-seaters three pairs of eyes
looked to that flank and the section was not evenly guarded,
because number four was far more vulnerable to attack than
the leader or number two; however, this criticism was not true
of two-seaters, because the four observers maintained a careful
lookout behind and, as far as possible, below. Except for one
manoeuvre, the pilots found that line abreast was a fairly safe
drill, for they could move into echelon or line astern without
undue risk. The left turn, pivoting on their leader, was easy,
but the right turn was very awkward, and they had to watch
each other very carefully to hold the correct spacings. All
manoeuvres in line abreast were much simplified when later
the leader led from the centre, but this position was not considered when formation flying was in its infancy.

Line astern is the easiest pattern to fly, because it is the air
equivalent of the children's game of 'follow my leader'. The
pilots found no difficulty in following their leader through a
series of aerobatics provided that he flew accurately and allowed
them a fair margin of speed. It was a very safe drill, because

the pilots turned and wheeled after each other and not at the same time, as in line abreast. Because the forward and upward view from their biplanes was restricted, they flew stepped up

from front to rear, which had the added advantage that if anyone lagged behind he could convert height into speed and catch up by diving towards his leader. It was considered a good bombing formation, because if the two-seaters flew close together their bombs would straddle the target. However, for single-seaters the tremendous disadvantage was that numbers two, three, and four spent a lot of time watching the aeroplane ahead and had little opportunity to keep a careful look-out; consequently it was a most vulnerable combat formation, and number four usually bore the brunt of an attack.

Echelon drill was practised because hand signals could easily be passed from pilot to pilot, but they found it difficult to keep an even spacing, and any slight alteration of the leader's course threw out the others. Also if for any reason the leader suddenly turned inwards there was grave danger of a collision, and it was soon found that echelon was not as safe a formation as either line abreast or line astern.

Formation leaders pondered about the best way of tackling large numbers of enemy machines and, for the present, based their tactics on a theory advanced by F. W. Lanchester, an authority on the theory of flight. Lanchester's law, also called the end-squared law, said that if five machines met seven German machines the aim should be to divide the seven into two bodies of four and three, and attack first one and then the other party. Since $5^2 = 4^2 + 3^2$, the five machines had every prospect of success, whereas if the five attacked the seven simultaneously they should be beaten.

From this brief résumé of the early air fighting one can see that the early months of 1916, when Ball served in 13 Squadron, was a period of tremendous transition for the R.F.C. Large scale formation flying was to change the character of fighting in the air from sporadic duelling to precision teamwork. Trenchard saw that space in which to manoeuvre in the air, unlike fighting on land or sea, is practically unlimited, and that any number of aeroplanes operating defensively would seldom stop a determined enemy from getting through. Therefore the aeroplane was, and is, essentially an instrument of attack, not defence, and his scouts would carry the fight to the enemy by means of offensive sweeps and escorts to slower machines. The normal battle unit was to be two machines, and squadron commanders were to build their formations upon pairs until twelve scouts could fly together. The scouts would operate in the best type of formation, thought to be line abreast, but the squadron commanders would continue to experiment as they received their new aeroplanes. Squadron formations would need more air space, would increase the collision risk, and add to the signalling problem; for a start, therefore, two or three pairs of scouts would fly together until more experience was gained.

During April, 1916, Ball and his observer succeeded in destroying a German two-seater. They were on patrol when their formation encountered five or six German machines. After some manoeuvring Ball got so close to an Albatros that he could see details of their opponents' faces beneath the goggles and helmets. Both observers opened fire, but the German gunner was killed after a few rounds and the enemy pilot was seen to crash land. In the same month they drove down two more enemy aeroplanes.

Ball took part in his share of bombing and reconnaissance missions, but he infinitely preferred to fly the Bristol Scout, for he had the keen eyesight, the quick judgement, the fast reactions, and the aggressive spirit of an air fighter. On the ground he spent much time working on his aeroplane, lowering the windscreen so that he obtained another mile an hour in the air, stripping his Lewis gun, and tuning the engine.

Ball's qualities, his passion to get at the enemy, his quest to improve his ability and his ambition to fly the single-seater, did not pass unnoticed by his superiors, and he was selected for training on scouts; during the following month he was transferred to 11 Squadron, who were just getting Nieuport Scouts. After a few flights in the Nieuport he was thrilled with its performance and thought it the perfect scouting machine.

Although team fighting was now the order of the day, some considerable time elapsed before 11 Squadron received their full quota of Nieuports, and often only one or two of these new scouts were serviceable for flying. Thus Ball often patrolled alone in his Nieuport, and this early experience influenced the rest of his air fighting career. He was becoming a dangerous man to meet in the sky, and at the end of May he began a long string of victories in his Nieuport when he destroyed two enemy aeroplanes.

Other squadrons were getting new, if not better, aeroplanes. One cynic said of his Farman Experimental 2b: 'I sat in a robust throne, rather like a bishop's seat in a cathedral, and my observer sat, or knelt, in a round nacelle about the size of an old fashioned footbath right in front. There he had a Lewis gun fixed to a tall pole and when he stood to use it the sides of the footbath came to his knees. After one or two observers had been tossed out of the footbath most of the others anchored themselves to the pole by a home made harness.' But the new Sopwith tractor two-seater, the famous 'one and a half strutter', was very popular, handled well, and carried an interrupter gear which allowed the Vickers machine gun to fire through the propeller. The Fokkers no longer ruled the air.

Young Ball had served his apprenticeship and was about to win his spurs. Meanwhile, two hundred miles away, at Verdun, Oswald Boelcke was being highly successful against French aviators.

Chapter 4

THE TEAM

WHEN the Germans were preparing for their attack at Verdun, in the autumn of 1915, some of their best scout pilots, including Boelcke, were sent to Metz and joined a unit possessing both scouts and bombers. All personnel lived in a train, containing offices, workshops, and spares, which could move at short notice from one sector to another over the well-developed railway network; naturally it soon became known as a 'travelling circus', but it was a fine example of that mobility which the Germans were to use with great success in later years.

Soon after Boelcke's transfer the Kaiser arrived on a tour of inspection. Some Fokker pilots patrolled to protect their Emperor from bombing attacks, but the keen Boelcke took off before the appointed time to give his aeroplane a thorough air test. Archie's black bursts warned him of the presence of French bombers, who dropped their loads over Metz at the very moment the Kaiser stepped from his train. Since he was at a lower height than his enemies, Boelcke could not intervene, but in his usual calm and deliberate fashion he began to stalk the retreating bombers. Seeing the pursuing Fokker, one of his opponents swung round to make a half-hearted attack and then rejoined his comrades. Boelcke was content to bide his time; he lessened the range, drew underneath the lowest bomber, and at eighty yards opened fire with careful, well-aimed bursts. His bullets found their mark, the bomber went into a steep dive with the German hard astern. Two Frenchmen broke formation to assist their stricken companion, and since he was fighting well over enemy territory, Boelcke used his superior speed to break off the fight. Later the German infantry reported that the biplane had crashed near the front lines, the pilot was dragged clear and the aeroplane completely destroyed by artillery fire.

Throughout that autumn and winter Boelcke scored against

the Allies. He destroyed another French biplane in the Champagne, and had a one-sided fight against a two-seater whose observer gallantly fired a shot gun at him until dispatched from a final range of five yards. He flew back to Douai to compare notes with Max Immelmann, and made a good start to 1916 by forcing down a British biplane, whose wounded pilot greeted him with a handshake, a smile, and 'Ah, Boelcke! We know all about you!' Another two-seater shot down into an apple tree especially pleased him, because he was able to examine the wreckage and saw that most of his bullets found his aiming point, the cockpit. But he was not a cold-blooded killer; he fought through force of circumstances, regretted the ghastly deaths of some of his foes, and spent much of his leisure motoring to various hospitals to cheer his victims and give them a few cigarettes.

Boelcke and Immelmann scored their eighth victories at the same time and were acclaimed as national heroes by a civilian population weary of reading the endless casualty lists of the ground fighting. Their duels in the air were a welcome contrast to the sordidness of the land battle, and their fights were suitably garnished and widely reported by the Press. In January they were each awarded a high decoration, the *Pour le Mérite*,* and two days later Boelcke celebrated his distinction by accounting for his ninth Allied aeroplane.

During the previous summer Boelcke had dived into a canal and rescued a French youth from drowning. His commanding officer recommended him for the German life-saving medal, and this was duly awarded. It says much for the character of the German pilot that he derived almost as much pleasure from this medal as from the *Pour le Mérite*.

I have already described how German scout pilots were not encouraged to patrol over Allied territory. During the early days of air fighting, when the Fokker and its gun were new, one can understand the reluctance of the Germans to hazard their secrets in case a Fokker was brought down on our side of the lines; but at Verdun the German airmen still patrolled on their

---

* A curious title for a German decoration, and so called because Frederick the Great, founder of the German Empire, could only speak French.

side of the lines, while below them their Fifth Army strove to crush the French. This strange philosophy is worth some reflection, for not only was it a contradiction of Trenchard's thinking but it was also to influence enemy scout pilots throughout the remainder of the First War and enemy fighter pilots during the Second War.

When the Germans began to concentrate for their thrust against Verdun it was natural that they should want to protect this build-up from the cameras and eyes of French reconnaissance pilots. The combat area of the German Fifth Army was divided into four 'barrage' zones, and small formations of aeroplanes patrolled these zones from dawn to dusk; the pilots were told that French aeroplanes were not to penetrate the barrage. The barrage patrols were flown by small arrow-head vic formations of three bombing or reconnaissance aeroplanes. The few available Fokkers were also used on these flights, because a

German instruction stated that the barrage had precedence over all other flying. These, indeed, were the tactics of the policeman pounding his beat, and the Germans soon found that the barrage system of defensive patrols absorbed most of their aeroplanes. Although the plan met with some success during the build-up period, it was an immediate failure once the ground fighting began, because the French airmen sought out their enemies and had no difficulty in penetrating the barrage.

Apart from the failure of the barrage system, this mis-employment of the German Air Service had other effects. The reconnaissance and bombing machines were prevented from getting on with the business of providing support to the Fifth Army; and some of these heavy two-seaters had a poor rate of climb, slender armament, and were totally unsuited for air combat. As for the Fokkers, they were at a serious tactical disadvantage when they were tied to these rigid patrol lines, because they lost a great deal of their flexibility. The lesson of the Verdun air fighting was that it is not possible to seal an air space hermetically by defensive tactics.

The Germans soon realised that the French must be halted and that the Fokker was the aeroplane for the job. But on this battlefront the French *escadrilles* were numerically superior to the Fokkers, which were scattered in penny packets on airfields ranging from northern France to the borders of Luxembourg. The Fokkers must be grouped together into special fighting units, and their job would be to gain air superiority over and beyond the Fifth Army so that the slow bombing and reconnaissance machines could fly in comparative safety behind the screen of scouts.

Two dozen Fokkers were swiftly assembled on suitable airfields and formed into temporary units known as 'Single Seater Fighter North and Fighter South Commands'. Once released from the rigid constraint of their barrage duties, the Fokker pilots fought back and were soon harassing the French on the ground and in the air. French airmen and soldiers demanded that their own scouts protect them from the Fokkers, and with the granting of this request French scouts had to resort to the defensive.

The grouping of the Fokkers was a move in the right direction towards specialised squadrons, but a stable organisation was still lacking. Profiting from the lessons of the air fighting at Verdun the Germans decided to keep the Fokkers together, and Boelcke, promoted to captain shortly before his twenty-fifth birthday, was ordered to form his own *staffel** of six scouts.

The organisation of the new flight would take some time and, pending the arrival of pilots and aeroplanes, Boelcke flew and fought single-handed from an airfield of his own choosing, a meadow at Sivry alongside the Meuse. His successes against the French mounted at about the same rate as those of Immelmann, who, from Douai, still fought against the British. When each had scored twelve victories the Kaiser ordered that messages of congratulation be prepared for his signature; he was

* The equivalent of a R.F.C. flight.

about to sign the letter to Immelmann when an aide announced the news of Immelmann's thirteenth victory, whereupon the Kaiser altered the text in his own hand, remarking, 'Immelmann can shoot faster than we can write!'

The race between the two German airmen ended when Immelmann, after fifteen victories, was killed, and it was announced that his scout had broken up in the air. Anthony Fokker, anxious to safeguard his reputation, announced that the Fokker was brought down by anti-aircraft fire; the R.F.C. claimed that Immelmann was shot down by Lieutenant McCubbin, 25 Squadron, but Boelcke, writing to his parents, confirmed that the monoplane fell apart.

Boelcke flew to Douai to pay his last respects to his friend, who lay in state in the courtyard of a hospital; he was deeply impressed with the dignity of the scene—the torches, the attendant crown princes, and more than a score of generals to honour the dead hero. As usual at Douai the R.F.C. were active and Boelcke fought on three separate occasions, but was unable to claim a victory. Irritated by this lack of success he delayed his return to Sivry and the staff began to make polite inquiries about his departure. After a few days the questioning became less amiable, and he was told to fly back immediately. Boelcke replied that the weather was too bad for flying, whereupon the staff had the last word with an explicit order to take the next train!

He found there was a good reason for the staff's agitation. Following Immelmann's death, and the shadow it cast on the nation, the Kaiser said that Boelcke, with eighteen victories, had done enough. It was almost the end of June, 1916, and Boelcke's interpretation of the royal edict was that he could fly until the end of the month. On 28th June he badly damaged a French machine, but did not report this combat, because he feared headquarters might take a different view about the terminal date of his long tour of duty. On the following day the staff began to make inquiries about a French aeroplane reported as destroyed by the German artillery. The game was up! Boelcke was credited with the Frenchman and grounded.

As a rest from the strain of combat flying, Boelcke was sent on a trip to Turkey, where he was given a tremendous reception from the German forces serving on that front. He had only been away a few weeks when news reached him of the British offensive on the Somme and of the complete air superiority won by Trenchard's re-organised squadrons. He was to return to France and raise his own permanent *jagdstaffel*** of fourteen scouts. This time he would be based near the Somme opposite the British; there would be some stiff fighting in the air, and he would have a free hand in the selection of his pilots. Here was his great opportunity to gather together a few proved fighters, to train the beginners, and weld the individual pilots into a fighting team.

On his return journey Boelcke was able to spend a few hours with his brother, Wilhelm, now stationed on the Eastern Front and flying against the Russians. After dinner the pilots and observers grouped themselves around the great man, who told them something of his flying adventures against the British and the French. Long into the night they discussed the latest reports of the Somme air fighting, where the English seemed to have so many machines that some could specialise in low bombing and strafing. At Verdun troops had revealed their positions to friendly airmen by signalling lamps and flares, and by spreading white cloth on the ground, and these 'contact' patrols reported to headquarters by wireless or by dropping a message; but English two-seaters on contact patrols often carried bombs and attacked German troops, which meant that German scouts would have to fly low over the battlefield to destroy the two-seaters. So, Boelcke said, they must be trained to fight at all heights from the ground to 12,000 feet—the ceiling of their latest scout.

They began to talk about some of their opponents. The French venerated their successful scout pilots, called them 'aces' when they each had five victories (the top scorer being known as the ace of aces), and gave them much publicity. The best scout pilots in the French Air Service were usually sent to a famous squadron such as the *Cigognes*, from the stork emblem painted on their machines. René Fonck and Georges Guynemer began their great fighting careers with the Storks, and after

* The equivalent of a R.F.C. Squadron.

Guynemer's nineteenth success his scout was exhibited in Paris, where his admirers covered it with flowers. Boelcke did not like the ace system, for it tended to make a man an individualist, not a member of a team.

For the first time Boelcke heard of the rising English scout, Albert Ball. This was unusual, for Trenchard maintained a discreet silence about his outstanding scout pilots, because he thought the work of the two-seaters was just as dangerous, and that it would create ill-feeling to glamorise the scouts. As a result, the British public did not know one scout pilot from another unless he received a high decoration or, like Ball, featured in French newspapers when, at the beginning of September, 1916, they told their readers about the single-handed daring of the Nottingham boy. Then the world knew that Albert Ball had destroyed thirteen machines, damaged several others, shot down an observation balloon, and held the Distinguished Service Order and the Military Cross.

They told Boelcke they rarely met any Russians in the air. Their only danger, apart from engine failure, lay from anti-aircraft and machine-gun fire, and they knew there was little chance of survival at the hands of the Russians if they were brought down. One young pilot, Baron Manfred von Richthofen, choosing his words carefully before his idol, described some of his adventures and how some of the half-savage Asian tribes panicked and fled when attacked from the air. It was all very different from the hurly-burly of the Western Front, where, Richthofen recalled, he had been privileged to serve alongside the captain, who perhaps remembered him?

Boelcke had not forgotten the ambitious, eager young officer who stood before him. He knew Richthofen came of a prosperous Prussian family, had joined the cavalry before the war, and had then transferred to the air service as an observer. They had met for the first time at Metz, when Richthofen, inspired by Boelcke's record, decided that he too must become a pilot and fight in a Fokker. The change was not easy, for he came to grief on his first solo and soon afterwards failed his flying test; yet he persevered and eventually was allowed to fly two-seaters, being considered too ham-fisted for the sensitive and easily broken scouts. But Richthofen so thirsted for aerial combat that he rigged a machine gun on his slow two-seater and somehow contrived to shoot down an Allied aeroplane. From France he went to Russia and now, Boelcke knew, was obviously offering himself for service in the new *jagdstaffel*.

What of the character and temperament of this twenty-four-year-old, slim, intense lieutenant? Would he fit into the new *jagdstaffel*, a hunting pack of expert scouts? He, Boelcke, knew something of Richthofen's background, his passion for stalking and killing deer and wild boar in the brooding pine forests of east Germany. Richthofen would know all about the careful stalk, the long wait for the quarry, how to hide himself, and how to kill cleanly, and if he learned to apply these skills in the air he might be good. He would probably keep a level head in the rough and tumble of a dog-fight, and if he had the luck to survive his first few combats he might develop into a ruthless killer, for he was a killer by nature, and there would have to be some killing before the British were repelled on the Somme. Boelcke made his decision; if brother Wilhelm gave him a reasonable chit he would invite Richthofen to join him.

The two brothers talked after the others had gone to bed. Richthofen, Wilhelm said, had made a poor start to his flying, but he was getting better, and his heart was set on becoming a scout pilot. He showed little concern about the mechanical efficiency of his aeroplane, and Oswald would have to watch this and make Richthofen get some technical knowledge inside his thick skull, especially about the care of his guns. But with further training he ought to do well as a scout pilot.

There was another pilot, Wilhelm continued, who would give his right arm for a crack at the British. This was Erwin Böhme, an old man of thirty-seven summers but an exceptional pilot, full of courage, very fit, and a splendid chap. Oswald would be well advised to take him along. Böhme was loyal and trustworthy, and it was not a bad thing to have an old wolf with the cubs.

On the following morning Oswald Boelcke rose early, dressed in his best uniform with the blue and gold *Pour le Mérite* gleaming at his collar, and packed for his journey to France. Then he went to the quarters of Richthofen and Böhme and formally invited them to join *Jagdstaffel 2*. Both men accepted. Thus it was that the trio made their separate ways to Lagnicourt, their new airfield. Their destinies were strangely linked. Boelcke, master scout, leader, and tactician, was about to reach the pinnacle of his career. Richthofen was to become his most brilliant pupil and Böhme his closest friend. Both were with him when he fell.

Chapter 5

THE HUNTING PACK

DURING the early morning of 1st July, 1916, when the shelling reached its climax, the British infantry rose from their trenches and advanced towards the German positions. Machine guns, which had forced both sides to adopt trench warfare, began their hammering, and the slowly advancing lines of khaki were mown down. Other groups and lines of khaki took their places until they, too, were slaughtered; then the reserves, company after company, battalion after battalion, until there were no more and the machine guns fell silent. For this was the first day of the Battle of the Somme when Britain sustained 600,000 casualties—the flower of her youth and manhood:

> *What passing-bells for these who die as cattle?*
> *Only the monstrous anger of the guns.*
> *Only the stuttering rifles' rapid rattle*
> *Can patter out their hasty orisons.**

For the airmen it was different. How fortunately different is perhaps best illustrated by the story of the R.F.C. pilot and his observer who had to make a forced landing in enemy territory, for on the following day a German aeroplane flew over the R.F.C. airfield and dropped a photograph of the machine, pilot, and observer surrounded by their captors; and on the back of the photograph was written *Your friends are well.* And perhaps the spirit of the aviators is illustrated also by the R.F.C. pilot who made a crash-landing well behind the German lines and came to rest amid heaps of picks and shovels belonging to a German working party; the pilot poked his head out of the cockpit, grinned at the astonished Germans and shouted '*Guten morgen!*'

During the early stages of the battle R.F.C. two-seaters, co-operating with the infantry and artillery over the front lines,

* From *Anthem for Doomed Youth*, by Wilfred Owen.

42

were seldom harassed by German scouts; and in the back areas, including the airfield at Lagnicourt where Oswald Boelcke was trying to get *Jagdstaffel 2* operational, R.F.C. offensive patrols pinned down the German scouts.

At the beginning of September only three of Boelcke's new aeroplanes had arrived, but the remainder of his quota of fourteen would soon be ferried from Germany. He wanted his team to be ready to fight within two weeks if they were to play a decisive part in repelling the British before the bad weather set in and restricted their flying. Two weeks to get the feel of the new aeroplanes, for formation flying, tail chases, dog-fights, gun testing, aerobatics, lectures, and discussions. Two weeks should be long enough for such a programme, especially as most of his pilots had already proved their mettle on active service.

For some time the enemy had realised that the Fokker monoplane was no longer a match for the latest British scouts, and the new German squadrons were equipped with better fighting aeroplanes. *Jadgstaffel 2* received a remarkable new biplane which soon outclassed all contemporary British scouts; this was the Albatros D II, which carried the formidable armament of twin Spandau machine guns firing through the propeller. Other squadrons were supplied with another biplane, the Halberstadt D II, and Boelcke was delighted to learn that Anthony Fokker had produced a biplane, the Fokker D III, which also carried the twin Spandaus. Of these three fighting biplanes the Albatros was the best, for its 160-h.p. Mercedes engine gave it a speed of about 110 m.p.h. and a ceiling of 17,000 feet. Two Fokkers were sent to Lagnicourt, and Boelcke flew these so that his pupils could concentrate on their new Albatroses. In early September he celebrated his return to the front and the beginning of his third year of air fighting with his twentieth victory.

Archie showed him the way to a slow B.E. escorted by three scouts. He stalked the British formation and dropped on the reconnaissance machine from a long, slanting dive, but the escorting scouts saw the Fokker and turned to protect their comrade. Boelcke found himself at a disadvantage, forgot his quarry, and concentrated on getting away. One of the R.F.C. machines followed him, and the German used every artifice to lure the Englishman away from the front lines. He slackened his speed and let his enemy draw closer; he dropped a wing and, feigning damage to his Fokker, fell in a controlled side-slip towards the ground. The unsuspecting Englishman closed for the kill. Boelcke side-slipped another few hundred feet and, with twisted neck, never took his eyes off the Vickers. At the right moment he opened the throttle, dived to pick up speed, and reefed the Fokker into a steep climbing turn.

The Englishman had never seen such a fabulous turn of speed. Gamely he followed the strange, fast biplane into the turn, and opened fire, but his gun stopped after two rounds. Fifteen miles on the wrong side of the lines with a useless gun and facing a superior adversary, the Englishman was extremely poorly placed; he tried every trick in the book, but Boelcke sat on his neck and peppered him. Some of his controls were damaged, others were jammed, the throttle lever was shot away from his hand. Boelcke's bullets ripped through his clothing, his fuel tanks were punctured, and he was saturated with petrol.

There was no quarter asked or given in this fight to the finish. There was no chivalry—of which much nonsense has been written—for an almost vanquished foe. Boelcke fought to knock down an enemy machine. The Englishman strove to save his life, and with desperate strength slammed his machine on to the ground, where it burst into flames. The circling German watched the vanquished pilot jump clear and tear off a burning garment. Boelcke set course for Lagnicourt, where his pilots laughed at his comical appearance, for his chin was blackened by burnt powder from the breeches of his twin guns. He told one of his officers to drive to the crash, collect his opponent, and bring him to the mess for a glass of wine and a chat, and this gesture should not be credited to a code of chivalry—it was simply good manners.

The R.F.C. pilot proved to be Captain Robert Wilson, whose dismay at the prospect of spending the rest of the war in a prison camp was somewhat tempered when he found his victor was the great German pilot. Boelcke generously showed Wilson round the airfield, and afterwards they discussed their combat and the air fighting over the Somme. When Wilson left he took with him the memory of a great man. As for Boelcke, he decided to make some notes about his two years of air fighting so that he could bring his pilots right up-to-date.

The following morning he began his talk with a few words about their new aeroplanes, which were better than any Allied machine, and he stressed this point to make them confident. His pilots must learn all about the rigging of the airframe, and have a sound knowledge of the powerful Mercedes engine, so that they could carry out elementary repairs if they made a forced landing. They had to know how to handle the Albatros; its best speeds at all heights, its fighting ceiling, its radius of action, the limiting speed in a dive, its turning qualities, and how to side-slip and go into a controlled spin.

He spoke about shooting, for many pilots got into good firing positions and then failed to get their opponents. He told them how Max Immelmann destroyed two aeroplanes with twenty-six bullets, and this was a record they must all try to beat. Gun stoppages were too frequent, and their lives would depend on whether or not they could clear a stoppage in a matter of seconds—look at his fight yesterday when Wilson's gun jammed after only two rounds.

One of the secrets of air fighting was to see the other man first. Seeing aeroplanes from great distances was a question of experience and training, of knowing where to look and what to look for. Experienced pilots always saw more than the new-comers, because the latter were more concerned with flying than fighting. In a big scrap the veteran fought his own duel, but he also saw a great deal of the other combats and what he did not see he sensed, so that his mind followed the ever-changing pattern of the battle. But the novice had little idea of the situation, because his brain was bewildered by the shock and ferocity of the fight.

Boelcke said he wanted them to fly in the same positions, with Richthofen on his right, Reimann next to Richthofen, Böhme on the left, and so on, for the best team would always win an air battle. His own Albatros had a red nose and a red rudder, so that whenever they became separated in a fight they could see his machine and re-form. He had selected a number of rendezvous points on their side of the lines, and whenever they could not find him they were to make for the nearest rendezvous and circle at their patrol height or just below cloud —never immediately above cloud, for their machines could be seen for miles against the white background. Any pilot failing to find a comrade at the rendezvous was to return home, and not hang about looking for trouble.

Usually the leader would see aeroplanes before the other members of the formation because he was only concerned with a little navigation and a lot of looking, while the others devoted a lot of their time to keeping station and cross-covering the sky astern. When the leader gave the 'enemy sighted' signal all pilots were to hold their positions until the combined attack was launched, when they would select individual targets and manoeuvre accordingly. But sometimes a pilot other than the leader would be the first to spot the enemy, and he was to draw ahead, rock his wings, and turn towards the hostile formation: this would attract the attention of the leader, who would overtake him and resume control. His method of attack would depend on weather conditions and the number and type of enemy machines. Sun, haze, and clouds could all be used to gain surprise, so there could be no hard-and-fast rule about attacks, but whenever possible he, Boelcke, would attack from above.

A dog-fight, continued Boelcke, attracted much attention, for the falling, burning aeroplanes, the smoke from crashes, and Archie could be seen for miles, and scouts from both sides would join the party. Leaders always tried to get in at the top of a fight because height gave them time—to decide how to attack—and a good speed when they dived. Twenty-five or thirty machines would soon be fighting, and perhaps a better name for dog-fighting was a free-for-all. For it was a series of rushes, attacks, breakaways, and feints, sometimes followed by brief respites when the contestants sparred for an advantage. Then the tormented circling began again, with each trying to turn inside the other, and victory going to the pilot who kept his head. Dog-fighting between aeroplanes of about equal performance was a contest of flying ability, because good flying meant complete control of the aeroplane throughout all movements. Perfect control meant a steady gun platform for quick, decisive shooting. Men went berserk on the ground with a rifle or machine gun and sometimes lived to tell their tales, but cool heads were required in the air.

Sometimes they would be 'jumped'—surprised—when they were to turn and meet the attack. They would never get away by elaborate antics, such as loops or half-rolls, but were to turn, and keep turning, until there was a chance of a shot. The most important thing in air fighting was a pilot's ability to make steep turns without losing height.

During the first two weeks of September Boelcke continued to fly alone while he waited for the arrival of all his aeroplanes. He increased his score to twenty-six, and one day, ever mindful of his pupils, skilfully fought a Vickers fighter so that the pilot landed it intact and the captured machine was used to demonstrate its blind spots, turning qualities, and armament. The news that the great air fighter, already a national hero, was back at the front inspired the whole of the German Air Service. During this time of expansion and re-equipment new German scout squadrons were formed at the rate of about two each week, although the German Air Service in the Somme area was still considerably outnumbered by the Royal Flying Corps.

Early one morning seven Sopwith 'one and a half strutters' flew over Lagnicourt; they were led by Captain G. L. Cruikshank, a most experienced pilot whose great ambition was to meet Boelcke in the air. Boelcke and Richthofen were just about to fly when the Sopwiths flew overhead and headed west; by the time the two Germans were airborne the Sopwiths were out of sight, so Boelcke set a course in the same general direction and eventually caught up with the Sopwiths, but at a lower height. Cruikshank, keeping a good lookout, saw a Fokker biplane well below and seemingly at his mercy; he gave the attack signal, dived on the Fokker, and probably hoped that its pilot was the legendary Boelcke. The remaining six Sopwiths followed their leader, who was well in front, and Boelcke, calmly watching the proceedings, calculated that there was time to engage Cruikshank before the rest fell upon him and Richthofen. Then followed a short, brilliant duel in which the Fokker always out-climbed and out-turned the inferior Sopwith; the end came when Boelcke hammered fifty rounds into his opponent from a final range of twenty yards.

Soon some of the new Albatroses were serviceable, and on 17th September Boelcke decided that *Jagdstaffel 2* would fight together for the first time. After a careful briefing the most experienced scout pilot in the world led four of his officers on a patrol and marked another milestone in our story of air fighting. For this was the beginning of formation fighting by carefully selected and specially trained officers who flew good aeroplanes. This was teamwork in the air, and it was a historic step, because from it the air forces of the world evolved a great deal of their subsequent training and tactics.

Boelcke soon found eight bomb-carrying B.E.s escorted by six F.E.2bs, two-seater fighters. For some time he stalked the R.F.C. aeroplanes, until at 10,000 feet he positioned his section between his enemies and their line of retreat. When the leader of the R.F.C. force turned for home Boelcke, beautifully positioned up-sun, headed towards them in a gentle dive, because during this first fight together he wanted his pilots to see their enemies in good time and exactly how he brought them to battle. The R.F.C. aeroplanes droned steadily westwards; the F.E.s were taken by surprise, for Boelcke was able to draw very close before attacking the leader's machine, which he recognised by coloured streamers fastened to the wing struts.

Having watched his leader open fire, Richthofen selected and rushed at his own target, a two-seater fighter with guns firing forward and aft. It was a blundering, ill-judged attack, because as he approached from astern and at the same height the observer of the two-seater was able to line up his sights and fire at the Albatros; when he broke away from his attack in a climbing turn the observer swung his machine gun on its mounting and sent streams of lead at the German. Then there was the front gun to think about, for the pilot of the two-seater sometimes stood his aeroplane on its tail to get a crack at Richthofen, whose several attacks were met with excellent flying and stouthearted resistance. Despairing of a quick kill, Richthofen drew away from his determined opponent and thought about his next move, and for the first time during the combat he remembered Boelcke's teachings; he would appear to accept failure, but he would shadow the two-seater from a lower altitude, ease into the blind spot, and attack from beneath its tail, where the observer's gun could not reach him.

Several of the R.F.C. aeroplanes had been shot down, and the fight had attracted reinforcements from both sides. It was a dangerous arena for a solitary pilot, but Richthofen gave no thought to his own safety. He overtook the two-seater without being seen, closed to a deadly range, and raked its belly with his twin guns. He swerved sharply to avoid a collision, and when he looked again the propeller of the two-seater had stopped and the dying observer was slumped in his seat. The crippled aeroplane, its pilot mortally wounded, reared and then fell in a series of side-slips and spirals as the pilot struggled to regain a vestige of control. Richthofen, cold and intent, circled and watched his opponent suspiciously, but the English pilot only thought of getting down before he lost consciousness; somehow he gathered his strength for the final effort, landed in a field, and jolted to a standstill. Richthofen landed in the same field and joined some German infantry who were running to the British machine. They gently lifted the two officers from the bloodstained cockpit. Both were unconscious. The observer opened his eyes, saw the grim, smoke-blackened face of his conqueror, smiled, and died. The pilot was taken to the nearest dressing station, but was dead on arrival. Richthofen climbed back into his Albatros, flew low over his cheering compatriots, and set course for Lagnicourt.

Back at the airfield he found the others at breakfast. Each member of the patrol had destroyed a British aeroplane, five in all, and they heard Richthofen's account of his duel with the two-seater. Boelcke listened intently, because it was apparent that his pupil had made several gross errors and was lucky to have got back alive. His first attacks sounded extremely ham-fisted; here was no careful deliberation of the circumstances, but a succession of wild rushes at the two-seater. Obviously he completely forgot to clear his tail from time to time and hung about the combat area too long, although his final attack seemed accurate and well judged. Finally, although it was a great temptation, Richthofen was foolish to make wide sweeps around his falling enemy, since a hostile scout could easily have approached unseen and finished him. Boelcke decided to have a quiet talk with Richthofen, but for the present, and in front of the others, a word or two of encouragement was the thing.

The first team success of *Jagdstaffel 2*, against a superior force and seasoned opponents, in aeroplanes which had just arrived, was a splendid tonic not only for Boelcke's unit but for all the newly formed scout squadrons. By the end of September Boelcke's pilots had destroyed twenty-five aeroplanes for the loss of three pilots; and further, the rapid expansion of the fighter arm of the German Air Service meant that many other pursuit flights such as Boelcke's were in action on the Western Front, while others were forming. For the first time in many months the superiority of the R.F.C. was seriously challenged. R.F.C. casualities increased, German losses decreased, and their reconnaissance and contact patrol units ranged farther afield. Trenchard was gravely concerned about the superiority of the enemy's aeroplanes and skilful pilots. Owing to heavy losses, he, Trenchard, was obliged to curtail his long-distance fighting patrols, bombing operations, and reconnaissances, although he still relentlessly followed his offensive strategy, well illustrated by such a sharp attack against Lagnicourt that Boelcke was obliged to move his unit to another airfield. Unless the R.F.C. was provided with more squadrons and better aeroplanes, Trenchard recorded, it would soon lose its hard-won ascendency in the air.

Oswald Boelcke, with forty victories, including twenty in less than two months, fell at the end of October when this first slogging ground battle of the Somme was drawing to a close. He spent his last night with his friend Erwin Böhme listening to gramophone records; they went to bed fairly early, because both were suffering from the strain of much fighting. On the following morning Boelcke flew four times without claiming a victory. During the afternoon there was a telephone call from the German lines asking for air assistance. Boelcke jumped into his Albatros, and with Böhme, Richthofen, and three other pilots steered towards the front lines.

Above the grey clouds they found two de Havilland Scouts on patrol. Boelcke no doubt thought this an easy contest, and dived to attack the leading de Havilland, but the R.F.C. pilots saw the Albatroses and the wild circling began. Another German patrol of six scouts joined the mêlée, so that twelve German pilots each climbed, dived, and turned to try to hold a bead on one or the other of the two de Havillands. In a dog-fight such as this, when the odds are heavily on your side, there is a great temptation to lower your guard, to get in close, and hammer your enemy until he falls. Too many pilots concentrate on one target and forget to keep a sharp look-out for friend or foe; too many aeroplanes converge, in a dangerous funnelling-like movement, on the single quarry, and the risk of mid-air collision is high. Both Boelcke and Böhme fired at the same de Havilland. As they fired they converged and did not see each other. Böhme's undercarriage touched Boelcke's machine, and the latter's wing-tip of thin wooden spars, matchwood, and fabric was torn away.

Fighting to control his machine, Boelcke descended in wide, easy sweeps. The two de Havillands were forgotten and made their escape as the apprehensive German pilots watched their leader disappear into a layer of cloud. When Boelcke was next seen, below the cloud, the damaged wing had fallen away, probably due to the effect of increased pressures in the turbulent cloud. The Albatros crashed to the ground, and it was thought that Boelcke might have survived had he been properly strapped in the cockpit. But the safety straps were found to be unfastened, and he either forgot them during the hurried take-off or unfastened them in the air the better to look behind. Thus perished the greatest air fighter and patrol leader the war had yet seen.

Oswald Boelcke was one of the first practical airmen, Allied or German, to grasp the full significance of the military aeroplane and to study, develop, and apply the tactics and doctrine of air fighting that formed a sound basis for later development. When, during the early months of the war, he began to fly against the Allies, air fighting was regarded as something of a sporting joust between gentlemen, and not highly dangerous. At the time of his death team fighting was becoming a specialised form of air warfare, and the formation of the scout squadrons, in which he played a major part, was to have a profound influence on the war in the air; in short, it was he who gave the expression 'scout pilot' form and content. By imperial command his beloved unit was renamed *Jagdstaffel Boelcke*, but his death was a severe blow to the German scout squadrons, who took some time to recover that spirit of aggression that marked his zenith in the air. His character was suitably expressed in a message accompanying a wreath dropped by the Royal Flying Corps: *To the memory of Captain Boelcke, our brave and chivalrous opponent.*

Chapter 6

'REMEMBER BALL'

WHEN the First War was half over an R.F.C. pilot was required to have some twenty-eight hours solo flying before joining his squadron in France. Whenever possible the novices were given more training with their squadrons, but sometimes, during periods of heavy fighting, they were thrust immediately into the arena; having scant knowledge of any combat techniques and possessing little air experience, it was not surprising that the combat life of the newcomers sometimes averaged only a few hours.

The authorities were worried about our inadequate system of training, and during the autumn of 1916 various measures were introduced to improve the quality of the student pilots. One of these was the transfer of experienced air fighters from France to the training units; among them was the victor of thirty fights in the air, Captain Albert Ball, D.S.O. and two Bars, M.C.

Like many others, Ball found that teaching others to fly and to fight was exceedingly monotonous after the exciting life in a squadron. Instructing was, and is, a great and difficult art; it calls for a special mental approach, and few great combat pilots have ever made outstanding instructors. Certainly Ball was far from content with his lot; he constantly badgered his superiors to let him get back to a squadron or, failing that, to have a crack at the German airships who were making life unpleasant in England. Not even if one passes overhead, was the reply: the Home Defence squadrons would take care of the Zeppelins, and Captain Ball was to get on with his instructing.

For some time there had been sporadic airship raids on England, which caused little damage and few casualties, but the public were very apprehensive of these sinister, brooding monsters which prowled the night skies for hours at a time. The Zeppelin threat made Britain take some stock of her inadequate air defences, and in 1916 the Royal Naval Air Service assumed guardianship of the approaches to Britain, while Home Defence squadrons of the R.F.C. were made responsible for other districts; this organisation, the forerunner of Fighter Command, also included searchlights, sound locators, and anti-aircraft batteries.

Lieutenant W. Leefe Robinson had caught the imagination of the country when during the early hours of 3rd September, 1916, he won the Victoria Cross by shooting down a Zeppelin illuminated by searchlights, which subsequently burned on the ground for nearly two hours. Later *Kapitänleutnant* Heinrich Mathy, the greatest airship commander of the war, fell at Potters Bar; another was sent down in flames at Billericay, and a fourth had to land in Essex. The airships then turned from the strong London defences to raiding the North and the Midlands, but more were brought down, and the Germans realised that their Zeppelins were losing the contest; they began to think about aeroplane raids, and in November London had its first bomber attack. It was made by one machine, a two-seater having a 225-h.p. Mercedes engine, and the first that was known of its presence was at midday, when small bombs began to fall near Victoria Station; the German observer took some photographs of military camps and airfields, but these fell into R.F.C. hands when the pilot landed near Boulogne with engine trouble.

But the air war proper was being fought over France, and Ball wanted to get back before the season opened in the spring of 1917. It was common knowledge that the new German scouts were better than those of the R.F.C., so much better that Trenchard had obtained some Royal Naval Air Service squadrons, from the Navy's command near Dunkirk, to lend a hand on the Somme. Because of their long and happy relations with British industry, the Navy often procured better machines, especially better engines, than did the R.F.C., and their Sopwith 'Pups' (80-h.p. Le Rhone engine) and Sopwith Triplanes (130-h.p. Clerget engine) were good fighting machines. Both these scouts were tractors, both were delightful to fly and popular with their pilots; the Pup had a speed of some 106 m.p.h. and a ceiling of 17,000 feet, while the Triplane was slightly faster and could reach 20,000 feet.

It was also common knowledge that the mantle of Boelcke had fallen upon other outstanding leaders, and Ball was anxious to re-enter the lists and pit his own skill against these men. Only two pilots had shot down more aeroplanes than he; these were Oswald Boelcke, with forty victories, and France's famous Georges Guynemer, with thirty-seven victories. Continually in his letters and conversations Ball expressed his great ambition to become the world's top scorer. This concern with their personal scores and their position on the scoreboard was characteristic of some of the great air fighters. Certainly it was an obsession with Richthofen, who solemnly presented himself with suitably engraved silver cups to mark each victory, and also with Ball, whose letters* often contained such phrases as 'only three more to be got and I am top of England and France again' or 'two more to beat the Frenchman'.

Towards the end of February, 1917, Ball was posted to 56 Squadron as a flight commander, and was soon busy preparing to move to France. The squadron was equipped with the latest scout, the S.E.5, a tractor-biplane whose 150-h.p. Hispano-Suiza engine gave it a top speed of about 120 m.p.h. and a ceiling of 18,000 feet. It carried two machine guns, and the Vickers

* *Captain Albert Ball, V.C.*, pp. 247 and 251.

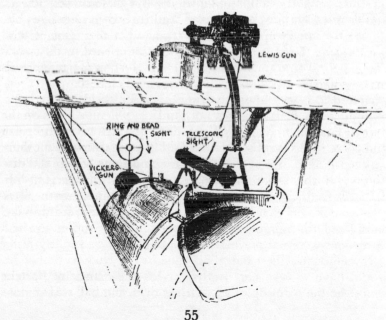

was synochronised to fire through the propeller by means of the new Constantinesco gear. The other gun, the reliable Lewis, was attached to the top mainplane and fired over the propeller; it could be pulled down on a quadrant mounting so that drums of ammunition could be changed in the air and the gun fired in this position. Once its teething troubles were over the S.E. became one of the finest scouts of the Kaiser's War; it was strong, manoeuvrable, stable, and had no vices—a good thing for the hastily trained youngsters who flew it in combat.

As a flight commander Ball would have far more responsibility than on his previous tour in France. He would be one of three junior commanders who, now that scout squadrons had eighteen machines, were each responsible to their squadron commander for a flight of six S.E.s, for the training of their pilots, and for the efficiency and care of their ground crews. Once in France, he would lead his flight on offensive patrols of about two hours duration. He would average about two patrols a day, and sometimes these would be flown in squadron strength with as many aeroplanes as possible.

Apart from the patrols planned and ordered by wing headquarters, squadron commanders of the R.F.C. had wide powers and were encouraged to plan and lead their own offensive missions. One squadron commander trained his new pilots with a late evening, low-level cruise parallel to the lines, with an occasional foray into enemy territory, which increased in depth as his boys gained experience; another, with a more seasoned unit, preferred to have a look at various enemy airfields in the hope of finding Germans taking-off or landing, while a third, whenever he failed to find enemy formations, split his team into pairs and encouraged them to attack suitable ground targets on their way home. The size of these freelance missions was at the discretion of the squadron commander, and experienced air fighters could operate alone. On the other hand, German pilots were encouraged to make volunteer flights, but two scouts were considered the minimum for a tactical unit, and individual operations were not normally permitted.

It seemed to Albert Ball that when he got back to France he would have to take part in two styles of air fighting. There would be the team fighting, and his own solitary, roving missions. Brother pilots who had seen his flights of last year said that he was the quickest scout pilot in France, but this mode of combat, he realised, would be quite impossible when leading his flight. A formation of four or five aeroplanes was far harder to hide against earth, cloud, or sun than a solitary machine and therefore surprise, the essence of a successful attack, would be more difficult. He would have to wait for stragglers and inexperienced pilots who could not hold a steady formation; when attacking from a diving turn or a wide curve of pursuit he would have to throttle back so that his flankers would have sufficient power in hand to keep abreast. This meant that a team attack would take far more time than the flat-out, stooping dive of a single scout. More time usually meant less surprise; and he had to remember that he must always look after his boys in a dog-fight and was morally responsible for getting them home.

Each day he would try to find time for a crack against the Huns on his own; there would also be many occasions when the weather would be unfit for formation patrols and he would be able to slip across the lines and see what was afoot. A lot of people tried to tell him that the day of the lone wolf was over, that formations would tend to get bigger and bigger, and that air battles with fifty aeroplanes on either side would be commonplace. Well, the bigger the Hun formation the better as far as he was concerned. Such tactics would concentrate the Huns into large, unwieldy, conspicuous gaggles, and they would be so busy watching each other that a man could be in and away before they knew what had hit them!

When they arrived in France Richthofen's name seemed to be on everybody's lips, for the German pilot sometimes averaged one R.F.C. machine destroyed each day. His victims were often two-seaters, B.E.s and R.E.8s (known as 'Harry Tates'), and his favourite attack was to fire from behind and below into the belly of the machine so that the R.F.C. observer could not fire at him. There were many who tried to belittle Richthofen's great achievements because of his lack of sportsmanship in singling out the B.E.s, and who held that any air fighter worth his salt would go for a scout rather than the slow, clumsy two-seaters. Such opinions were absolute nonsense, because Richthofen realised that the Royal Flying Corps was the servant of the British Army and that the main task of the R.F.C. was to provide various forms of reconnaissance for the soldiers; it was the British reconnaissance aeroplanes, not the single-seaters, which did the real damage, and since Richthofen's job was to get on with the winning of the war, he went for the two-seaters whenever possible.

Richthofen was no great exponent of aerobatics, and based his tactics on good flying and accurate firing from short ranges. In a dog-fight he was steady rather than brilliant, and yet when the occasion demanded, his inner compulsion to kill made him a cold, ruthless opponent, and this aspect of his character was well illustrated when he shot down one of our most experienced air fighters, Major L. G. Hawker, V.C., D.S.O. During some preliminary fighting Richthofen and Hawker became separated from their comrades and fought a duel that lasted thirty minutes and finished a few feet above the ground, when Hawker was mortally wounded.

He was ambitious, and with fourteen victories began to wonder why he had not been awarded the *Pour le Mérite*; after all, Boelcke and Immelmann had each won the same decoration with only eight victories! But soon after he was awarded the coveted decoration and given command of his own unit, *Jagdstaffel 11*. At last he was a hero of the Fatherland; but his burning ambition was whetted, not appeased.

As commander of his own *jagdstaffel* Richthofen had more opportunity than ever before to increase his score. He could authorise volunteer patrols and lead them when he thought fit. During March his pride was shaken when his machine was hit in a dog-fight and he had to make a forced-landing, but he was soon in the air again, and at the end of the month his score was thirty-one. The tempo of air fighting was increasing not only because of more and faster scouts and experienced leaders but also because both sides introduced elementary warning systems to help their pilots find enemy formations.

The Germans relied upon telephones and field glasses in the hands of trained observers spaced at regular intervals along the front lines. These observers reported the movements of Allied aeroplanes to various centres, where the information was filtered and then telephoned to the nearest airfield for possible action. It was a crude system, but it gave some warning of the assembly of large raiding formations and their height and course, and as some of the German airfields were only a few miles behind the lines, a section of their scouts about to take-off could act on this information. The enemy ground observers reported any low-level activity by our contact patrols or reconnaissance missions. They also watched the progress of dog-fights fought below 5,000 or 6,000 feet and confirmed claims of individual pilots, especially if they flew vividly coloured aeroplanes.

The R.F.C. knew it was possible to find the direction from which wireless waves were received, and wireless interception stations were set up to listen for enemy machines. These bearings were telephoned to wing headquarters, where the cross bearings were plotted on a map, and the position of the enemy machine was telephoned to a nearby squadron where scouts were ready to take-off. The interception stations also placed white strips of cloth on the ground which gave R.F.C. pilots, when they flew overhead, the latest bearing and the number of enemy machines. Air fighting was becoming less haphazard than before.

Richthofen and his men seemed to be here, there and everywhere. In the air he was a marked man because when flying with his squadron his scarlet Albatros stood out like a blood-red hawk among pigeons. His opponents dubbed him the 'Red Knight' and *Le Petit Rouge*, and his pilots, fearing for his safety, asked for permission to paint their own machines; this Richthofen allowed, but with the reservation that his was to be the only all-red aeroplane. His brother Lothar, who also served in *Jagdstaffel 11*, flew a red scout with yellow control surfaces, while another pilot favoured the same colour but with black controls. Other German scout squadrons were quick to follow suit, and soon the most extraordinary colour schemes were seen in the air.

One Albatros was painted an almost feminine pink, and the pilot who flew it had a round, girlish face. The R.F.C. pilots soon dubbed it 'The Pink Lady', and for a short time she was as legendary as the tottering Virgin atop of the church spire at

Albert whose fall would signal the end of the war. The super-
stition about the Pink Lady was that she was flown by a beautiful German girl determined to avenge her lover who had been
killed in the air fighting. The story was quite untrue, because
when the Pink Lady was eventually shot down her dead pilot
proved to have a very distinguished record.

During April Richthofen shot down twenty R.F.C. machines,
and the intensity of the air fighting can be judged from Leefe
Robinson's encounter with the Baron. Robinson was leading six
of our new 120-m.p.h. two-seater Bristol Fighters (250-h.p.
Rolls-Royce engine) when he met Richthofen at the apex of
five Albatroses. Four Bristols were brought down, and of the
two that got back one was much shot about. Robinson was
made a prisoner (he died of influenza shortly after the war
ended), and Richthofen became the world's top scorer with
forty-three victories. His ambition was to top the hundred mark,
and he was to come near to it.

'Bloody April', the greatest ordeal ever endured by the Royal
Flying Corps and the second period of German air superiority,
was about half over when 56 Squadron began to fight. Naturally Trenchard wanted his new scouts to have a go at Richthofen, and it was decided that a flight of old pusher F.E.s would
fly over Douai, lure Richthofen and his men into the air, when
the S.E.s would drop from the sun and have a party. The
pushers were led by Lieutenant Tim Morice (who won his
M.C. soon afterwards, and a D.S.O. in the Second War), and
when they arrived over Douai the Baron and his men, true to
form, climbed to attack the pushers. All was set for the new
British scouts to pounce, but they never arrived, and the F.E.s
were in serious trouble.

Morice put his pushers into a defensive circle and hoped this
would give them some protection until help arrived. The Baron,
in his red machine, flew round the pushers just out of range,
while he decided how to attack, shook his fist at Morice, and
made rude signs with his fingers. Suddenly a juicy Hun two-
seater droned straight and level beneath the pushers and one
R.F.C. pilot, seeing the chance of a victory, left the circle, and
chased the Hun. Quick as a flash, the Baron was into the gap
and the fight was on.

Some of the Albatroses followed Richthofen, while others circled above and kept guard. Two pushers were soon shot down. Morice's observer managed to damage a couple of Huns before the Baron appeared from nowhere, head-on, with his twin Spandaus blazing. Their instrument panel was blown to bits, and pieces scattered all over the cockpit. The radiator, immediately behind Morice, was punctured in several places and blew out such vast quantities of steam that he thought the water-cooled engine would soon seize-up. Richthofen had aimed and fired wonderfully well, but both pilot and observer were unhurt, so Morice dived away, turned towards the British lines, and was immediately set upon by a brace of Fokkers. The Fokker pilots, who were waiting to finish off any damaged R.F.C. machines, were not very good and the observer, looking backwards over the engine, was able to judge each attack and tap his pilot on the side of his helmet to indicate which way to

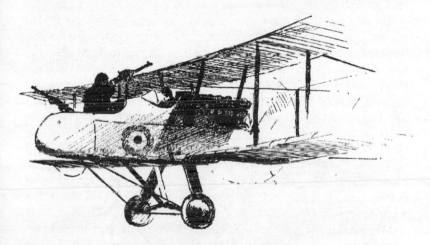

turn and meet the attack. But even when they turned to face the Fokkers they could not do very much, for they were out of ammunition, so they fired Very lights and the Fokkers sheered off.

The pusher was forced lower and lower, the engine got hotter and hotter, the enemy scouts still attacked, and Morice's excited observer struck him several sharp blows on the head. They were dangerously low with a faltering engine, but the lines were only a hundred yards ahead. Morice had to work desperately hard to keep control, and after a particularly hard blow from his alarmed observer he responded with a tremendous clout on the jaw, and seconds later they crashed among some British gunners. Before they could struggle from the wreckage an irate, red-faced colonel rushed up and shouted: 'You've ruined my telescopic sight! The only —— telescopic sight in France!' and then seeing their plight. 'I say, are you chaps all right?'

But Albert Ball showed that the Albatros was not invincible when, flying alone, he spotted a few of these enemy scouts, tackled the nearest, and sent it down in flames, and although the remaining enemy pilots gave him a hard time, hitting his machine many times before he got away, the encounter made little difference to his simple tactics, which were always to attack the enemy—regardless of their height and numbers. He

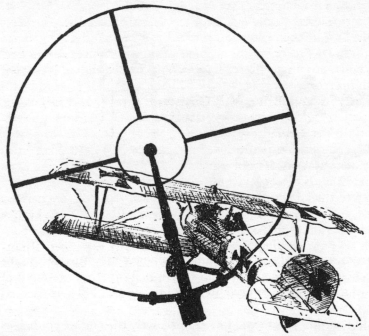

had no apparent fear and was very confident of his own ability. Towards the end of April he averaged a Hun a day, and when he brought back a damaged machine he immediately climbed into another and returned to the fray.

Ball never flew for pleasure, but only on patrols or to test his machine. On air tests he sometimes threw an old newspaper out of the cockpit and fired at this small target as it drifted down. Sometimes he removed the machine guns from his S.E., took them to his room, and attended to them as other men would care for a pair of sporting guns made by James Purdy.

Shooting down eight aeroplanes in six days, Ball's victories mounted at about the same rate as those of France's ace of aces, the frail Georges Guynemer. There was a certain rivalry between these two great pilots, which became more intense when their personal scores neared the half-century mark. Both men were individualists, and both were excellent shots. Both pilots were contemptuous of heavy odds, but Guynemer took even more risks than Ball, and several times only a kindly providence saved him from destruction. His famous Spad, *Vieux Charles*, was often riddled with bullets, but such was his hatred for the Germans that he took little notice of his comrades' advice for more caution. Day after day he tackled strong enemy formations and his crash-landings, after being shot-up in dog-fights, increased with his score.

Early in May Ball passed Guynemer's score, and this called for a tremendous celebration. Hurried invitations were phoned to all the local squadrons and nearby army units. The bar officer produced suitable quantities of champagne. The squadron band was alerted, and the old songs and the new flying songs were sung. Some officers spun in, and others were detailed to get them to their beds. Ball fetched his violin, lit a red magnesium flare, and started to play. Other flares were lit, and it was hardly surprising that some of the hutted quarters were burnt down.

It was an excellent party. Now there only remained Richthofen, who had just shot down four in one day and had brought his score to fifty-two. He would like to meet the Baron! He had seen him in the air, but had never managed to get a bead on him. Once Maxwell and he had splitarsed with a dozen Huns, including an all-red Albatros, but there was no hope of getting him in their sights. There were reports that the Baron had been sent on leave and that his brother, Lothar, had assumed temporary command of *Jagdstaffel 11*; if this were true it would be a good thing to pass the Baron's score before he returned to the fighting.

Ball, forty-four victories, was delighted to see the Germans were flying in larger formations than ever before, because they could be seen from greater distances. Trenchard had, however, to counter these massed enemy formations and on the evening of 7th May, 1917, it was decided to send up two scout squadrons, including 56, to patrol Richthofen's airfield at Douai.

There was a lot of cloud, both layered and heaped, so that on the climb to patrol height they dodged and threaded their way through slowly moving rifts and canyons. This sort of combat flying, sometimes in cloud and sometimes in the clear air sandwiched between banks of cloud, was highly dangerous. They never knew if an ambush lay round the corner, and when they popped out of the white bubbling vapour their chocolate-coloured S.E.s were most conspicuous.

It was impossible for them to remain together. Soon the ten S.E.s split into three sections and patrolled independently. Ball found a gap at 7,000 feet and steered a course towards Douai; two other pilots were still with him. As they got deeper into enemy territory the cloud below broke up and they caught occasional glimpses of the ground, but as the evening wore on the visibility worsened.

As expected, *Jagdstaffel 11* was in the air. Lothar von Richthofen was leading in his red-and-yellow Albatros, but he had wisely split his force into three sections. The six sections, three British and three German and one lone Spad, threaded their way through the valleys, ravines, and towering alps of the evening sky. When they flew to the west they steered towards a vivid layer of golden light, but when they turned about it was much darker. The sections met, skirmished, fought, broke away, and re-formed. An S.E. fell away, spinning, an aileron came off, and the pilot jumped to certain death, if not already dead. A red-and-green Albatros went down in flames. The leaders tried to hold their small sections together. Curtains of rain further reduced the visibility, and there was more luck than judgement in such close terrier-like fighting.

Some pilots, having lost their leaders, returned. 56 Squadron was badly split up, but this had been foreseen, and the rendezvous was over Arras. Ball fought his way there, re-formed the squadron, now numbering only five, and flew on after his enemies. They found four German scouts, and in the dog-fight became separated once more. Alone, young Ball flew his indomitable patrol. He fired some flares, and these attracted another flight commander, Captain 'Billy' Crowe, who joined up, but Ball did not appear to see him.

In the fading light they flew through some cloud, and when they emerged Crowe saw Ball chasing an enemy machine, which disappeared into more cloud, followed closely by Ball. Crowe followed too, but on breaking cloud could see neither friend nor foe and, wisely, went home.

Ball was never seen alive again, and for some years the circumstances of his death remained a mystery. But later it was found that his scout was brought down by a machine gun mounted on the tower of a church, and the Germans buried him near Lille—where he still lies. Others had fought more cautiously than lion-hearted Albert Ball. None had fought harder. He relied above all on the surprise that comes of daring. His courage did more than anything else to revive the morale of the R.F.C. He was posthumously awarded the Victoria Cross. He was such an inspiration to those who followed that one of the leading scout pilots of 1918 pinned on his instrument panel a card bearing the words:

> *He must fall*
> *Remember*
> *BALL*

Chapter 7

THE CIRCUS

THE casualties suffered by the Royal Flying Corps during 'Bloody April' 1917, while supporting the British Army at the Battle of Arras, were the highest of the First War. Encouraged by Richthofen's victories, the enemy scout squadrons fought bravely and pushed the air fighting from their rear areas to the front lines. But at the beginning of May their efforts fell off, and the Kaiser's War never saw a similar period of German air supremacy.

More R.F.C. squadrons were forming, and the flow of better and faster machines continued. 56 Squadron received its first S.E.5a, whose 200-h.p. Hispano-Suiza engine gave it more speed and a better ceiling than the previous model. Those squadrons who had fought for some time had gained much valuable experience in the handling and servicing of their aero-

planes; engine troubles and gun stoppages were fewer than before. Meeting less opposition in the air, Trenchard ordered his scouts to carry out low-level attacks against opportunity targets such as enemy troops, transports, and machine-gun positions.

I have already explained how during the Somme fighting of the previous year the R.F.C. introduced contact patrols and how, as a secondary duty, the two-seaters carrying out these patrols were permitted to bomb or strafe targets of opportunity. The introduction of scouts to such low-level bombing and strafing was an important development in the story of air fighting, because scouts were now dual-purpose. To give them more striking power in their new role a few small bombs were carried on the lower mainplane, which gave the pilot a choice of weapons—machine guns or bombs—against different targets.

These low-flying attacks fell into two categories. Those which gave immediate support to our troops required careful planning and co-ordination between the troops and the pilots if the best results were to be obtained. Low-level bombing and strafing had a demoralising effect on German troops, but rapid follow-up action by our infantry was necessary before the effects of the air attack dissipated. Trenchard, that steadfast disciple of offensive action, advised his pilots 'to cross the line very low and then shoot everything . . . to harass the enemy and spoil the morale of his troops'.* Such operations were dangerous because the pilots had to fly low over areas where both machine-gun and rifle fire were highly concentrated; none the less, they did their best because they knew they were helping their comrades on the ground. In 1917 this type of air support was known simply as ground strafing; today similar missions are known as close air support operations.

The other type of low-level attack took the pilots well beyond the trenches. They crossed the lines at a reasonable height, where only Archie could reach them, eased down their scouts to a hundred feet or so above the ground, and attacked reserve troops, transport, barges, low-flying aeroplanes, parked aeroplanes, hangars, and workshops. They were not so dangerous as close support flights, because there was less small-arms fire in

* *The War in the Air*, Vol. IV, p. 129.

the rear areas; today they are known as harassing and indirect air support operations.

Scouts used on either close or harassing operations were called bomb-loaded fighters, but much later, during the Second War, they received a far better name, fighter-bombers. Trenchard realised that here was perhaps the most flexible instrument of air power, because the low-level operations did not interfere too much with the scout's primary task of air fighting. Bombs could be jettisoned before a dog-fight, but if the enemy could not be found in the air the patrol was not wasted as all manner of targets could be beaten-up on the way home.

The Germans attached such importance to close air support operations that they formed special units, *schlachtstaffeln* (battle flights), each of six two-seater aeroplanes whose crews were trained to attack targets with machine guns, bombs, and hand grenades. Whenever possible the *schlachtstaffeln* operated in formations of not less than four aeroplanes. At this time the difference between German and British thinking on this subject was that the enemy raised special units, while Trenchard regarded it as a secondary duty of his scout squadrons.

The S.E.s of 56 Squadron were often used as fighter-bombers and, since their airfield was only some forty miles from that housing Richthofen's *Jagdstaffel 11*, it was only natural that the high-spirited youngsters should try and attack the Albatroses on the ground. They soon found that such attacks called for great skill, not only to overcome the problems of low-level navigation but also because enemy airfields were very active and their scouts were flying in greater numbers than ever before. Sometimes as many as twenty were seen sweeping the battle area, and this was a big change in tactics from their usual eight or nine.

These first big formations were dubbed 'Richthofen's Circus' because the red aeroplanes of *Jagdstaffel 11* were present on these occasions. However, the records show that these early sweeps were temporary groupings of various units. Shortly afterwards, convinced that they were tactically correct, the German Air Service formed the first permanent *jagdgeschwader** of scouts,

* *Jagdgeschwader Number One* (*J.G.1*), comprised *Jagdstaffeln 4, 6, 10,* and *11*.

whose job was to win the air battle. Like Boelcke's old unit at Metz, *J.G.1* was given ample transport and personnel so that it could move rapidly from one sector to another. As the aeroplanes of the four squadrons were painted all the colours of the rainbow, 'Circus' was indeed an appropriate name. Manfred von Richtohfen was recalled from leave to command and lead it.

In addition to their scouts German bombers were flying in large numbers, as that experienced air fighter James McCudden, aged twenty-two and now employed as an instructor, discovered by chance on a hazy day in June. He landed his Sopwith Pup at Croydon, where he was told that a hostile formation had crossed the coast and was heading for London. He took fifteen minutes to fly back to his own airfield in Kent, where a machine gun was fitted to its mounting on the Pup. Grabbing three drums of ammunition, he took off, climbed through the clouds, and spotted some anti-aircraft bursts, which directed him to fourteen twin-engined Gothas, who, at 15,000 feet, were holding a steady formation on their homeward journey after bombing the City and the East End of London. The Gothas seemed to be as fast as the Pup and, although McCudden chased them over the North Sea, he could not close to a killing range and had to be content with some ineffective long-range shooting. This was the first big daylight raid against London, and the Gothas killed one hundred and sixty-two people. For all that ninety two British machines went up to attack all the Gothas returned safely. So great was the public clamour that two of the most efficient fighting squadrons were temporarily withdrawn from Flanders to repel any similar raids.

Soon after this raid McCudden was sent to France on a Refresher Course; the idea of this short detachment was that experienced instructors should visit and fight with a squadron for a few weeks so that they could bring themselves up to-date with the latest trends in air fighting, which they could then pass on to their pupils. McCudden found himself at an airfield which housed four squadrons, including 56, and there was a constant coming and going of S.E.s, Pups, Spads, and the new Sopwith 'Camels', which were the first R.F.C. Scouts to carry twin side-by-side Vickers machine guns. McCudden thought the Camel a match for any enemy scout, but it had one or two vices and was tricky to fly.

Apart from McCudden's present assignment, he was vastly interested in the different squadrons, for he would soon be coming back to France for his third tour. He thought that 56 Squadron was the best outfit he had ever seen. They had excellent aeroplanes, a sound ground organisation, and a wonderful orchestra. But, above all, the warm interlocking comradeship could be felt immediately he entered their mess, and this was largely the result of the brilliant records and personalities of the flight commanders, especially Gerald Maxwell, who had taken over Ball's flight. There were several promising youngsters, including Rhys-Davids, with seven victories, and McCudden resolved to join this happy team. Meanwhile, he had to bring his knowledge of air fighting up-to-date.

The most noticeable change since McCudden's previous tour of duty in France was that there was more team fighting and less individual scouting over Hunland. When things were slack pilots could patrol alone, but except for engine trouble, they were not allowed to break formation and go Hun-hunting. The flight was the tactical unit, and most of the patrolling by friend and foe was carried out by flights of five or six machines, but the trend was towards bigger formations, and sometimes the Germans put thirty or forty scouts into the air.

These big enemy packs were not seen very often, and then usually during the late evening when Richthofen assembled his Circus and patrolled on his side of the lines looking for trouble. R.F.C. scout leaders led from the bottom of their formations, where everyone could see and follow them, but one evening the Baron, in his all-crimson Albatros, was seen to dive from the very top of the pack and shoot down a British machine. Other British pilots had seen the same ruse, and although Richthofen was also seen at the bottom of his Circus, he sometimes delegated the lead to a trusted deputy while he remained on top with a few selected comrades to collect easy victims.

Thirty or forty enemy scouts would be difficult to handle, and even when they were in a good attacking position the best leader in the world could not hold them together in any subsequent flight. Since the Circuses assembled only in good weather they could be seen for miles, and there was less danger from small enemy patrols tucked away in the sun. The Circuses looked frightening, but the real fighting took place when flight met flight.

McCudden learned that to counter the Circuses R.F.C. scouts sometimes flew in squadron strength of fifteen or sixteen machines. Until wireless linked all scouts the greatest number of machines one man could control was about six, but three flights could be co-ordinated, if not controlled, by a leader. Experienced leaders thought that the best squadron formation was of three flights, each flight flying its usual vic pattern. The squadron commander led the lowest flight, and the other two flights were higher and echeloned two or three hundred yards away on either side. The highest flight was the above guard, or reserve, and only came down when a fight below was getting out of hand.

Soon McCudden's wish came true, and he was posted to 56 Squadron, as a flight commander. He found the evening patrols were popular with both sides, for the air was less turbulent than when the sun was high, and the lowering sun offered little tactical advantage to either side.

A big dog-fight resulted from the assembly of many small formations and McCudden, who gave much thought to these things, liked to cruise his little band well over Hunland and then, hoping for surprise, headed towards the Ypres Salient, where the British lines thrust towards the enemy. Once, from afar, McCudden saw bunches of black specks, well silhouetted against a golden band of evening sky, moving slowly across the horizon, and when he got nearer he thought about fifty aeroplanes were sandwiched between 12,000 and 18,000 feet and many more below. This particular air battle, typical of those fought over Polygon Wood at this time, seemed to have a base five or six miles across where the fighting seemed fiercest. Then the contest tapered away to a narrow apex, where it burst open, like the anvil head of a thunder cloud, as eighteen or twenty scouts jockeyed for height; and like a cumulus cloud the air battle drifted slowly across the countryside, its shape ever changing as sections climbed and dived, joined and separated, fought and broke away.

The highest scouts looked like the new Fokker Triplanes,*
seven or eight of them painted red in kind, but each bearing
small distinguishing marks—a white tail, a blue rudder, green

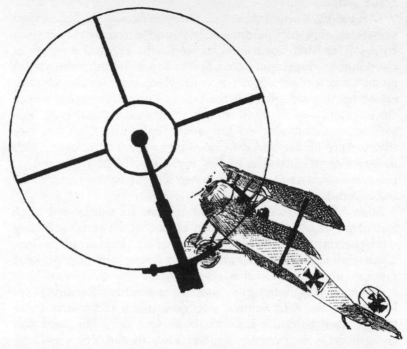

ailerons—to set them apart from their master, whose crimson
machine could not be seen; but all very experienced from the
way they threw their mounts around the sky. The Triplanes had
a fabulous climb and also an ugly reputation for falling to pieces
when heavily stressed.

McCudden worked his way round the fringes of the battle.
He wanted to bring off one of those rarities, a formation attack
on four of the new Pfalz† scouts, but his flight was jumped and
badly split up by four or five Triplanes, and McCudden had to
resort to a long spin to get out of serious trouble. He recovered

* A single-seat triplane (110-h.p. Le Rhone engine), with twin Spandau
guns and a ceiling of 18,000 feet.
† A single-seat biplane (160-h.p. Mercedes engine), with twin Spandau
guns and a ceiling of 17,000 feet.

at 7,000 feet, where the milling, turning machines looked like a beehive, cleared his tail and slipped away, for caution was his watchword, and he never allowed bloodthirstiness to cloud his better judgement.

Once a pilot was separated from his section, these massive dog-fights were very dangerous, as Richthofen discovered when eight of his Albatroses attacked six slow F.E.s. The R.F.C. two-seaters adopted a defensive circle, and this was a cunning move, because most of their blind spots were covered either by the aeroplane ahead or that behind. As usual, the circling machines attracted others, more German patrols arrived, and some Sopwith Triplanes came to help the two-seaters. Two F.E.s and four German scouts had already gone down when Richthofen, manoeuvring to get on the tail of a F.E., was hit by a bullet which ripped open his skull and splintered the bone. Temporarily blinded and paralysed, his red Albatros spun down out of control but, regaining his senses, he was able to crash-land before he fainted again. Within a few weeks he was fighting once more.

Soon afterwards one of Richthofen's ablest lieutenants was shot down in one of the greatest air fights of the First War. This was Werner Voss, the experienced commander of *Jagdstaffel 10*, who had flown with Boelcke. Searching for his forty-ninth victory, Voss was alone in his silver-blue Fokker Triplane when he fastened on to a solitary S.E. Meanwhile McCudden, who had re-formed his flight after destroying a two-seater, was about to attack six Albatroses, when he spotted the Fokker glued to the tail of the unfortunate S.E. Abandoning the Albatros, McCudden attacked Voss from one side, while Rhys-Davids, quick to seize the opportunity, opened fire from the other. Realising his danger, Voss evaded the seven S.E.s with great skill; he could not escape the faster S.E.s by diving away, and neither could he exploit the climbing qualities of his Fokker, because already a Spad formation was circling overhead holding off the six Albatroses. The only hope for Voss was to turn inside the S.E.s until the arrival of more patrols, and then to escape during the usual shambles.

Assistance did arrive in the form of a red-nosed Albatros whose pilot attempted to guard Voss's tail and the German ace, not content with defensive tactics, took some snap shots and hit some of the S.E.s. After some minutes, however, the Albatros was shot down, and again the S.E.s concentrated against Voss. Once McCudden saw five of his pilots firing simultaneously at the German, who flew with wonderful skill. Eventually the gallant Voss was forced down to a low altitude, and McCudden, having drawn apart to change a drum, studied his opponent and noticed that the Tripe's movements were somewhat erratic. Then Rhys-Davids, guns blazing, got behind Voss, and the Tripe fell into a steep dive, struck the ground, and exploded.

So perished Werner Voss in a magnificent fight against odds. That evening the pilots of 56 Squadron debated the identity of their stout-hearted foe. On the following morning they learned that he was Voss, and when congratulated the young Rhys-Davids echoed all their thoughts: 'Oh, if I could only have brought him down alive.'

The winter of 1917 brought the customary grey skies and poor visibility, and the air fighting slackened, but when the weather was suitable the enemy sent over reconnaissance two-seaters who, flying alone at 20,000 feet, thought themselves immune from the attentions of R.F.C. scouts, whose fighting ceiling, like that of German scouts, was 2,000 or 3,000 feet lower. Single-seater combats rarely took place above 16,000 feet and, as the weather became colder, fewer German scouts were seen at this altitude. Even so McCudden found that the S.E. was a reasonably warm and comfortable machine, and on a cold day he could remain aloft for two hours. He thought that something should be done about the impudent Hun two-seaters and, by tuning his engine and saving weight here and there, he found he could coax his machine to 20,000 feet. He paid special attention to his guns and synchronising gear, because icing would mean more stoppages than usual.

McCudden found that the Army had improved on their wireless interception system of reporting enemy air activity. All the information was now centralised, and enemy air movements were continuously plotted throughout the day at various control posts. Patrol leaders had only to telephone their control post to obtain detailed and up-to-date information and, if they operated from one of the recently constructed advanced landing grounds, sited close to the front lines, the time taken to intercept was reduced, and the number of combats increased.

These two-seaters, McCudden reasoned, did not fly to fight, but to carry out some important reconnaissance mission. The best time to attack was when the enemy observer was taking photographs and the pilot was fully occupied flying an accurate course. It was vastly different from the swift thrust and parry, the hurly-burly and the intoxication of scout fighting. It called for cunning, patience, and endurance, all of which he possessed in abundance, and sometimes he would stalk a Hun for an hour before sliding, unseen, into a firing position. It also called for flying skill, for often he had to climb through much cloud to get at his enemies. He flew alone on these patrols, because even two S.E.s had difficulty in sticking together at this height, and one machine, making flat skidding turns, exposed less reflecting wing area than two. The form was to sit high in the sun, spot the Hun, let him cross the lines, and knock him down on our side of the lines. Then McCudden liked to land alongside his victim to talk with the German airmen, and to collect a souvenir before the Tommies stripped the machine.

Some of these two-seaters carried armour plating and were difficult to bring down. The morale of the crews was very good, and when attacked they usually fought well. McCudden shared Ball's opinion that an enemy two-seater when properly handled was more than a match for a single scout. The scout pilot should not allow the engagement to develop into a shooting match, but should surprise the Hun, kill the observer, and finish off the defenceless pilot.

Having achieved surprise, the finest pilot on earth was no good unless he had the nerve to sit just behind and below the Hun and fill him with lead. The scout pilot must position himself in the blind spot, usually fifty feet below and seventy or eighty yards astern. When the Hun turned it was essential to keep exactly astern of him; otherwise the enemy gunner would get a bead on the scout, who must first turn in the opposite direction before attacking again. Sometimes the Hun would reverse his direction of turn, or he would dive away. When he

changed direction the scout waited until his opponent's wings
were level and then opened fire; or if he dived away the stand-

ing gunner was often blown flat along the fuselage by the slipstream and the scout sat behind and fired.

Although McCudden led his flight on many offensive patrols
during these winter months and shot down some enemy scouts,
his great successes were against the larger machines. During
December he established a record by bringing down four two-
seaters in one day, and a few days later he destroyed three and
damaged a fourth on the same patrol. That he was seldom hit
by return fire is a tribute to his great skill and courage. Whether
flying alone or leading his flight, he always fought with a cool
head, respecting the fighting qualities of his enemies, always
sought an ideal attacking position, and was sufficiently cunning
to avoid or break off combat when the odds were against him.
Strangely enough, he only saw the Baron in the air once, when

he rushed to help a Sopwith Pup being harried by a beautifully handled red Albatros. The Pup was shot down before he could intervene, and Richthofen, apparently satisfied with one kill, disappeared to the east.

Early in 1918, with fifty-seven victories, McCudden concluded this great third tour of operations. Gerald Maxwell, twenty-one victories, had already gone to England and, to McCudden's dismay, the popular Rhys-Davids, twenty-three victories, had been last seen heading towards some Huns. McCudden shot down his squadron's 250th Hun, and his own flight claimed seventy victories for the loss of four pilots—a fine testimony to their leader. During this tour he had won a Bar to his Military Cross, as well as the Distinguished Service Order and Bar, and now he was awarded the Victoria Cross. Rarely has this supreme decoration for gallantry been better earned in the air.

Because of his achievements, his modesty, and his willingness to pass on his experiences to others, James McCudden was very popular throughout the Royal Flying Corps. Before he left France he was dined out by his brother officers and was delighted because so many officers from other squadrons were present. He told them that he had simply tried his best to uphold the name of 56 Squadron.

Many toasts were drunk that evening and one, 'To von Richthofen, our most worthy enemy', well illustrates the sentiments of our scout squadrons. For after his three years of air fighting the able and wily Richthofen, sixty-three victories, still remained at the head of *J.G.1*.

Chapter 8

'A RED EAGLE—FALLING'*

WHEN James McCudden returned home he found that both enemy airships and aeroplanes were attacking at night, but, like Ball, his requests to 'have a go' were refused. On cloudless nights searchlights and anti-aircraft fire helped the defending pilots to find the Zeppelins, and firing into the big slow airships was not difficult. They were also attacked over the high seas, for in addition to her aircraft carriers the Royal Navy carried scouts on other ships, and Flight Sub-Lieutenant B. A. Smart flew a spectacular mission when H.M.S. *Yarmouth*, a light cruiser steaming off the Danish coast, turned into wind to launch her Sopwith Pup against a Zeppelin which could be seen some miles away. Smart, who was relieving the usual pilot, had not previously flown from the ship, but he took off without mishap from the special flying platform, only about forty-five feet long, climbed to 9,000 feet and shot down the airship in flames; then he landed on the sea and was rescued while his Pup sank.

After a disastrous raid against Britain, when unpredicted gale-force winds blew them well off their courses and five Zeppelins, from a force of eleven, failed to return, the airship offensive faltered and the enemy increased his moonlight bomber raids against London and south-eastern England. Multi-engined Giants, carrying a crew of five and cruising at 80 m.p.h., reinforced the older Gothas. These bombers were hard to find, for they were not easily held in the searchlights and presented a small target to both airmen and ground gunners. Occasionally a pilot found himself near one of the bombers, but, on a dark night, the enemy had only to turn sharply away and he was lost in the darkness.

Eventually, as pilots gained more experience, the latest scouts were used at night both at home and in France. While defending the Abbeville area for some months, Camel pilots

* Motto of 209 Squadron.

of 151 Squadron brought down sixteen German bombers, including a five-engined Giant carrying a crew of nine, without loss to the squadron. At home, improved sound locators for measuring the heights and ranges of the Giants, together with better communications, made for an improved defence system, which was put to the test when forty-three enemy bombers crossed our coasts. In the light of the moon eighty-four defending machines ascended and accounted for three bombers; another three were brought down by gunfire, and two more failed to get back.

An attrition rate against the bombers of more than twenty per cent was thought to be highly successful, but it was painfully obvious that should the bombers come across on dark nights R.F.C. single-seater scouts and two-seater fighters would have a difficult time. The writing was clearly on the wall that the scout was not the best machine for night fighting, because its sole occupant could not cope with all the problems of navigation and interception; and it was first appreciated at this time that night fighting was a highly specialised business and called for properly trained and equipped squadrons.

Hitherto, messages between those in an aeroplane and those on the ground could only be received and transmitted by wireless telegraphy, in Morse code, which was a lengthy business, since the observer had to decode and record the message or instruction. However, towards the end of the First War the movements of home-defence machines were controlled, through a transmitting station at Biggin Hill, by radio telephony, which enabled the ground controller to speak to scout pilots. If the reception was often of dubious quality, and if the pilots could not reply to the controller, or speak with each other, the introduction of radio telephony was an advance—but it would be many years before distinct speech could be received and transmitted in the air.

The air defence of Britain, however, was overshadowed by events in France, where the German Army had already begun a great offensive and advanced across the hideous desert of the old Somme battlefield to try to separate the British and French Armies and capture the Channel ports. As Allied troops fell back the position became so desperate that Field Marshal

Haig issued his famous 'backs to the wall' order, and R.F.C. scout squadrons were told that their first duty was no longer air fighting but bombing and strafing. Behind the lines enemy dispatch riders and staff cars were coursed by scouts, like hares by greyhounds, and some German soldiers were struck by the wheels of our low flyers.

Thanks to their ability to switch units from one place to another, the German Air Service outnumbered the R.F.C. during this second great struggle on the Somme, and a great many enemy machines, including the enemy battle flights, sometimes quartered the battlefield at a few hundred feet. This gathering of both friendly and enemy aeroplanes at low heights meant that the upper air was temporarily empty; some very stiff fighting took place lower down, and Captain J. L. Trollope, a Camel pilot, set up a record by shooting down six machines in one day.

Studying the tactics of the German scout squadrons during these critical days, R.F.C. patrol leaders could find no set pattern of operations in support of their successful ground offensive. The enemy scouts seemed elusive, and in an attempt to bring them to combat British bombers attacked their airfields to flush them into the air; they were sensitive to these attacks, reacted violently, and some big dog-fights took place. Sometimes all their scouts seemed to fly very low; and then they inexplicably switched to high Circuses, whose leaders seemed content to send down small numbers against lower R.F.C. formations. This, after almost four years of war, was indeed a strange concept of air power, for had the German Air Service undertaken a vigorous offensive, instead of flying a series of seemingly haphazard scout missions, it might have played a decisive part in this Somme offensive, which failed eventually in front of Amiens.

Once the heavy ground fighting abated the Circuses were seen more frequently, and because their squadrons formed the habit of joining together over some landmark or other, it seemed as if big, layered enemy gaggles suddenly appeared in the sky. Some enemy squadrons were re-equipped with a splendid Fokker biplane, the D VII, whose outstanding B.M.W. engine gave it a speed of more than 120 m.p.h., a ceiling of 26,000 feet, the best rate of climb of any fighter in France, and enemy pilots seemed to throw it about like a leaf in a high wind. Once again the Germans had a technical superiority in scout aeroplanes; without it they would have been hard pressed during these closing months of the war. They were also ahead of the R.F.C. in providing parachutes for their pilots and, although some failed to open, a considerable number of enemy pilots saved their lives when they baled-out from burning aeroplanes. Despite their imperfections, these early German parachutes boosted morale because, for the first time in air warfare, a pilot stood a sporting chance of getting down in one piece without his aeroplane.

Having resumed normal offensive patrols in flight or squadron strength, R.F.C. pilots saw either too many of the enemy or none at all. Obviously strength had to be met with strength, and the R.A.F.* often assembled fighting formations of two or three squadrons to counter the Circuses. Sometimes squadrons formed up over their airfield and flew wing patrols; and sometimes three or four independent squadrons patrolled a certain area at the same time and supported each other. The lowest squadron searched for and attacked enemy machines, the intermediate squadron, or squadrons, protected the scouts below, while the highest squadron, the above guard, screened the wing from high surprise attacks. Henceforth fighting formations of three or four squadrons were to become fairly common, but the great majority of R.A.F. missions were flown by five or six machines.

It was at this time that the German Air Service suffered the loss of its great scout pilot, Baron Manfred von Richthofen, for on 21st April, 1918, he was brought down, and the manner of his death illustrates the air fighting as the First War drew to an end.

Richthofen had left his airfield with only six machines, but he was joined in the air by one of his squadrons, and eventually, at 12,000 feet, he led his mixed formation of Fokker Triplanes and Albatroses westwards over the Somme valley until they were over the front lines. Normally he patrolled farther back over his

* The Royal Air Force, amalgamating the Royal Flying Corps and the Royal Naval Air Service, was formed on 1st April, 1918.

own territory, but another German ground offensive was imminent, and he had to prevent British two-seaters from photographing the preparations. Before they took off he had warned his gentlemen to keep a special look-out for the two-seaters, and to watch the stiff easterly wind which drifted them towards the enemy.

Much cloud and poor visibility made navigation difficult, but occasionally he caught a glimpse of the Somme and was able to pinpoint his position. Suddenly four Tripes broke away and dived steeply on a pair of R.A.F. two-seaters. Richthofen circled and watched the fight well below. The two-seaters were well handled and gave a good account of themselves, but British anti-aircraft fire soon attracted eight Camels to the scene, and Richthofen turned his fifteen multi-coloured scouts to engage the Camels.

As usual there was a hard core of stern fighting and manoeuvring, with some skirmishing on the flanks. Confident in his own ability to turn inside any adversary, he pirouetted his all-red Fokker through the jumble of twisting, turning aeroplanes. A side-slip here, a steep turn there, a dive and zoom, he watched the ever-changing pattern of the fight and waited for a good opportunity, which he seized when he saw a Camel, flown by Lieutenant W. R. May, diving away from the dog-fight. May was a beginner, his two machine guns had jammed, and he got out of the dog-fight at the first opportunity and made for home.

Richthofen went after May, but the latter's flight commander, Captain A. R. Brown, a Canadian of 209 Squadron, saw the Triplane on the tail of the Camel and gave chase. By this time both machines were near the ground. May was aware

of his danger and tried to throw off the red Triplane, but Richthofen, oblivious of the other Camel behind, calmly waited, as he had so many times before, to get May in his sights at the decisive range. Meanwhile Brown fired a burst from his twin machine guns. Too late, Richthofen turned in his cockpit, and it seemed to Brown that he crumpled before the Fokker crash-landed some two miles inside the British lines. Help was at hand, but when Richthofen was lifted from the cockpit he was dead. His opponents regretted that he did not survive the war.

During the early summer a French counter-offensive met with unexpected success. Well-equipped Americans joined the Allies in a series of decisive advances, and as the tide of battle turned there were signs that the German troops were weary and disorganised. The German scout squadrons, however, flew hard and fought well. *J.G.1*, renamed in honour of Richthofen, fought under a new 'Circusmaster', Wilhelm Reinhard, who was killed when flying a new fighter. A few days later, in June of 1918, the third and last commander of the *Richthofen Jagdgeschwader* was nominated, Oberleutnant Hermann Göring. A leader of proved worth, with twenty victories and holding the *Pour le Mérite*, Göring's experiences and tactical thinking during these closing stages of the First War must have influenced his remarkable concept of fighter operations in the next contest, when he led the Luftwaffe.

Göring began his military career in the Army, but, suffering from arthritis, found that he could not use his hands or feet properly. Reared in the strict German military tradition, and possessing an iron will, he could not bear the thought of missing the remainder of the war, and he became an observer in the German Air Service. Later, recovering from his affliction, he learned to fly, and eventually became a reasonably successful commander. Like Richthofen, Göring was also content to operate his scouts defensively, but he possessed a more aggressive temperament than Richthofen, and his pilots stayed to fight as never before. But perhaps this change of attitude was due not only to Göring's appointment but also to the fact that since the war was going against them they sometimes fought savagely and regardless of cost.

For the Royal Air Force, too, these summer months, when the enemy first began to crack, were a period of extremely hard work. Pilots and observers realised that the long and bloody struggle had reached a vital climax and that they had the chance to strike a decisive blow. It was a time of opportunity. A time when leaders such as Captain 'Mick' Mannock, 74 Squadron, pressed their attacks right home.

During his early days in France Mannock had not impressed his superiors, who thought he was unduly cautious in air combat. For his part, Mannock was shattered by the lack of finesse in air fighting, and when he recovered from the novice's usual bewilderment in his first few dog-fights, and learned to see aeroplanes in the air, he still thought that R.F.C. tactics and teamwork were extremely crude. On his first tour, which lasted nine months, he destroyed six German aeroplanes, won the M.C. and Bar, and became a flight commander. His pilots liked to fly with him because he took great pains to explain his methods, both before and after a patrol. Now, during the last few months of this conflict, he was proving such an outstanding tactician and such a brilliant leader that some of his contemporaries claimed he was the greatest fighting pilot of the First War.

Mannock saw very clearly that air fighting was an affair of formations, calling for much leadership and tactical judgement. He was a ruthless leader, who actually fired over the top of one of his own machines when he saw the pilot, who had been previously warned about his lack of aggression, slipping away from a fight. He was the master of team fighting, gunnery, ambush, and decoy, and his golden rule was *always above, seldom on the same level, never underneath*. He was a splendid teacher and intensely popular with his pilots, to whom his usual greeting was 'All tickets please, gentlemen!'

He told his pilots that the best way of attacking enemy scouts was from astern, so that they got a simple, non-deflection shot. He made them practise aerobatics until they were masters of their S.E.s, but warned them that even if their loops looked pretty over the airfield, they were useless in combat, since there was no advantage in floating upside-down, near the stall, over Hunland when the Fokkers were about. He did not believe in a lot of dog-fighting. The Hun should be got in the first dive, and if he was missed they must manoeuvre for another firing position. In combat the steep turn was used far more than any other manoeuvre, but the half-roll was also very useful, for if they missed their man in their first dive they could zoom higher, half-roll, and return to the attack.

Mannock's own score mounted steadily towards the half century, and he was awarded the D.S.O., which was soon followed by a Bar. But he worked up a great hate against the Germans which sometimes clouded his judgement, for once having made an enemy two-seater crash-land, he proceeded to strafe his defenceless enemies, explaining later that 'the swines are better dead!'* Unfortunately, like others before him, he began to think too much about his personal score and often wrote to his friends about beating McCudden and Richthofen.

After a brief leave in England he was promoted to major and returned to France to command 85 Squadron. He wept at the idea of leaving his beloved 74 Squadron, and was obsessed with the thought that he would soon be killed. Although Mannock's second tour was not far advanced, there can be little doubt that the tension, the combats, the losses, the long hours of waiting on the ground, the Archie he could not fight, and the machine gun fire he could not see, had all taken a heavy toll of his highly strung nature. He had reached a degree of mental tiredness beyond which lies the realm of fear, and this he strove to conquer on his return to fighting.

Fashioning and leading his new command, Mannock was the very antithesis of his predecessor, Billy Bishop, who, not caring for team fighting, specialised, like Albert Ball, in single-handed exploits and, defying one of the cardinal rules of air fighting, surprisingly lived to tell the tale. Indeed, on one of his solitary forays Bishop won the Victoria Cross when he beat up an enemy airfield at dawn and shot down three Huns as they took off. Bishop often fought in this fashion and, although these were heroic tactics, he was a lucky man to return to his native Canada with seventy-two victories. Meanwhile, Mannock was fully occupied with teaching his pilots the finer points of the

* *The King of Air Fighters*, p. 193.

game, showing them how to fight together and sometimes leading a wing patrol of 74 and 85 Squadrons. With his hands so full, and bolstered by the affection of his officers and men, it seemed as if he had recovered from his recent bout of depression. He heard that James McCudden was about to begin another tour at the head of 60 Squadron, and Mannock was eager to compare notes with him at the first opportunity.

When learning to fly a pupil is carefully taught that should his engine fail immediately after take-off he must never turn back to try to regain the airfield, but should carry out a forced-landing straight ahead. The reason for this teaching is that the speed just after take-off is only slightly above the stalling speed, and a turn, inducing heavier wing loads, stalls the aeroplane so that it loses height and sometimes spins. McCudden, taking-off from a French airfield on the last leg of his journey, tried to get back when his engine cut, but his machine fell to the ground, and this great fighting pilot was killed.

Mannock was acutely distressed by McCudden's death, and swore to avenge him. His personal antagonism against the Hun was stronger than ever before and, violating his own creed, he began to take grave risks when he followed his enemies down to the ground to make certain of their destruction. His end was inevitable, and towards the close of July, when flying at tree-top height, he was hit by ground fire and fell in flames. Mick Mannock had seventy-three victories and he was posthumously awarded the Victoria Cross.

Sopwith 'Dolphin' and 'Snipe' scouts, with 200-h.p. engines, speeds of more than 200 m.p.h., and ceilings in excess of 20,000 feet, helped to deal with the Fokker biplanes, but the majority of R.A.F. fighting squadrons were still equipped with the well-proved Camels and S.E.s. Towards the end of the war much attention was devoted to improving communications in France, both for air fighting and ground strafing, and a wireless central information bureau was developed and made responsible for collecting and distributing information about likely targets. Observers in reconnaissance two-seaters reported ground targets, and enemy air activity, by wireless telegraphy to the bureau, which passed the news to the headquarters of interested squadrons; the observers also fired red lights to attract any friendly machines who might be near by.

The Allies retained their initative on the ground and during their Amiens offensive, in August, the close air support of the British Army was further developed when a squadron of Armstrong-Whitworth two-seaters was allocated to the Tank Corps to try to deal with enemy anti-tank guns and pave the way for the tanks. For some time there had been an interchange of officers between the squadron and the tank units, and some experiments were made with radio telephony, but those in the tank could hear the airmen only when they were very low and within a quarter of a mile. Tests with wireless telegraphy were more successful, but it was too late to perfect these communications, and air observers had to keep in touch with the tanks during the Battle by visual signalling and by dropping messages. Later, in the Battle of Bapaume, more squadrons cooperated with the tanks and did some useful work; such was the importance placed on this form of support that a special armoured ground fighter, the Sopwith 'Salamander', was built, but only two arrived in France before the armistice.

Little more remains to be said about air fighting in the First War. The Allies continued their pressure against Germany until she surrendered on 11th November, 1918. Falling back from airfield to airfield, their supply organisation disrupted, short of aeroplanes and pilots, the enemy scout squadrons fought as best they could until the end, and their story is reflected in

the exploits of the *Richthofen Jagdgeschwader* in these last weeks of the fighting. For sometimes its pilots spent ten hours in the air, and suffered losses which reduced the number of serviceable aeroplanes in the space of a few days from fifty to eleven. Hermann Göring rallied the remnants; but more pilots were lost, the *Geschwader* was fought almost to destruction, and finally withdrawn from operations. Eventually, with replacement pilots, it returned to the fray, but the *Richthofen Jagdgeschwader* —for so long the spearhead of German fighting formations— never had an opportunity, in that war, to recover its former glory.

Chapter 9

THE LUFTWAFFE

M ANFRED VON RICHTHOFEN's brother Lothar, with forty victories, survived the war, but was killed in 1922 when piloting a passenger aeroplane. Their cousin, Wolfram von Richthofen, fought until the armistice, and his eight victories brought the family score to one hundred and twenty-eight; later he studied engineering and tried to settle down in his troubled homeland, but he found civilian life boring and did not hesitate when, in 1923, there was an opportunity to join the Defence Ministry.

Although Germany was forbidden to have an Air Force, she was allowed to retain a Defence Ministry, and here were secreted some experienced and dedicated ex-officers, including Richthofen, who planned the shape of things to come. Since she was allowed a civil airline, *Deutsche Lufthansa*, and the industry to support it, the next step in her record of deceit was to conceal military aircrews in the unnaturally swollen ranks of *Lufthansa*. Gliding was encouraged to the extent that she soon had a tremendous potential of air-minded youth. She arranged to train her pilots abroad, and Hermann Göring, having been treated in Sweden as a drug addict, was allowed to brush up his flying with the Swedish Air Force; perhaps the supreme irony of this clandestine policy was the establishment of a secret flying school in Soviet Russia.

In 1931 Adolf Galland was a slim, dark youth of nineteen and a glider pilot of some ability. Eventually he and his three brothers all became fighter pilots, but in these lean, depressed years of bread queues, the dole, and bloody street fights, there were few opportunities to learn to fly, and when the boy applied for pilot training with *Lufthansa*, he and nineteen others were selected from some 4,000 applicants.

Having completed their elementary flying, they were offered a secret training course for military pilots, and all accepted, not only because they had an inner urge to fly, but because

Germany's cause seemed good and just and appealed to their strong nationalism. Then followed a visit to Italy, where, disguised as the Duce's airmen, they were given some training by the Italian Air Force, which, except for some excellent aerobatic instruction, did not impress the young Germans. Returning to Germany, Galland received more training, including instrument (blind) flying on multi-engined transports and, as a co-pilot, began to fly on the airline route to Spain; at this time he was a well-trained fighter pilot with some three hundred hours in his log book.

The advent to power of Adolf Hitler and his Nazi Party provided the necessary political background for further expansion of the still unborn German Air Force. An Air Ministry was created with Göring as Minister; Government subsidies were available for aeroplane firms, and the expansion programme called for 4,000 aeroplanes by September, 1935. It only remained for the existence of the Luftwaffe to be openly declared, with Göring as its commander-in-chief.

The glory of the old days and the magic of Manfred von Richthofen's name were not forgotten, and the *Richthofen Geschwader* was re-formed near Berlin, where Galland was posted after narrowly escaping the more mundane duties of a flying instructor. Experienced pilots spent much time practising for numerous air displays, and Galland fitted his machine with a special carburettor to improve its inverted flying characteristics. One day, flying too low and too slow, he crashed and came to a grinding halt with his head stuck in the instrument panel; his left eye was weakened, and much surgery did not improve his countenance. Later, when attempting to land, he had an argument with a lighting standard and the machine was written-off. There were hints of an inquiry, and he was subjected to a strict eyesight test, which he overcame by the familiar ruse of memorising the chart.

The Spanish Civil War began in the summer of 1936, and although the Great Powers had agreed to a policy of nonintervention, Italy and Germany soon supported Franco. Air support for the Republicans was provided almost exclusively by Russian units under the command of Russian officers. Realising that such a limited conflict would provide an ideal proving ground for his Luftwaffe, Göring ordered some Junkers 52 bomber-transports and a handful of Heinkel 51 biplane fighters to be flown to Spain by volunteer pilots. This assistance was soon increased by the formation of a tactical air force, known as the Condor Legion, which consisted of bomber, fighter, ground-attack, and reconnaissance squadrons, together with supporting anti-aircraft, communications, medical, and supply units, all of which were highly mobile and could be moved rapidly from airfield to airfield. Wolfram von Richthofen was the Legion's chief of staff, and the driving force behind some of its highly successful operations.

German bombers attacked Spanish harbours to prevent the landing of supplies, and important bridges to stop the movement of arms and troops. One of these bridges was near the Basque town of Guernica, and on 10th April, 1937, wave after wave of aeroplanes attacked the place for more than three hours. Being market day, Guernica was full of people. The town burned all night, and more than 1,600 people were killed. In his autobiography* Galland states that the bridge was undamaged and the town destroyed owing to the primitive bomb-sights and the inexperience of the bomber crews; but at the Nuremberg trials, after the Second War, Göring admitted that the action was a deliberate experiment in aerial bombardment for his young and untried Luftwaffe.

The German bombers were escorted by Heinkel 51 biplane fighters, which were soon found to be inferior to both the Russian Rata, a low-wing monoplane fighter with four machine guns, and the American Curtiss biplane flown by Republican pilots. It was fortunate for the Legion that Franco at this time wanted more close air support for his troops, which was provided by the out-moded Heinkels, and, pending the arrival of better fighters from Germany, the air fighting was left to Germany's allies.

Remembering the battle flights of the old days on the Somme, Richthofen introduced similar techniques for his ground-attack units, which were now renamed *Schlachtflieger*. The work of these units was hampered by the lack of reliable radio communications, but to some extent Richthofen overcame

* *The First and the Last*, page 25.

this problem by setting up observation posts on suitable hills, from which he could watch the ebb and flow of the land battle and, by means of a landline to an advanced landing ground, 'scramble' his close-support sections.

Göring decided that the maximum number of his most promising young officers should be 'blooded' in Spain. Lieutenant Galland duly arrived when the war was about a year old. He joined a ground-attack unit and often flew in a tight vic formation at almost ground level and, because they had no proper bomb-sights, released his six small bombs when his leader vigorously nodded his head. Their close formation of Heinkels meant that they obtained a concentrated bomb pattern against enemy troops and fortified positions, which they named 'the little man's bomb carpet'. Sometimes they dropped primitive, yet effective, fire bombs, which were made by fitting special igniters to petrol cans. Before they returned to their airfield they strafed other targets with their two machine guns and then, if the tempo demanded, refuelled and re-armed with engines still running. During the long summer days when the light was crystal clear they flew long before the sun painted the sombre hills; and they flew again and again, half-naked, their bodies oil stained, their faces blackened from the gun ports, until the light began to fade.

As the war progressed better aeroplanes arrived from Germany, including the famous Junkers 87 ('Stuka') dive-bomber, whose screaming stoop terrorised all and sundry until its highly successful operational life was cut short by Fighter Command. The secret of this two-seater was that because its dive-brakes allowed it to dive steeply at a steady speed of about 350 m.p.h., the two 500-kilo, or four 250-kilo, bombs were released so accurately, some 3,000 feet above the target, that a good pilot could get his bombs within twenty or thirty yards of his aiming point. The Stuka carried two fixed forward guns and one free gun firing to the rear. Navigation and target identification were easier than in a single-seater because there were two pairs of eyes. Characteristic Teutonic thoroughness specified that the Stuka carry a siren, which delivered an ear-piercing shriek during the steep drive. Whenever there was little air opposition it was a formidable and precise weapon.

Richthofen, promoted to command the Condor Legion, made sure that the efforts of his airmen were closely integrated with infantry attacks. Some few minutes before an infantry attack went in a dozen twin-engined bombers, Heinkel 111s, attacked enemy ground positions while some twenty fighters circled overhead. Each vic of three bombers made three separate attacks, while two squadrons of dive-bombers, flying in a loose echelon formation, cruised serenely on the flanks of the battle waiting for the smoke and debris to clear. The Stukas peeled-off in rapid succession, plunged from the sky, released their bombs, pulled-out, and climbed and circled in line-astern to repeat the treatment, except that on the next attack they strafed with machine guns. So, in less than half an hour, the long line of Stukas rose and fell a dozen times and, appropriately, the Spaniards called them '*La Cadena*' (the chain).

Immediately after this softening-up process the tanks and infantry began their advance, supported by a few loose formations of fighter-bombers, who flew a few hundred feet above the battlefield and pounced on such items of enemy hardware that had survived the previous bombing. Whenever any pockets of enemy resistance were reported to Richthofen's control post more fighter-bombers, or Stukas, were ordered to the scene to quell the opposition, while overhead the fighters continued their protective patrols. And so it was until the day was won, and the standard of Nationalist Spain hoisted on the field of battle.

In little more than a year Galland flew three hundred Heinkel missions, and for all that his aeroplane was shot-up on several occasions by ground fire, he saw little air combat, because Republican fighters were taken on farther afield by another excellent German aeroplane, the Messerschmitt 109B, superior to all else in Spanish skies and the forerunner of a long series of great fighters from the same stable. A single-seater, low-wing monoplane, with three 7·9-mm. machine guns, its 670-h.p. Jumo engine gave it a top speed of almost 300 m.p.h. at 13,000 feet; it made its debut a few weeks before the Hawker Hurricane, and some months before its chief Second War antagonist, the Supermarine Spitfire. These three high-powered, cabin monoplanes marked the end of the long reign of the biplane fighter.

Galland's tour of duty in Spain ended in the summer of 1938, just as the squadron he commanded was about to receive Messerschmitt 109s. He was sorry to leave Spain, for had he stayed he would have seen some real fighting in his new Messerschmitt. Like Manfred von Richthofen, Galland was a keen hunter, and he regarded the strafing and bombing of ground targets as a sort of poaching where his weapons were not decently and cleanly used; indeed he longed to be a fighter pilot where the true hunter could express his skill and judgement. Regretfully he handed over to the slim, immaculate, keenly intelligent Werner Mölders, twenty-five and a devout Catholic, who, fully exploiting the superiority of his Messerschmitt, destroyed fourteen Republican aeroplanes in the few remaining months of the Civil War and so became the Condor Legion's top scorer in Spain.

One of the most important lessons from the air fighting of the Kaiser's War was that the best formation for combat was the open, abreast style, with a spacing of fifty or sixty yards between each scout, so that pilots could keep station with each other, fly near their leader without the risk of collision, search the surrounding sky against the possibility of surprise attack, and turn inside each other to face an astern attack. This formula was learned by both British and German pilots under the constant and unforgiving hammer of battle, was recorded in a thousand memoirs and memoranda, and was seemingly lost with the cease fire. For when the Messerschmitts began to fight in Spain they flew in a close wing-tip to wing-tip formation totally unsuited for combat because of the lack of manoeuvring space and the absence of cross-cover.

Why had the Luftwaffe forgotten this crucial tactical doctrine? Obviously their staff officers had failed to study the history of the German Air Service, and here there is some excuse, because for many years, when the Luftwaffe was concealed from the world, their Air Staff were very properly far more concerned with the creation of their own autonomous Service than with digesting historical records and studying the lessons of the past. Also, many German fighter pilots were influenced by some training they received in Italy, where the Italians, being splendid aerobatic pilots, invariably flew in tight vics of three aeroplanes when practising for their numerous fly-pasts and aerobatic displays. But in Spain the German fighter pilots realised that their close formations were too vulnerable, and they soon adopted a far better style of fighting.

This perfect fighter formation—for it has survived into the jet age—was based on the *Rotte*, that is the element of two fighters. Some two hundred yards separated a pair of fighters, and the chief responsibility of number two, or wingman, was to guard his leader from attack; meanwhile the leader navigated and covered his wingman. The *Schwärme*, of four fighters, simply consisted of two pairs and was exactly the same abreast pattern as that devised by Oswald Boelcke long ago, except that the spacing between aeroplanes had increased from about sixty yards, the turning radius of Boelcke's Albatros, to some two hundred yards, the turning radius of a Messerschmitt 109.

There was an important difference of principle, however, between the old and new formations, since the number of machines in the former varied between three and six, according to aeroplane serviceability, while in Spain the Messerschmitt pilots found that owing to their increased speeds, greater turning radii and the restricted view, especially behind, from their enclosed cockpits, it was essential to build their formations around the smallest fighting unit, the pair, for a lone pilot was more vulnerable than ever before. Flying in this fashion, a Messerschmitt squadron stretched some one and a half miles across the sky, and each *Schwärme* flew at varying heights, so that the starboard group, deployed down-sun from the leader, could search into the sun and guard the rest from surprise attack. These staggered heights gave cross-cover in all directions, and also made the fighters far less conspicuous in the sky.

The Messerschmitts carried radio telephones and, for the first time, fighter pilots could receive and transmit clear and distinct speech. When he manoeuvred before attacking, Mölders could keep his team fully in the picture—a tremendous improvement over the previous methods when a leader signalled his intentions by rocking his wings or firing coloured lights. So far air fighting had been inarticulate. In Spain it became articulate; this made for better teamwork in the air, and closer control from the ground. For the air fighters it was a big step forward.

Sometimes Mölders led his *Schwärme* from the flank, so that he could break away easily and get into a good attacking position, but usually he led from the centre. He shot down most of his victims when he led his men on fighter sweeps over enemy airfields; the object was to lure Republican fighters into the air so that the higher Messerschmitts had every tactical advantage. He took infinite pains to train his pilots, and often made sure that a newcomer had an easy shot at his first opponent, lending a hand when necessary, and so building-up team spirit and morale. Unlike most of his contemporaries, he was unselfish about his personal score, and often gave an easy victory to one of his new boys.

Sometimes, when the Republican fighters rose to the bait, large air battles took place, and Mölders found that when 'bounced' from the sun Republican fighters went into line astern and adopted a defensive circle which kept them together but prevented mutual support. Mölders countered this impotent manoeuvre by attacking with one *Schwärme*, while another gained height and then took on the first Republican pilots to break out of the defensive circle.

Mölders thought that his Russian opponents were not well trained and that their tactics were primitive. They flew in tightly packed sections of a few aeroplanes, and seemed loathe to venture beyond the front line. They were not aggressive, but seemed content to wander over the battlefield strafing targets of opportunity. To some extent one can understand their behaviour, for the main task of all Russian aeroplanes in Spain was support of the ground forces.

Victory for Franco ended the Spanish Civil War, and the Condor Legion returned to Germany, where the lessons of air warfare were carefully studied. The radius of action of the Messerschmitt 109 was considered insufficient, and drop tanks, which could be jettisoned before a fight, were ordered. The three light machine guns were found to be inadequate for modern air combat; the four guns of the Curtis P.36 and the heavy weapons used by the Italians were thought so commendable that the 20-mm. Oerlikon cannon was developed for the Messerschmitt. Experienced German fighter pilots thought the salient features of the ideal fighter to be (in order of precedence): a high speed and a good climb to engage, manoeuvrability to get out of trouble, fire-power to knock down an opponent in a few seconds, and a good radius of action so that the fighter could be used offensively.

Bombing by new and fast Heinkel 111s had been almost entirely limited to short-range, close-support operations, when the few escorting Messerschmitts rarely saw Republican fighters; as a result of this freedom of action enjoyed by the bombers the belief grew, and not only in Germany, that the fast bomber would always get through and would soon devastate any country despite its fighter defence.

In Spain, for the first time in history, an Army and an Air Force fought to a joint air–ground plan, where centralised control gave the Condor Legion such flexibility that it was able to concentrate its striking power and paralyse the opposing ground forces. Richthofen, the driving force, had fashioned his command into a highly successful tactical air force, and once back in Berlin, he argued his case for more tactical air forces to fight not in air battles, but jointly with the ground forces in air–ground battles. He was opposed by those high ranking officers of the Luftwaffe who foresaw that more tactical air forces would inevitably mean less resources for the strategic bomber force, but Richthofen so won the day that *Luftflotten*** were formed, consisting of bomber, reconnaissance, fighter, and ground-attack squadrons, and strategic bombing came to be regarded as a short-term and often short-range affair. For, influenced by their successes in Spain, the German concept of modern war was for their bombers to attack enemy airfields and industrial centres as the immediate prelude to air–ground operations, which would consist of great masses of armour rolling deeply into enemy territory, supported by fighters to cope with the remnants of an opposing air force, more fighters to scout ahead of and on the flanks of the armoured columns, dive-bombers to reduce the ground opposition and attack all road and rail communications and to terrorise the civilian population, fighter-bombers to quarter and harass the surrounding countryside, taking out practically anything that dared move, paratroops to secure the flanks, and for all these violent, irresistible thrusts to be actively supported by Quislings and a Fifth Column. This was a new type of mechanised war, and it was known by a new and appropriate name—*Blitzkrieg*—Lightning War.

* *Luftflotte*—Air Fleet.
　　Fliegerdivision (Later Fliegerkorps)—Air Division (later Air Corps).
　　Geschwader—usually consisted of three *Gruppen* and ninety aeroplanes.
　　Gruppe—the basic flying unit of the Luftwaffe; consisted of three *staffeln*, and was similar to an R.A.F. wing.
　　Staffel—contained nine or ten aircraft, and was smaller than an R.A.F. squadron.

Chapter 10

FIGHTER COMMAND

THE Royal Air Force of the early 'thirties has often been truly, and not unkindly, described as 'agreeably amateur' and 'the best flying club in the world', and young Douglas Bader found life very good when, in 1930, he flew with 23 Squadron from Kenley, which before this age of two-mile runways was an agreeable grass airfield perched on the wooded Surrey hills. He and his brother officers lived well in the spacious mess, comfortably ministered to by a well-trained staff. On most evenings they donned mess kit and dined together, the candlelight gleaming on the polished silver of squadron trophies and the portraits of Ball, McCudden, Mannock and other immortals smiling down on them. Pay was such that even the most junior officers possessed battered cars, in which they ferried their girl friends about the countryside. A chap was entitled to plenty of leave, and sport went hand-in-hand with flying, especially if, like Bader, he played cricket for the R.A.F., rugger for the Harlequins and the Combined Services, and had the chance of a cap for England.

After breakfast the young officers strolled out of the mess, past the tennis courts and the beautifully tended gardens bright with flowers, and across a stretch of tarmac towards the flight hangar, where half a dozen gaily painted Gloster Gamecocks were parked in a neat line. Propellers began to spin into noisy life, and the delightful smell of burnt mineral oil mingled with the heavy scent of new-mown hay.

Those officers who were detailed for flying changed into white overalls, chatted for a few moments with their flight commander, signed the authorisation book and the serviceability log, and climbed into their cockpits, where fitter and rigger assisted with the new standard parachute and the safety harness. Soon they were in the air and practising solo acrobatics, team aerobatics, fighter attacks, and forced landings. Sometimes they flew cross-country to another airfield where someone was talked into buying lunch and when they made the return trip they were careful to be down by half past three, for the flight sergeant looked very sour unless the hangar doors were firmly closed by tea-time. Occasionally, when moon and visibility were suitable, there was a little night flying, when they floated over the Thames and hoped the searchlights would illuminate their target; each year the squadron flew to Sutton Bridge, where they fired at towed targets and competed in the gunnery contest.

There were few tactical lectures, a serious approach had not yet been made to instrument flying, and squadron training seemed based on pretty aerobatics and tight formations rather than on the lessons of air fighting. But for the pilots this was the golden age of flying, when their bright, stubby biplanes, only a few miles faster than the S.E.5, handled beautifully and, in the rare event of an engine failure, could be safely put down on a soccer field. One young pilot, on being admonished by his flight commander for a poor landing, replied, 'Well, sir, I was landing with my left hand in case my right ever gets shot off!' Aerobatics gave ample scope for brain and artistry, and there were opportunities for skilled pilots to excel, for Harry Broadhurst and Teddy Donaldson to fight out the gunnery contest, and for Dick Atcherley and Dermot Boyle to perfect the art of pure flying.

The annual Display at Hendon expressed the junior Service's lighthearted approach to life. The Prince of Wales arrived in his private aeroplane to join the vast crowd that watched air refuelling, autogiros for Army co-operation, bombers from some of the Auxiliary squadrons trailing smoke across the sky, teams of dumpy, chequered fighters, tied together with coloured rope, looping and stunting over the airfield and landing in immaculate formation with the rope unbroken, parachute dropping, flying boats, bombers bowling over giant skittles with small practice bombs, dog-fights with blank ammunition, and the shooting down of a balloon. Imperialism was unfortunately portrayed when the fighter boys beat-up with flour bags a native fort whose coloured occupants were about to commit some dastardly crime. After the natives had abandoned the fort it was destroyed by means of a small quantity of explosive which went off with a large bang. Unfortunately, on one occasion the timing of the various events went astray and the fort was demolished just as Dick Atcherley was flying upside-down a few feet overhead. The blast blew him the right way up and Atcherley and the Display proceeded.

There was much competition between the fighter squadrons to get an aerobatic team into the Hendon Display. In 1931 Douglas Bader was one of the *élite* chosen to represent his squadron, and the 175,000 spectators thrilled, declared *The Times*, to 'the event of the day . . . the most thrilling spectacle ever seen in exhibition flying!' Much of Bader's aerobatic training was carried out alone, and sometimes it did not seem to make sense that he was allowed to fly upside-down at Hendon, with his head almost brushing the grass, when his training had to be performed much higher. There was a great temptation to really get down to it just above the tree-tops, and such breaches of flying discipline were frowned upon because the odd chap wrote himself off. Bader had already received strong warnings from his squadron commander when he 'rolled' a few feet above the clubhouse at Woodley Aerodrome, but this time he broke more than the regulations, for he lost height, dug-in a wing, and crashed. After months in hospital he was fitted with two tin legs and discharged from the Service, which did not see him again until the shooting began.

When the Luftwaffe was rapidly growing Britain rated, thanks to our peace-at-any-price policy, as the world's fifth air power and when, in the mid-'thirties, the R.A.F. was expanded to meet the German threat our plans not only included the regular forces but fortunately provided for a cheerful and growing band of week-end flyers. The bomber squadrons of the superb and exclusive Auxiliary Air Force were converted to fighters, so that by the outbreak of war no less than one-third of our fighter squadrons were Auxiliaries, and this *corps d'élite* was reinforced as the expansion proceeded by another enthusiastic community of amateur pilots, the Royal Air Force Volunteer Reserve.

The next step was to replace the old biplanes with modern fighters, and the Air Staff was keenly interested in the evolution of the splendid monoplanes which enabled Flight Lieutenant Waghorn, piloting a Supermarine S.6, built round a Rolls-Royce engine, to fly at 328 m.p.h. and win the Schneider Trophy Contest against the best foreign entries. Britain had only to win once more to make the Trophy hers for ever, but at this crucial stage Government support was withdrawn as an economy measure and development of the Supermarine world-beaters ceased.

Just as it seemed that the Trophy would be denied us the late Lady Houston came to the rescue and put £100,000 in the kitty a few months before the 1931 Contest. There was little time for the designer, Reginald Mitchell, to improve on his S.6, but, with a specially boosted Rolls-Royce engine in the S.6B, Flight Lieutenant John Boothman clocked 340 m.p.h. and, thanks to Lady Houston, won the Trophy outright for Britain. Later the same year Flight Lieutenant Stainforth flew the same machine at 407 m.p.h., and that speed still stood as a British record fourteen years later.

Later, when an Air Ministry specification called for a mono-plane fighter with a closed cockpit, a retractable undercarriage, four Browning* machine guns mounted in each wing, a speed of not less than 275 m.p.h. at 15,000 feet, an endurance of one and a half hours, and a ceiling of 33,000 feet both Supermarines and Hawkers were able to respond quickly with detailed draw-ings, and one prototype monoplane from each firm was ordered.

But time was running short for Reginald Mitchell, who knew he was dying of cancer. Convinced of Germany's evil inten-tions, Mitchell did not spare himself and, as his beautiful aeroplane took shape, so his life wasted away. His aeroplane was small and clean and, although it had a fuselage like the Schneider racers, the wing form was curved and pleasing to the eye. Every day he could be seen in the workshops contem-plating the progress of his machine, walking round and ex-amining its graceful lines, rejecting this, approving that, talking with the mechanics and then going back to his office, where he would sit for hours, face cupped in hands, elbows on the drawing board, pondering the latest problem.

* The Browning machine gun carried 1,200 rounds, sufficient for fifteen seconds fire, and the pilot aimed through a reflector sight in the cockpit.

The rugged and sturdy lines of the Hurricane, designed by Sidney Camm and the logical outcome of a long string of fighting aeroplanes, first flew in November, 1935, and such was its performance that six hundred were initially ordered into production. Mitchell's slender, ballerina-like monoplane, happily named the Spitfire, took the air a few months later, and the watchers of this historic event say that when the pilot opened the throttle the fighter shot forward as an arrow from a bow and left the ground (judging by the standards of those days) after an incredibly short run. Its undercarriage folded neatly into the elliptical wings and soon it was out of sight; but before landing, the designer saw his dream come true when the pilot demonstrated its superb handling qualities; soon a contract was issued for four hundred and fifty Spitfires.

During the Battle of Britain there were more Hurricane than Spitfire squadrons, and so the former bore the brunt of the fighting. Sidney Camm saw this honourable partnership and to this day continues to design splendid fighters. More than 20,000 Spitfires were eventually built, but Reginald Mitchell died in 1937 and saw only his first Spitfire fly. He left behind a legend, and his dedicated work helped his country to win a victory which ranks with the greatest battles in our history.

Having got the Hurricanes and Spitfires into production, the next task was to improve the warning system so that the fighters would have sufficient time to scramble and intercept enemy raids; fully aware of the paucity of the old sound locators, the Air Ministry, in 1934, formed the Committee for the Scientific Survey of Air Defence to look at the problems. Sir Henry Tizard, a notable scientist and a former R.F.C. pilot, presided and at their first meeting it was decided to seek the advice of R. A. Watson-Watt, Superintendent of the Radio Department of the National Physical Laboratory, who, from his researches about the tracking of thunderstorms, later told the Committee that it might be possible to detect aeroplanes by reflected radio waves which could be seen and measured on a cathode-ray tube.

The story of the British development of radar has been told many times, and it will suffice to say that although scientists in America, France, and Germany were also on the scent, Watson-

Watt's work was so encouraged and developed that when it
came to the fighting Britain led the world in the practical
application of radar, with twenty coastal stations which could

'see' medium-altitude formations up to one hundred miles away
and determine their course, speed, and approximate strength.
Since radio waves are limited by the earth's curvature, these
coastal radars could not see aeroplanes making low approaches
over the sea, and so a further chain of stations was eventually
constructed which scanned the lower altitudes, but at the
expense of greatly reduced range. In theory friend could be

distinguished from foe by the former transmitting a special signal that was missing from a hostile echo.

With the expansion of the R.A.F. the Air Defence of Great Britain organisation was replaced by Fighter Command, whose first commander-in-chief, Air Marshal Sir Hugh Dowding, commonly known as 'Stuffy', had already been closely associated with the introduction of the eight-gun fighters and the application of radar to defence. Dowding's first and most important task was to train his day fighter force, but he was also keen to modernise his night fighter force, for night fighting was still very much of a hit or miss affair, and there had been little advance in the art since the Gotha raids of twenty years ago. The commander-in-chief wanted his night fighters to carry radar sets so that hostile aeroplanes could be tracked down and attacked in the dark; he favoured a twin-engined fighter to carry the radar because of its unobstructed nose and good endurance, and he thought it should carry a radar operator, since the pilot would have his hands full flying and fighting.

The day squadrons had to be organised into a flexible force that could assemble quickly and fight at any place within the radar shield. Radar had to fill two roles, the reporting of hostile raids and the control of fighters. The secret of all this was sound and duplicated communications linking all the components of air defence. Eventually improved communications, including radio telephones, made it possible to centralise the control of many fighter squadrons.

Radar supplied intelligence about hostile formations, and interception became more and more scientific and less like finding a needle in a haystack. Radar and radio provided the means of close control from the ground, and fighter pilots, fighting within the radar shield, would have far less freedom of action then the scout pilots of the First War. Now fighter squadrons could be used economically, so that the cathode tube had the effect of multiplying the fighter strength several times. Radar gave additional power to the defence, and while British strategy continued to be based on the bomber offensive, Fighter Command provided an invaluable guard which gave Britain, for the first time in the history of air warfare, the means of defending our island home.

Flying on training exercises, it seemed to some fighter pilots, not in the know, that suddenly they were intercepting other formations over the east coast, and they did not understand the reason, except for gossip about the mysterious masts at Burnham-on-Crouch, which, it was said, sometimes stopped nearby cars!

Unfortunately, Fighter Command's tactical training was based on the theory that the air threat to Britain would be hordes of German bombers flying in close formation, and not escorted by fighters, since the Messerschmitt 109 could not reach our shores from airfields in Germany. Apparently those who assessed the nature of the threat did not take into account either the possibility of more adjacent airfields becoming available to the Luftwaffe, or that Willi Messerschmitt might double the range of his angular-looking fighter by fitting long-range drop tanks under the fuselage and wings. Dog-fighting was a thing of the past, and rigid air fighting tactics were introduced which, by a series of complicated and time-wasting manoeuvres, aimed at bringing the greatest number of guns to bear against the bombers.

RED SECTION   YELLOW SECTION

The tactical unit was the tight vic of three fighters, and from it the Air Fighting Development Establishment worked out six types of formation attacks against unescorted bombers on which squadron training was based. For example, Fighter Attack Number Three was the prescribed drill when two sections of fighters met three bombers. Having sighted the bombers, the flight commander ordered 'Yellow section, line astern, go' and yellow leader eased his section behind his flight commander, red leader. The flight commander had to judge his turn behind the bombers and, to get round the corner, he said 'Aircraft, line astern, go' followed by 'Number Three Attack, turning starboard, go' so that all would know the form. The next step was to get the fighters back into vics for a co-ordinated attack, so, having completed the turn, the flight commander said 'Aircraft, form vic, go' when it was estimated that if the bombers had obligingly continued to fly straight and level the first section of fighters would be well placed behind them with an overtaking speed of some 40 m.p.h. Having got within range, the red leader ordered 'Red section, fire, go' and he engaged the leading bomber, while his wingmen took on their opposite numbers until they were told to break away. Meanwhile yellow section, having waited in the queue, attacked after red section.

Some of the other prescribed attacks were even more complicated and time-wasting than the one I have described above, but all were based on tight vic formations and on opening fire together, so that a wingman found it impossible to keep a good look-out and to watch both his leader and his target. These formation attacks, although excellent for precision flying and squadron discipline, were useless for air fighting, for even in the Kaiser's War the tempo of air combat did not allow time for elaborate manoeuvres in tight formation. Eventually Fighter Command got back to a sensible style of fighting, but the last words too many splendid fighter pilots heard were 'Number . . . Attack, go'.

The lessons of the First War had not been completely neglected, but there was a strong reluctance to associate the new fast monoplanes with the biplane era, especially since we British have so often accused ourselves of planning for the last war. Dog-fighting had gone for ever, and it was old-fashioned to discuss it, for the moderns held that high-speed manoeuvring in Spitfires and Hurricanes was impossible because of the effects of 'g' on the pilot.

Many young pilots were unhappy about their tactics and wondered how they would cope if hordes of Messerschmitts accompanied the bombers. A great fighter pilot, the softly spoken, splendidly unflappable South African, 'Sailor' Malan, thought the tight formations and pretty aerobatics of little training value, and his views were endorsed by other bright junior officers such as Johnnie Kent and Bob Tuck. But there was a regrettable gap between these practical flying men and some of their commanders, who had reached high rank but were seldom seen at high altitudes. The youngsters talked about fighting tactics with the old-timers, but for some extraordinary reason the best flying club in the world considered it bad form to discuss one's profession after tea (I was mildly rebuked by a senior officer for talking 'shop' over a glass of beer when the Battle of Britain was at its climax). Generally speaking, the only people in touch with tactical problems were the squadron pilots. This was an unsatisfactory situation, for the essence of leadership in the Royal Air Force was, and is, that every leader from flight commander to group commander should know and fly his aeroplanes.

In the spring of 1938 Hitler and his Nazis were on the march, and they rehearsed some of their *Blitzkrieg* techniques during their bloodless occupation of Austria. Czechoslovakia was next on the list and was Hitler's 'last territorial claim in Europe'. In the autumn of that year the radars watched the Prime Minister's aeroplane return from Munich bringing news of the unsavoury agreement whereby Britain backed the French Government, who abandoned her faithful ally, Czechoslovakia, and left her to her fate. The policy at Munich was fiercely contested at home by those who held that if Britain had taken a firmer stand at Munich, France would have followed the lead. However, the Luftwaffe was much stronger than the Royal Air Force, the Germans were well ahead in their re-equipment programme and had numerous Messerschmitt 109 wings, while the R.A.F. had only five Hurricane squadrons and the Spitfire had barely entered squadron service. There can be no denying that Munich gave the R.A.F. a valuable breathing space. Had Fighter Command taken on the Luftwaffe at this time, the old British biplanes would have been swept from the skies.

During the following year Hitler prepared to conquer Poland, but to secure his eastern flank he concluded a pact of non-aggression with Russia. On the morning of 1st September,

1939, the world saw the new and terrible military strength of Germany when it was thrown against Poland. It was still dark when Galland and hundreds like him clambered into the cockpits of their ground-attack aeroplanes. Polish headquarters, barracks, troops, armour, and dispersed aeroplanes were close-support targets, while farther afield the bombers hit many Polish airfields and soon gained air superiority. Richthofen, commanding *Fliegerdivision VIII* and supporting some of the great Panzer thrusts, as they were called, was able to devote all his attention to the careful and systematic elimination of each and every obstacle which might obstruct the rapidly advancing German forces. Whenever the gallant Poles sought to make a

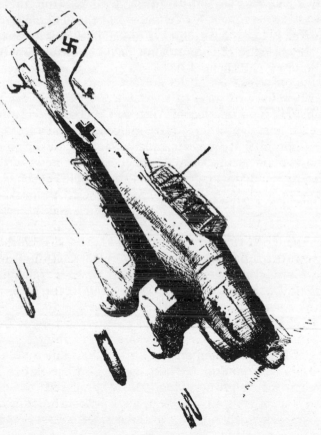

stand the versatile dive-bombers and fighter-bombers were called up, while the fighters, finding little joy in the upper air, often joined the happy throng below. Transport aeroplanes were used to bring up supplies for the forward armour, already far ahead of the infantry, while fighters leap-frogged from airfield to airfield and the tempo of operations rarely slackened.

After two weeks of bitter fighting the Polish Army ceased to exist as an organised force, despite their gallant cavalry, who were not lacking in valour when the merciless time came to pit lances and swords against tanks and armoured cars. Warsaw continued a hopeless yet magnificent resistance until, after days of savage, unopposed bombing and shelling, the city was reduced to rubble and the radio ceased playing the Polish National Anthem, which told the world that Poland had been conquered in one month. Yet her ordeal by *Blitzkrieg* was not in vain, for, because of their solemn pledges, the British Empire and France found themselves once again at war with Germany.

Chapter 11

BLITZKRIEG

ONCE again British troops and squadrons went to France, and waited for the Germans to attack. Allied strategy for the coming battle was complicated by the neutrality of Belgium, Holland, and Luxembourg, and greatly influenced by the military thinking of the French, who had built the heavily fortified Maginot Line, whose sally-ports, anti-tank traps, and big guns stretched for miles along the Franco-German border, but surprisingly stopped at the Ardennes because the French thought that hilly terrain of dense woods and narrow roads quite unsuitable for fast-moving armour. When the German Army attacked it would batter itself to pieces against the Maginot Line, while farther north Allied forces would advance into Belgium and hold a front from Antwerp to the Maginot Line.

The Air Component of the British Expeditionary Force consisted of some Lysander squadrons for Army co-operation and tactical reconnaissance, Blenheim squadrons for strategic or deeper reconnaissance, and a few Hurricane squadrons for air defence. Because the French had few modern bombers, the Advanced Air Striking Force, also based in France, contained a few Battle and Blenheim squadrons supported by some fighters.

Army–R.A.F. co-operation in the land battle virtually began and ended with the slow two-seater Lysanders, whose crews took photographs and plotted the fall of shells for the gunners. This makes strange reading when one thinks of the very close co-operation that existed between the Army and the R.A.F. in the First War, when the principles of air support were thrashed out. But just before the Second War the Government view was that another conflict with Germany would largely be fought in the air and at sea, although, if need be, a small B.E.F. would serve with the French Army as a token of British co-operation in the land fighting. Thus R.A.F. squadrons in France found themselves taking part in air–ground operations for which, except for the Lysanders, they had not been designed, equipped, organised, or trained.

A number of British radar sets were also sent to France, and these were intended to be part of a proper air defence system, but the organisation was such that sometimes enemy aeroplanes flying near the radars in France were unseen, although they were plotted by radars in England. Consequently R.A.F. fighters in France could never fight as efficiently as home-based fighters, for the two air defence systems did not compare.

It was soon found that the single-engined Battle bombers were desperately ill-equipped to stand up to Messerschmitt 109s, for they were slow, unwieldy, and their vulnerable bellies were unprotected by either their forward- or backward-firing guns; but the fitting of a dozen guns could not disguise the fact that the Battle could not live with the Messerschmitt. Mercifully, they were withdrawn from daylight missions, and for the next few months were flown at night on reconnaissances and dropping propaganda pamphlets which called upon the Germans, if they read them, to bring the war to a speedy conclusion by over-throwing their despotic Government.

It was found also that the enemy had early warning coastal radars when twenty-two Wellington bombers flying near the German coast in four formations, without either fighter screen or escort, were seen by an experimental *Freya* radar, and a strong force of *J.G.1* fighters were scrambled and intercepted them. Ten Wellingtons were shot down, two ditched in the sea on the way home, and a further three force-landed after crossing our shores. But, after a thorough examination of this, and similar disasters, the R.A.F. still held obstinately to the belief that unescorted daylight bombers could fight their way to the target against strong fighter opposition and suffer few casualties. *J.G.1*, however, took the more rational line that such tactics were no less than criminal folly.

The R.F.C. had discovered, years before, that bombers had to have a fighter escort if they were to survive on day operations, and even when Trenchard operated his bombers within the protection of a loose fighter screen, he found it essential to provide a fighter escort. On the other hand Trenchard sometimes sent out a few strategic bombers well beyond the front lines without fighter protection, and made little effort to command the air beyond the front areas; bomber losses in daylight were small, largely because the German fighter defence against long-range bombers was extremely rudimentary, and so the R.A.F. drew the wrong conclusion and thought that day bombers flying in tight patterns could depend upon their own guns to penetrate enemy defences. When fighters were available they would free-lance in the vicinity of the bombers and 'cleanse the sky' of enemy fighters.

In the few fighter clashes the Messerschmitt 109 proved to be superior to the Hurricane. The trouble with the Hurricanes was that they were fitted with wooden fixed-pitch propellers, which were designed for efficiency at high speeds. But at great heights the pitch of the propeller could not be adjusted to bite into the thin air; and when pilots dived after the 109s they were in 'second gear' when they wanted their highest speed. Fortunately, for some time Dowding had been demanding variable-pitch propellers, and these were gradually fitted to the Hurricanes; but the 109s still flew higher. Moreover, the Messerschmitt engine had a 'negative-g' carburation system which enabled the fighter to dive steeply, while R.A.F. Merlin engines, lacking this device, cut-out when the control column was pushed hard forwards. So it was a good thing that, on Dowding's insistence, both Hurricanes and Spitfires were fitted with armour plate behind the pilot, for this protection saved many lives.

On 9th April, 1940, 'the Phoney War' ended when Hitler invaded Denmark and Norway. The Danes could offer no resistance, and the small Norwegian Air Force was soon destroyed, despite the British contribution of a small expeditionary force supported by two fighter squadrons. The obsolete Gloster Gladiator biplanes of 263 Squadron were embarked on the aircraft carrier *Glorious*, and eventually the pilots, led by Squadron Leader 'Baldy' Donaldson, one of three famous brothers, all of whom were fighter pilots and all of whom won the D.S.O., flew from *Glorious* to a frozen lake in Norway, whose edges were already beginning to melt from the spring sunshine and whose surface was not improved by much bombing. There were no radars and no warning system, so the pilots took off when they saw the black crosses and somehow shot down a few aeroplanes, but at the end of the second day Baldy's force consisted of one serviceable Gladiator. Ground crews and pilots sailed home in a merchant ship and, undismayed, were given more Gladiators and embarked on *Furious* with the Hurricanes of 46 Squadron, commanded by Squadron Leader 'Bing' Cross. Once more the pilots of 263 Squadron flew from an aircraft carrier and began operations from a hastily constructed airfield in Norway. The destined base of 46 Squadron, however, was flooded by the spring thaw, so *Furious* returned to Scapa Flow, where the Hurricanes were transferred to *Glorious*; soon *Glorious* arrived back in Norwegian waters, where 46 flew off and eventually joined 263 Squadron.

After some days Donaldson was ordered to fly his remaining Gladiators on to *Glorious*, while the Hurricanes, which had never landed on a carrier, were to be destroyed where they stood. Cross, however, knowing of the desperate shortage of Hurricanes, visited *Glorious* and made arrangements with her captain to try to get down after the Gladiators.

All the pilots came in to a safe landing in the brightness of an Arctic midnight. Trying to operate fighters outside a proper air defence system, the two squadrons had done their best under appalling conditions, but the Germans were not yet finished with them, and just as Cross was sitting down to a cup of tea 'action stations' was sounded. He made his way to the flight deck and estimated that two out of three salvos from the battleships *Scharnhorst* and *Gneisenau* were hitting *Glorious*. Soon the 'abandon ship' order was passed from man to man, *Glorious* went down, and of the ship's company only thirty-nine, including Cross, survived.

When it was clear that victory in Norway was only a matter of days, many Luftwaffe units flew south, rested for a brief spell, and at dawn on 10th May, 1940, attacked Allies and neutrals alike, so that the once empty skies over France and the Low Countries filled with aeroplanes as the now familiar *Blitzkrieg* pattern unfolded. Bombers, escorted by long-range fighters, attacked more than seventy Dutch, Belgian, and French (including R.A.F.) airfields. Some of these attacks lasted for almost an hour and were so successful that the Dutch and

Belgian Air Forces were practically written-off. In Holland the Germans were careful to leave some landing areas undamaged and, when the bombers turned for home, scores of Ju. 52s, with strong fighter escorts, dropped thousands of tough and experienced paratroops. The seizure of Holland had begun.

More bombers, fighter-bombers, and dive-bombers attacked Allied troops, strong-points, ports, and railways, and some enemy pilots flew nine missions on this day. Other fighters, fighter-bombers, and dive-bombers gave close support to powerful columns of tanks and motorised troops, guarded by ample flak, while reconnaissance aeroplanes scouted ahead and called in the close support formations whenever there was the slightest opposition. At night enemy bombers had a free hand.

To try to stop the enemy columns the Battles and Blenheims flew again in daylight, and to evade the Messerschmitts they sometimes carried out their attacks at tree-top height. Although more Hurricane squadrons had arrived in France, the fighter screen was not big enough to protect the bombers, who had to contend with both Messerschmitts and flak. During these desperate first days of the German advance it was the flak which took the heaviest toll. Enemy rapid-firing automatic weapons were accurate up to some 5,000 feet, while lower down the hordes of machine guns added to the hazards faced by the crews. The theory of the low-level attack was sound enough provided the gunners did not have time to traverse and aim their weapons; but the Battles were so slow that, of thirty-two sent out on 10th May, thirteen were lost and all the rest damaged. On the next day only one of eight returned from attacking armour in the Ardennes. On the following day five Battles attacked two bridges near Maastricht and all were brought down. Indeed, one crew who escaped from their crashed and burning aeroplane were sternly lectured by a German officer about the folly of attacking such a target two days after its capture. Did they not appreciate that the flak would be ready and waiting?

Light bombers flying from England fared little better than the Battles, for, on one mission, five out of six Blenheims fell to Me 109s; and on another mission, eleven out of twelve Blenheims succumbed to the same type of fighter.

These losses were hard; but worse was to come when, four days after the attack began, a strong enemy spearhead, supported by clouds of Stukas, crossed the Meuse at Sedan—the ominous name which has figured in three wars against Germany and now filled all Frenchmen with despair. On this day all Allied bombers were ordered to attack the enemy bridgehead, but some French formations fared so badly that their remaining missions were cancelled. Then came the turn of the Advanced Air Striking Force. Seventy-one light bombers, in small formations of four aeroplanes, made concentrated attacks against five bridges and enemy columns near Sedan. Hurricanes were instructed to patrol the area, but these fought some distance from Sedan. When the light bombers made their approach they were set upon by hordes of Messerschmitts and many were destroyed. Others fell to flak, and more were shot out of the sky on the way home; only thirty-one returned. Five days of daylight operations had cost about half the R.A.F.'s bomber strength in France, and some squadrons had to be taken out of the line. When, after a few days, bombing was resumed, the attacks were largely carried out at night, and if the targets were harder to find and the bombing less effective, the crews enjoyed some expectation of life.

Light bombers flying from England provided most of the daylight support over the battle area, but, owing to the lack of communications and the speed of the German advance, mobile targets reported by the B.E.F. were seldom in the same place when, many hours or even a day later, the bombers turned up. There was no longer any punch in the daylight attacks. Fortunately, because of these grievous casualties, the concept of unescorted bombers was drastically revised. The R.A.F. simply reverted to the R.F.C. tactics of almost a quarter of a century ago, and began to give their daylight bomber formations a close escort of fighters.

As the terrible German combination of aeroplanes and armour blasted its way through the Low Countries and France, fighter pilots of four countries took on the Messerschmitts as best they could. But the French were poorly placed in their Moranes, and any sting in the small fighter arms of Holland and Belgium had been much reduced by the bombing. When

Adolf Galland shot down three Belgian Hurricanes he was not greatly thrilled about his first victories, because they had proved so easy and his Me 109E so superior in combat.

The Hurricanes were reinforced by more squadrons, but most of their pilots had never fired a shot in anger, their tactical training was indifferent, and 615 (County of Warwick) Squadron had flown to France in Gladiator biplanes. Fortunately they were given Hurricanes just before the balloon went up. The Gladiators, flown by staff officers, were parcelled out to different airfields for local defence, and legend has it that one staff officer shot down a brace of 109s and another a pair of Heinkels, but, alas, there is no recorded confirmation.

There were many Messerschmitts and few Hurricanes, and so the dive-bombers had a splendid time during these early days of the fighting, when the screaming Stukas seemed to have a personal antagonism for everyone on the ground. For it seemed to civilian and soldier alike that disaster came with the Stukas, that after the noise and the bombing and the machine gunning, the tanks rolled on and on through France. The Stukas meant death, confusion, and terror. To the French the dive-bombers were not part of the *Blitzkrieg*, they *were* the *Blitzkrieg*.

Within a few days Dutch resistance was almost overwhelmed and, to hasten the progress of submission, two attacks, each of twenty-seven Stukas, demonstrated the irresistible quality of Teutonic air supremacy by an attack of utter ruthlessness against Rotterdam, while the ultimatum demanding the surrender of that city had still nearly three hours to go. There was no opposition, the centre of the town was set on fire by the first few dive-bombers, and a thick pall of smoke made a nice aiming point for those waiting behind. Retribution followed that night, when, for the first time in this war, Bomber Command attacked targets in Germany.

Retribution for some Stuka pilots also followed when 151 Squadron, led by Baldy Donaldson's brother, the small, aggressive, bouncing Teddy, patrolled over the battle area, under a reinforcement scheme in which U.K.-based Hurricanes flew daily from French airfields and then returned home. Teddy was undoubtedly one of the best shots in the business and was also a splendid aerobatic pilot; he did not know the meaning of fear and was aching to have a crack at the Germans. Possessing excellent eyesight, Teddy saw a bunch of aeroplanes milling about far below. Suspecting a trap, he dived his red section to investigate, very wisely leaving yellow and blue sections to guard against Messerschmitts. Recognising the Stukas, he followed the rules, ordered Fighter Attack Number One, and opened the squadron's account with a sharp burst into the belly of a dive-bomber which began to burn.

The precise, peacetime drills of Attack Number One were forgotten as the other two pilots of red section each sorted out a Stuka and opened fire. White smoke streamed from one dive-bomber, and the Hurricane pilot thought he had killed the rear gunner, who, however, got a very good burst into the Hurricane as it broke away. Teddy, watching for another opening, thought the Stukas were well handled and, although they were slow compared to the Hurricanes, they tried to escape by steep, vertically banked turns, while their rear gunners continued to fire vigorously at the Hurricanes.

The dog-fight lost height, and Teddy counted sixteen or seventeen Stukas who dodged round trees and farm buildings to try to escape. Soon six Stukas were burning on the ground and another five were badly damaged, at a cost of some Hurricanes slightly damaged by *flak* and a bullet through a pilot's sleeve.

Other Hurricane squadrons shot down many Stukas. The latter then began to fly in larger numbers escorted by twin-engined Messerschmitt 110s and still higher 109s. Other enemy bombers were also heavily escorted, and packs of free-lancing 109s roved well out on the flanks. Hurricane pilots thus found themselves fighting for their lives against the Messerschmitts before they could get at the bombers; for they were so few and the odds so great—four Hurricanes against thirty Dorniers and twelve Messerschmitts, eight against sixty Stukas and thirty Messerschmitts, three against one hundred Stukas escorted by sixty Messerschmitts, stepped-up behind. Many Hurricanes were destroyed before they could get at the enemy bombers.

France was disintegrating before the onslaught. Undisciplined groups of French and Belgian soldiers began to swell the throngs of refugees. German soldiers in captured Allied uniforms added to the confusion, and there were rumours of enemy paratroops dressed as nuns. Here and there the retreat was fast becoming a rout, and the British Expeditionary Force had begun a fighting withdrawal that was to end at Dunkirk.

When, after ten days of fighting, the fighter squadrons of the Air Component were ordered back to England, nearly two hundred destroyed or damaged Hurricanes were left behind, and these represented one-quarter of Fighter Command's strength of modern fighters. Dowding's home-based force of some forty squadrons was well short of the fifty-two he thought necessary to defend these islands, but he was under much pressure to send more squadrons to France, where, without the backing of a proper system of air defence, they would have fared like the two squadrons in Norway. Dowding was allowed to plead his case before the War Cabinet, who no doubt had to strike some balance between moral support for France and unsound military measures, for Dowding felt his audience was not sympathetic to his views; after some time he produced a graph showing the wastage rate of Hurricanes, placed this before the Prime Minister and said, 'If the present rate of wastage continues for another fortnight, we shall not have a single Hurricane left in France or in this country.'* On the following day Fighter Command sent the equivalent of a further four Hurricane squadrons to France, but these, the Cabinet decided, were to be the last fighter reinforcements.

Dunkirk was an ideal target for the Luftwaffe, for, unlike Warsaw, it lay on the coast and could be easily found when visibility was poor. Allied troops struggling into the town abandoned and burned many vehicles on the outskirts, and the smoke was another beacon for the bombers now gathering for the kill.

The enemy's daily programme usually opened with a few tactical reconnaissance aeroplanes searching for our positions, and there followed, shortly after dawn, a deluge of Stukas against shipping in the harbour. At breakfast-time fifty Heinkels, with more escorting Messerschmitts, bombed the

* *Leader of the Few*, p. 191.

docks and, when the sun was at its zenith, more Heinkels attacked, followed by Stukas, who dive-bombed and then machine gunned the beaches, now filling with exhausted men. A great gaggle of Junkers bombers and twin-engined fighters worked over the town in the mid-afternoon, and the Stukas were again hard at it for the last thirty minutes of daylight. German artillery was only four miles from Dunkirk, so that shelling and mortar fire filled the gaps left by the bombing; and the ground situation further worsened when the Belgians surrendered, leaving a gap in the defences. Little wonder that the first evacuation ship to leave Dunkirk was bombed, shelled, and machine gunned before it reached Dover with many of its soldiers either wounded or dead.

Dunkirk is only a few miles across the English Channel, so that a Spitfire flying from Manston could spend some forty minutes over the town before returning with a safe margin of patrol. Fighter squadrons began to fill the airfields of south-east England, but their pilots had little idea that we were getting out of France. Indeed Douglas Bader, back in the Service and a flight commander on Hurricanes, tells how on the third day of the evacuation he landed at Martlesham and, anxious to find out the score before leading his flight over Dunkirk, stumped over to another flight commander and demanded the form. 'Haven't got a clue,' was the reply. How tragic that the hundreds of fighter pilots who fought over Dunkirk did not know that the game was up! How sad that the bomber crews, sent off to attack enemy columns near Dunkirk, did not know that the shelving beaches, where a man could wade to a small boat, were filling with tired and exhausted men and that a strike pressed home more fiercely than usual might have saved many lives.

At Dunkirk the initiative lay with the Luftwaffe because no one could anticipate the timing of the attacks and enemy bombers could rapidly concentrate over the town. For all that the radars in England constantly saw large gaggles, R.A.F. airfields in Kent were too far away for fighters to intercept from ground readiness; and when the bombers came in low there was no radar warning whatsoever. Accordingly Air Vice-Marshal Keith Park, a tall lean New Zealander, thrice decorated for gallantry in the First War and now commanding 11 Group, had no option but to resort to the wasteful system of standing patrols, and each of his thirty-two fighter squadrons flew up and down the beaches at 16,000 feet or so for forty minutes and was then relieved.

Occasionally a squadron fought immediately it arrived near Dunkirk, and the pilots, having used all their ammunition, withdrew to re-arm. Sometimes R.A.F. formation leaders attacked such large numbers that all that a few Spitfires could hope for was one pass at the bombers before the 109s were upon them. Park therefore increased the strength of his patrols to two squadrons, and later to four squadrons, but this meant even longer periods when the men below were without fighter protection and had to suffer heavy bombing and a murderous hail of machine-gun fire.

Sometimes the early morning mists of these dramatic June days cleared from Luftwaffe airfields in France before those in south-east England, and the Germans again had it all their own way. Sometimes cloud or thick black smoke from the burning oil tanks hid the town and the drama below from R.A.F. fighters, but whenever a Spitfire or Hurricane chased an opponent down to the sea every available Allied weapon opened up at both aeroplanes, for everything with wings was understandably regarded as hostile by the men on the beaches.

First light on 4th June saw the Germans only two miles from the beaches and the last ship leave Dunkirk, and those on board testified to the fine bearing of the French troops who were left behind. The B.E.F. and its Allies had fought and held off the enemy for nine days, and the Royal Navy, the Merchant Navy, and a host of amateur yachtsmen had achieved the near-impossible by bringing home more than a third of a million men who would fight again. Bomber, Coastal, and Fighter Commands had upset the Luftwaffe to the extent that another Warsaw was prevented. Fighter Command could have done more, had Dowding thought fit to use all his squadrons, but this would have left much of England wide open to air attack, and he was desperately aware that the air fighting had already cost him more than half his total strength.

After Dunkirk the German columns swept southwards,

accompanied by precise close air support and the usual bombing of airfields and communications. Paris was occupied, and the remnant of the French Air Force was largely destroyed. The Germans pushed on towards the Spanish frontier and the Atlantic, and what remained of the fighter squadrons of the Advanced Air Striking Force prepared to cover another evacuation.

While the Hurricanes flew from airfield to airfield the airmen made their way along the crowded roads as best they could. The departure of one party of airmen from a hamlet was seriously delayed while an ardent French inventor tried to explain his anti-aircraft device which would revolutionise air warfare, and more airmen only barely escaped capture because one of them was haggling with a local café owner over the price of an Austin Seven. On 17th June, however, all Frenchmen were ordered to cease fighting, and on the following day a few Hurricanes flew the last patrols to cover our final evacuation from Brittany.

Unfortunately, at Dunkirk R.A.F. fighter pilots claimed more than three enemy aeroplanes shot down for every one actually destroyed, and this led to wild reports about the superiority of British fighters. The regulations stated that before an aeroplane could be claimed as destroyed it must be seen to crash, or to be going down in flames, or its pilot bail out. But one burning aeroplane or one parachute spilling out was often briefly seen by many pilots when they twisted and turned five miles up. Very few fighters were fitted with ciné cameras, and, although the intelligence officers tried to sort out and verify the various claims, there was little co-ordination and cross-checking between different squadrons, especially when they flew hard.

Mölders often fought over Dunkirk, where the Defiant, a two-seater fighter, gave him a nasty shock because it had a four-gun power-operated turret which had a good arc of fire on either flank. At a range of half a mile the Defiant looked not unlike a Hurricane and when, during its first combats, the Germans allowed it to come alongside, it gained a spectacular but short-lived success. But the turret proved little compensation for the Defiant's indifferent performance, the Germans soon had its measure and, like the Lysander and the Battle, it was fought out of the sky.

Mölders sometimes bounced a few Spitfires who, flying in their neat, tight vics, failed to see the German ace in the sun; but once the R.A.F. pilots had broken out of their pitiful formations they fought with a skill and determination which Mölders had never met. Like the Hurricanes, the Spitfires could not fly as high as his 109E, and he could out-dive both British fighters, but when he stayed for the close fighting he found the Spitfire could out-turn him. And, although he did not have a high opinion of French fighter pilots, it was a Morane that almost finished his career.

Sweeping the Amiens area one evening, Mölders took his formation into a fight already waging between six Moranes and some twenty Messerschmitt 109s, and the Germans had every advantage. Mölders fired at a Morane, which made off, and then rejoined the circling 109s and searched for another Frenchman. Suddenly there was an explosion in the cockpit. Everything went black, the throttle was shot to pieces from his hand, the stick plunged forward, and the aeroplane went down in a vertical dive. Mölders tried to get out, grabbed the release catch, and the cockpit hood flew off. Fortunately for him his Messerschmitt levelled out of its own accord and gave him a fleeting chance to unfasten the safety belt, get up from the seat, and jump clear. His parachute opened, and as he floated down he watched his favourite 109 plunge down, crash vertically into the ground, and burn. He never saw his opponent, and on reaching the ground was taken prisoner by the French.

After Dunkirk enemy ascendancy in the air was such that Adolf Galland was nearly shot down by a brother officer. Galland often flew a specially camouflaged olive-green 109, experimenting to see if it were less conspicuous than the usual blue model. Flying alone one day, Galland heard a young fighter leader explain on the radio to his pilots the best way to shoot down a Hurricane. 'Below us,' said the German, 'is a Hurricane, I will destroy it. Watch closely. I dive and approach from behind.' Galland listened, full of admiration as the other continued, 'My range is five hundred metres, three hundred, two hundred . . . the fool is asleep. I close to fifty metres.' Suddenly Galland saw flecks of light fly over his cockpit and realised he was the target. He dived away cursing!

After the armistice Mölders and many like him were released by the French and would fight again. Mölders, with twenty-five victories, and Galland, with seventeen victories, were each awarded the Knight's Cross and promoted. The R.A.F.'s top scorer in France, with some fourteen victories, was Flying Officer 'Cobber' Kain, 73 Squadron, a happy, strapping, fearless boy from New Zealand, who had fought bravely against tremendous odds, and showed that man for man R.A.F. fighter pilots could stand up to the best of the Luftwaffe. Kain was a rarity in the fighter world, because he was a 'collector' of different types of German aeroplanes. He seemed more interested in destroying different makes of aeroplanes than in accumulating a large score, and his log book records victories over Messerschmitt 109s, Messerschmitt 110s, a Junkers 88, a Stuka, a Dornier 17, and a Heinkel 111. He was desperately keen to bag a Fieseler Storch, a slow-flying two-seater communications aeroplane, and spent many hours quartering the area well behind the combat zone until he found his Storch and knocked it down. Posted to England as an instructor a few days before his squadron left France, the young New Zealander killed himself 'beating-up' his own airfield. Sweeping low over the grass, he began to flick-roll to the left, but after the third roll the Hurricane lost speed, spun, recovered with a burst of engine, then stalled again, hit the ground, and burst into flames.

Except for sporadic periods over Dunkirk, the R.A.F. never got air superiority over France, and when they arrived home British troops were bitter and resentful about the hammering they had taken from the air. In the pubs of Kent and Surrey there were some ugly scenes and disparaging remarks about the whereabouts of the 'glamour boys'. Today, after all these years, and when time has mellowed the sharp outline of personal experience, one can plainly see the great accomplishment of the three Services who, despite appalling difficulties, brought off a combined operation and made it possible for Britain to continue fighting.

If there were to be more land battles supported by aeroplanes, then the Army and the Royal Air Force would have to reach a better understanding. Aircrews would have to learn about the lot of the fighting soldier and what it means to be at the receiving end of a dozen dive-bombers, and the soldiers would have to realise that air action does not always take place before their eyes. Meanwhile, the fighter squadrons had much to learn and a lot to relearn. Those nostalgic, amateur, flying-club days of the 'thirties were gone for ever.

Chapter 12

'THE SENIOR OFFICER PRESENT'

A FIGHTER pilot flying at a great height off the North Fore-land during that fine high summer of 1940, when each day seemed full of blinding light and colour, saw the calm waters of the Channel splintered here and there by the wakes of a few tiny ships hugging the English coast. Before him the Pas de Calais stretched from the coast until it faded into a blue haze, and here lay the crack fighter squadrons of the Luftwaffe, some only thirty miles from Dover. Flying five miles above the Channel he would not see the scores of airfields which dotted the landscape between Hamburg and Bordeaux and which housed two air fleets, *Luftflotte 2* and *Luftflotte 3*, while *Luftflotte 5* rested on Danish and Norwegian bases. This powerful air armada, containing some 2,800 combat aeroplanes, was thus disposed along a wide front so that air attacks could be de-livered against Britain from many directions. The airfields were well stocked for the coming assault, while the refreshed and well-disciplined crews, flushed with victory, inspired by Nazi fanaticism and a blind faith in their *Führer*, listened to the loudspeakers blaring the martial strains of '*Bomben Auf En-ge-land*' ('Bombs on England'), and waited for Göring to give the signal.

When he turned westwards down the Channel he saw the flat lands of Kent, the chequered fields and chalk downs of Sussex gapped by tiny rivers, and, on the far horizon, the rolling country of Hampshire and Dorset. He was too high to pick out the hamlets and villages crouching under down and wold, but he fleetingly remembered them and knew that all this splendour would soon be the backcloth of bloody combat. He remem-bered, too, other perilous times in the long history of his country, when other invaders had faced the narrow waters of the Channel; but this time it was different, because all would be won or lost in the air. And when he came down towards the crawling earth he saw the white cliffs at Beachy disentangle themselves from the haze, and a few seconds later he recognised his airfield lying at the foot of the downs and fitting into the landscape as easily as a thrush on her nest.

Fighter Command had lost almost three hundred pilots during the fighting over the Continent, and their replacements were very inexperienced, but the Command had borrowed some excellent pilots from the Fleet Air Arm. The first American volunteers were joining their squadrons, and the few Belgians included a pilot who had fought with the Condor Legion and was considered something of a Messerschmitt expert, but he failed to return from his first encounter with the yellow-nosed fighters. Canadian, Polish, and Czechoslovakian squadrons would soon be ready.

Dowding's squadrons were based throughout the land from Caithness to Cornwall, and their day-to-day operations were controlled by four fighter groups who were subordinate to Fighter Command; the groups were divided further into sectors, each a geographical area containing a sector station and satellite airfields. 11 Group, bounded by Lowestoft, Dover, Bournemouth, and Northampton, contained eighteen day fighter squadrons and four night fighter squadrons, while 12 Group's thirteen squadrons defended the Midlands and could, if need be, reinforce 11 Group. Farther north, twelve squadrons, including six obsolete Gladiators, guarded the industrial cities of the north-east and Scotland, while four squadrons were deployed in the west country. A further eight non-operational squadrons would take their places in the front line after more training.

Fighter Command was about the same size as that force which had been reckoned a sufficient defence against the Luftwaffe bomber arm operating unescorted from Germany: Dowding could put some six hundred fighters into the sky, but he would keep some squadrons in reserve, and fighters based in Cornwall were too far away to be used against raids on London and the Midlands. If, as seemed probable, enemy formations would cross the coasts between the Thames Estuary and Bournemouth, the fighter pilots of 11 Group would bear the brunt of the fighting. It was estimated that about one-third of the Luftwaffe's strength would always be out of commission for repairs and inspections. This meant that they could mount raids involving some 1,800 aeroplanes. Hence Dowding's pilots would face heavy odds; but if radar, the magic eye, saw, and went on seeing, his fighter pilots would be fully briefed on the tactical situation from take-off until they opened fire. Radar gave them eyes which saw for about one hundred and twenty miles, whereas German pilots, having no radars in France to back them, could only see four or five miles and would know little about the ebb and flow of the air battle.

Fighting tactics were still a long way behind those of the Luftwaffe, but some squadron commanders took a big step forward when they forgot the Fighter Attacks and trained their pilots to fight in pairs. The vulnerable vics of three were discarded, and replaced by sections of four consisting of two pairs, not four individual fighters; sometimes these sections

'weaved' to try to cover the blind spot behind the last man, 'tail end Charlie', in each section. Other squadrons provided two 'weavers', who flew to and fro above the rest of their comrades to protect them from the bounce. The tactics of fighting men have been described, ironically, as 'the opinion of the senior officer present', and this phrase aptly reflects the state of Fighter Command's tactics immediately before the Battle of Britain.

Within the squadrons there was much talk about deflection shooting, for powerful engines of more than 1,000-h.p. gave the Spitfire I and the Messerschmitt 109E top speeds of nearly 400 m.p.h., which meant that during a fight there was not a lot of time to adjust one's aim. The reflector sights were a great improvement on the old ring and bead sights, for the horizontal range bars were movable and, when they touched the wing-tips of an enemy aeroplane, the pilot knew he was within effective range. But he had still to judge how much 'lead', or deflection, was required to hit his opponent. The average standard of shooting in Fighter Command was not high, for too little attention had been devoted to gunnery instruction, and the kills in any squadron always seemed to fall to the same three or four pilots, while the remainder had to be content with a 'probable' or a 'damaged', because they hose-piped their

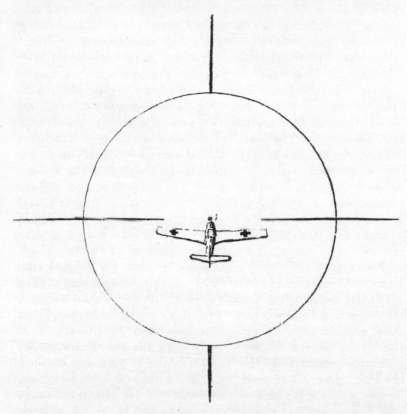

machine guns from skidding aeroplanes, opened fire from absurd ranges, and could not estimate their amount of forward allowance. The average pilot of those days could usually hit an enemy aeroplane when he overhauled it from dead line astern and sprayed his opponent with eight machine guns, but give him a testing deflection shot at angles of more than a few degrees and he usually failed to make a kill.

Because the average fighter pilot was not a good shot it was usual for the machine guns to be harmonised to give a fairly large 'shot-gun' bullet pattern at the best firing range, and this 'area of lethal density', as it was called, gave the poor marksman the best chance of destroying his adversary. But although the shot-gun grouping catered for the rank and file, it handicapped splendid shots such as Sailor Malan, Harry Broadhurst, and Teddy Donaldson, who sometimes closed to excellent killing ranges only to find that the area of lethal density was not particularly lethal, because the harmonisation of their guns did not give a sufficiently heavy concentration of fire to destroy an enemy bomber within a few seconds. Accordingly, expert shots harmonised their guns to give a 'spot' concentration of fire, and Sailor demonstrated their hitting power when, one moonlight midsummer night, he watched the searchlights near Southend holding enemy bombers in their beams for several minutes. The German aeroplanes seemed to be flying fairly low, and since the light was sufficient for an experienced day fighter pilot to stalk and attack his quarry, Sailor asked and received permission to take off. He climbed towards a Heinkel making towards the coast at 8,000 feet and well illuminated by the searchlights. Opening fire from two hundred yards, the South African kept his thumb firmly on the 'tit', saw his bullets strike home and, his windscreen covered with oil, broke away at fifty yards. He watched the German spiral down and then climbed after another Heinkel, also 'coned' by the searchlights. This time Sailor fired short two-second bursts as he closed; when the enemy turned he fired again with the exact amount of deflection required, for the Heinkel began to burn and crashed in flames near Chelmsford. Highly satisfied with his two kills, Sailor returned to base and telephoned his charming wife, who was waiting for the arrival of their first child, whose godfather would be Winston Churchill.

There was also much squadron gossip of how best to get on the tail of a 109, of the merits of astern, head-on, beam, and quarter attacks, and of the use of sun and cloud cover. A sound knowledge of these things could decide the issue of an air battle. The best squadron commanders invited themselves to other fighter airfields, and over a glass of beer chatted about the latest form in the world of air fighting. So it was that some pilots knew about the German habit of using their fighter escorts in stepped-up layers, of the vulnerability of the 109 when attacked from behind, and its half-rolling evasive tactic followed by a steep dive to the deck. They knew that all depended on teamwork, that they must never fight alone, and that when they found themselves alone they must never fly straight and level. They were taught never to follow an opponent down over France, because there would be more below, and too many good pilots had been last seen diving after a 109. The good squadron commander made sure his men knew these things, but other pilots were not so fortunate.

The training schools were working hard to replace pilots lost during the Dunkirk fighting, and before a new pilot joined his squadron he spent a few days at an operational training unit, where he flew some twenty hours on a Spitfire or a Hurricane. Here was a splendid opportunity for inexperienced pilots to be brought right up-to-date about air fighting, especially as the instructors had fought in France. But the knowledge a man acquired was largely a matter of self-instruction.

During August I spent a few days at one of these units, and although the instructors were good fellows they were few and we were many, and they seemed content to teach us to fly the Spitfire but not to fight it. We searched desperately for someone to tell us what to do and what not to do, because this, we fully realised, would shortly mean the difference between life and death. We knew we were about to face a period of great personal danger, and that if we survived our first few fights we would be of some value to our squadrons. But our problem was how to get through half a dozen fights? We wanted a man of the calibre of Boelcke or Mannock or Mölders or Malan to explain the unknown and to clear our confused and apprehensive minds; but on this occasion the right senior officer was not present.

Someone told us that an excellent novel, published at ten shillings after the First War, was well worth reading because it contained all the lessons of air fighting. So we sent a pilot to London to search the second-hand bookstalls and get half a dozen copies. The booksellers, it turned out, knew what we were after, but the book was out of print and recent demand had pushed up the price to three pounds! But our emissary returned not entirely empty handed, for he took the precaution of buying himself a bullet-proof vest to better his chances when he joined his squadron.

Since he commanded 11 Group, Keith Park would bear much responsibility in the coming battle. Park had watched the progress of air fighting from the early inarticulate days to the present time, when radar and radio gave him a large measure of minute-to-minute control over his squadrons. He was a practical airman and no stranger to the cockpit of a Hurricane, from which he had seen the last ships leave Dunkirk. He was a thoughtful man and an excellent staff officer, for his reports are models of excellent descriptive writing. He was one of the few officers of air rank who flew combat aeroplanes, and because of his love of flying he was keenly interested in the fighting tactics of his pilots, which he knew were in the melting pot. Shortly, he would begin to improve the training and tactics of his squadrons, but he had only been in the chair a few weeks and there had been much to occupy his time. Now he prepared to be Dowding's first lieutenant and tactical commander for the coming struggle, should it be fought over the south-east. At his headquarters, near Nottingham, the genial Trafford Leigh-Mallory, commanding 12 Group, made his final preparations should the Luftwaffe attack the Midlands.

There was one ominous gap in their defences which they could not plug and which, if properly exploited by the opposition, could do great harm. Already Göring had sent small formations of Stukas and covering 109s at low level across the Channel to attack small shipping convoys hugging the coast, and fighter pilots at cockpit readiness on Hawkinge airfield had seen the white geysers from exploding bombs before they got the order to scramble. The country lay naked and exposed to this form of approach and attack.

Bombing is often called 'strategic' when we hit the enemy, and 'tactical' when he hits us, and it is often difficult to know where one finishes and the other begins. But this time the issue was clear cut, for the group commanders were the tactical commanders, while at Bentley Priory the strategist Dowding, whose bleak countenance masked a strange and emotional character, waited for his long stewardship of Fighter Command to be put to the test.

Operation *Sealion*, the strategic plan for the invasion of Britain, followed the usual pattern of *Blitzkrieg*, except that the air fighting over Dunkirk had made Göring realise that the R.A.F. would prove a harder nut to crack than some air forces who, without the magic eye, had been surprised and largely written-off on the ground. Once again the Luftwaffe would be used as a big stick to bludgeon all opposition, and the panzers would cross the Channel, as they had crossed the Meuse, with strong packs of dive-bombers and fighter-bombers taking the place of artillery, and gain foot-holds on suitable beaches between the Isle of Wight and Dover.

The Luftwaffe would destroy the fighter defences in the south and then extend their offensive farther inland, so that the bomber fleets could roam unopposed over England, taking out the old cities, reducing civilian morale, and paving the way for invasion against a British Army short of modern weapons. The enemy planners estimated that four days of intensive operations would subdue our southern air defences, and a further four weeks would be required to write-off the remainder of the R.A.F. *Adler Tag* (Eagle Day), scheduled for early August, would mark the beginning of the attack against 11 Group and, if all went well, the panzers would cross the Channel four or five weeks later.

There was little wrong with these plans, for the Germans realised that the Luftwaffe had made possible their rapid Continental victories, and only air power could surmount the natural advantages of England's island position. In early July, barely two weeks after the Franco-German Armistice, Göring issued the first of many directives to his three *Luftflotten* about the air war against England, but there was much detailed discussion between the planning staffs, and much coming and going between Göring and his senior commanders. Obviously it would be some time before the detailed plans were approved, and during this period Göring decided to bring R.A.F. fighter squadrons to battle by a series of attacks against harbours and shipping which he hoped would progressively reduce England's air defences.

Thinking about the coming air battles, Göring doubtless remembered the old days when the scout squadrons were
assembled together into the first *Jagdgeschwader*, led by the great
Manfred von Richthofen, and of how this step simplified the
operational training of fighter pilots and the planning of
fighter operations, for he ordered that his single-engined and
twin-engined squadrons should be grouped together under
tactical fighter commands, known as *Jagdführer*, which were
similar to the R.A.F.'s fighter groups except for the radar.

Would Göring allow the magic eye to see, and go on seeing?
Would he, like Drake, who fought beneath the high guns of the
Spanish Armada, send his formations at such a height that
they could not be plotted and resisted? Had his scientific
advisers told him that the radar horizon could not follow the
curve of the earth, and that if he sent his formations across the
Channel fifty feet above the waves there could be no proper air
defence? Was he told that even the Stukas could venture low

across the Channel and take out the radar stations, whose masts stood out like beacons on our coasts? Did he know that radar stations could be easily jammed or spoofed?

Had Göring studied the effects of his recent bombing attacks, and had he realised that airfields, unlike densely built-up cities, were difficult to knock out? Did he remember that an aeroplane on the ground, full of fuel and ammunition and unable to evade or shoot back, was a sitting duck and one of the most vulnerable of all military targets, and that most of its life was spent in this position? Did he recall that the fighter could best exploit its basic qualities of speed and surprise when it was used offensively, or would he be bedevilled by his own experiences, twenty-two years ago, when he rarely crossed the front lines and was content with defensive tactics?

Had Göring, like Dowding, done his homework faithfully and well? Would he, like Dowding, be content with the strategic direction of the battle, leaving the problems of fighting tactics to the men who knew best? Or would he act the part of 'the senior officer present' on every available occasion?

Chapter 13

'BOMBEN AUF EN-GE-LAND'

From their massive air fleets the Germans were able to mount raids which varied from single unescorted bombers attacking shipping off the Suffolk coast to mixed formations of more than one hundred fighters and bombers in the central Channel. The day usually began with single aircraft making shipping and weather reconnaissances, and these were followed by two, three, or four raids separated in time and widely varying in composition. Usually 109s provided the close escort, but occasionally the twin-engined 110s guarded the Dornier and Heinkel bombers and the Stuka dive-bombers. Sometimes a few 109s took advantage of low cloud, slipped across the Channel, dive-bombed Dover harbour, and tested their cannons and machine guns against the barrage balloons.

Once the gaggle had formed up, with the fighters stepped-up behind, the bomber leader flew straight towards his target, delivered his load, and made for France at high speed, leaving a rearguard of fighters to hold off any opposition. The heaviest day's fighting during these few weeks of probing and sparring over the Channel saw four separate and strong raids against a west-bound convoy passing through the Straits of Dover and involved three hundred German aeroplanes, apart from strong 109 patrols, who from noon until dusk were never absent from the Channel.

The Germans intended that this conflict should be a fighter contest, and the bombers were dangled as an attractive bait over the Channel to lure Hurricanes and Spitfires into a hornet's nest of high, waiting Messerschmitts. It mattered little how many of the small coasters plying through the Channel were damaged or sunk, for sinking ships was not the primary object of their air battle, and no doubt the British would survive even if their coasters were denied these narrow waters. What did concern them was how the R.A.F. reacted to the raids and how best to decoy Spitfires and Hurricanes so that Fighter Command could be steadily reduced during these few weeks of high summer before the invasion.

When the attacks began in early July bombers and fighters flew in equal numbers, so that a wing of 109s provided close escort to some twenty-five bombers or dive-bombers. It was soon apparent that the air fighting took place under conditions which favoured the attackers, for they always enjoyed the advantages of numbers and height. Werner Mölders led his wing on many of these forays and often bounced Spitfires who were climbing to get at the bombers, but who, if they survived his first surprise attack, gave a good account of themselves in the ensuing close-fighting. Mölders usually positioned his close escort at some 4,000 feet higher and about a mile behind the bombers, but it sometimes happened that small, hard-hitting Spitfire formations struck at the bombers before the close escort could lend a hand. Mölders also found that he could not come to grips with large numbers of R.A.F. fighters, and he was concerned about their elusiveness and the suddenness of some of their attacks, as were the bomber boys.

The Stuka could not live over the Channel unless it was protected by fighters, but the very nature of dive-bombing made this aeroplane exceedingly difficult to escort. Because of her dive-brakes the Stuka dived at a steady speed, but when the clean 109 dived its speed soon increased, and the escorting fighters were separated from the dive-bombers. Sometimes after the bombing the fighters failed to find the dive-bombers and the fighter pilots could only search for a short time, otherwise they would be short of petrol for the return journey. Thus the Stukas often found themselves alone, and occasionally they were badly mauled by the defending Spitfires and Hurricanes, whose pilots were always ready for a 'Stuka Party'.

Unaccustomed to such rough treatment, the Stuka crews called for more fighter protection, and the *Kommodore* of the fighter units decided that the proportion of escorting fighters to bombers should be doubled; in addition, a wing of 109s, called a reception escort, was to patrol in mid-Channel to protect the harrassed Stukas, and free-lance fighter sweeps would trail their coats off Dover. Also, the Luftwaffe organised an efficient rescue service to recover crews who had either baled-out or ditched in the sea.

German crews wore 'mae-wests', carried dinghies, fluorescine markers and flares, and a number of rafts were moored in the Channel containing first-aid supplies, dry clothes, food, and radio. Launches patrolled off the French coast, and a fleet of Heinkel seaplanes carried out excellent work and saved many lives from both sides. The white Heinkels carried the Red Cross, and the Germans were incensed whenever one was set upon and destroyed by R.A.F. fighters. 109s began to escort the seaplanes, Spitfires, then attacked the 109s, reinforcements followed from both sides of the Channel, and sizeable air battles developed.

The high summer began to fade: July passed, and during early August it was time for Göring to take stock. Four weeks, sufficient time to conquer half Europe, had gone since the beginning of the Channel fighting, and although his bombers ranged over England almost every night, causing protracted air-raid alarms, some loss of production and suffering few casualties, Göring must have known that the day struggle was not going according to plan. The much vaunted Messerschmitt 'Destroyer' fighters, the 110, was proving a failure as an escort fighter, being vulnerable to the more manoeuvrable Spitfire and Hurricane, and 109s frequently had to help the twin-engined fighters out of a tight spot.

So far the Germans had barely used one-third of their available strength, but the three *Luftflotten* had now prepared their detailed plans to destroy the R.A.F., and would soon increase the pressure. After Göring had expressed his views the plans were finally approved and aimed at destroying the Royal Air Force in the same way as the Polish and French Air Forces. But a firm date for Eagle Day was still lacking, a spate of directives from Göring further amended the plans, and the *Reichsmarschall* summoned the able commanders of his two most powerful air fleets, Sperrle and Kesselring, to his fabulous country house at Karinhall for a final meeting. Eventually 10th August was selected, and although this date was postponed because of unfavourable weather, it did not prevent some preliminary blows at Fighter Command when on 12th August

Portsmouth dockyard, shipping, six radar stations, two forward airfields, and an emergency landing ground were battered by raids that varied from some of the strongest formations yet assembled to a solitary aeroplane which bombed the radar site at Pevensey. The main attack was postponed from hour to hour, and such was the confusion that some units took off during the morning of Eagle Day, 13th August, instead of the afternoon.

During the following days, *Luftflotte 2* attacked airfields in the south-east of England, *Luftflotte 3* operated against the south, while *Luftflotte 5* spread the R.A.F. defences in the north-east. The majority of these attacks fell on targets within five miles of the coast, between the Solent and the Thames Estuary, where every airfield was attacked, regardless of whether or not it operated fighters, including heavy raids on the Coastal Command airfield at Gosport and the Fleet Air Arm bases at Ford and Lee-on-Solent. The airfields at Croydon, Detling, Eastchurch, Hawkinge, Lympne, Manston, Martlesham, Thorney Island, and West Malling were attacked, sometimes frequently, and occasionally the Luftwaffe ranged well inland and bombed the flying training airfields at Brize Norton and Sealand, near Chester, the bomber airfield at Driffield in Yorkshire, the maintenance airfield at Colerne, and Fighter Command's vital sector stations at Middle Wallop, Tangmere, and Biggin Hill.

Kenley was hit by a low-level raid of nine Dorniers, followed immediately by a bombing attack from 12,000 feet. The high attack was intercepted, and some bombers were brought down. However, the low attackers, who flew just above the tree-tops, reached their target without loss and proceeded to carry out some extremely effective low bombing and strafing, during which a Dornier was brought down by the ground defenders. In all about one hundred bombs were dropped on this sector station, which cratered the runways and destroyed hangars, workshops, and sick quarters, badly damaged many other buildings, wrecked several fighters, lorries, refuellers, and transports, and killed some personnel.

Between 13th and 18th August some thirty-four airfields and five radar stations were attacked and some, such as Manston and

Hawkinge, were bombed several times. Raids on the forward airfields were often made by Stukas, who approached at their usual height, flew once round the circuit for a quick survey, peeled-off, and made steep attacks from the sun. Dorniers and Junkers 88s, escorted by fighters, penetrated farther inland and released their bombs from medium altitudes.

So far, the Luftwaffe had attempted in various ways to weaken the defences by maintaining pressure on one area, by feint attacks, and by continuing operations in one locality immediately they had ceased in another. Now, however, they began to mount simultaneous and widely separated heavy raids to spread the defences further, so that two-pronged attacks hit airfields in Essex and Sussex at the same time. Bombers still usually operated in wing strength, but occasionally two wings flew together against targets of special importance.

There was no control from the ground, and each German attack was a set piece, planned in detail beforehand, so that it was impossible to improvise, or change plans, once the aeroplanes had taken-off. The big raids took a long time to build-up, for the bombers did not carry suitable radio for communicating with the escorting fighters, and their assembly had to be made in fair weather over a town such as Boulogne or Calais. Sometimes, in poor weather, or when two or three raids assembled in the same area, the fighters could not find the bombers, and the latter came across the Channel with little or no fighter protection. Weather played a big part in these raids, for the navigation leader steered the force by dead reckoning, that is by checking his pre-planned tracks with prominent landmarks on the ground below, such as towns, rivers, and railway junctions; and, in 1940, there was no such thing as 'blind bombing': the only means of hitting a target was for the bomb aimer to see it from the air.

In mid-August, owing to their heavy losses, the Stukas were temporarily withdrawn from the battle. Concentrating against the twin-engined bomber raids, which usually came in between 11,000 and 18,000 feet according to cloud cover, R.A.F. fighters exploited the gap of a few thousand feet between the bombers and their escorting Messerschmitts, and sometimes trounced the bombers before the higher 109s could interfere.

Bomber casualties increased, and the German fighter tactics were highly criticised by their bomber crews, who held that their escorting fighters should fly at the same level, and not several thousand feet higher. The fighter leaders, however, were opposed to this suggestion, because if they flew alongside the bombers they would either have to cut down their speed or weave round their charges. Enemy fighter pilots did not want to be tied rigidly to the bombers; they wanted freedom to manoeuvre, and a height advantage to surprise R.A.F. fighters. Here were the ingredients of a first-class row, but the controversy about enemy escort tactics was settled, temporarily, when the close escorts were instructed to fly at the same height and alongside the bombers.

Meanwhile, *Reichsmarschall* Göring closely followed the progress of the battle, for the estimated four days to subdue Britain's southern air defences would soon be gone. His Intelligence reported that the bombing was good, and that Fighter Command had evacuated some forward airfields. Accordingly there were more high-level meetings at Karinhall and, on 19th August, more instructions about the conduct of the air battle.

Day and night operations, Göring ordered, were to be directed exclusively against the Royal Air Force. Daylight operations were aimed at inducing big air battles in which Fighter Command would be defeated; if the Hurricanes and Spitfires failed to react to the raids they would be destroyed on the ground. Shipping was only to be attacked in the most favourable circumstances. Airfields successfully attacked were not to be bombed on the following day.

A bomber wing must always be supported by three fighter wings, one of which would fly ahead and clear the target area, while the second and third carried out the duties of close escort and high escort respectively. But only part of the fighter arm was to be employed as escort to the bombers; the remainder were to fly free-lance operations so that they would engage British fighters on favourable terms and indirectly protect the bombers.

Whenever possible fighters were to attack R.A.F. aircraft on the ground, and these low-level attacks were to be protected by other fighter formations. Attacks by single aircraft using cloud cover were to be flown only by highly trained volunteers. Fighter pilots were to pay less attention to the shooting down of balloons. New pilots, led by veterans, were to gain experience over the Channel before flying over England.

Stocks of twin-engined fighters were low, and they were only to be used when the range of single-engined fighters was inadequate or to cover 109s during their withdrawal. There must never be more than one officer in any crew.

No radar site, the *Reichsmarschall* instructed, had yet been put out of action, and the attacks were to cease.

During the following four days a spell of bad weather prevented the assembly of large raids, and the Luftwaffe had to be content with high-altitude fighter sweeps over Dover, a few sharp fighter-bomber attacks against Manston, and some scattered bombing raids. Similarly the night effort, influenced by the weather, varied between twenty and two hundred bombers, who reconnoitred and harassed large areas of England, with little interference from the defences.

After the early morning haze had disappeared on Saturday, 24th August, an almost continuous stream of bomber and fighter units joined together over the Pas de Calais and assembled into bombing formations, close escorts, high cover escorts, target supports, fighter sweeps, and reception escorts.

At breakfast-time the bombing began with a small, unopposed raid against Great Yarmouth, and shortly afterwards five strong patrols, numbering about one hundred aeroplanes in all, reconnoitred south-east England, from the coast to Biggin Hill, and were challenged only by a brace of Spitfires. Two hours later, during the mid-morning, two separate raids, each consisting of a bomber wing, well protected by 109s, missed their primary target, Manston, and dropped their bombs near Canterbury. Only a few minutes elapsed before a Heinkel wing, escorted by twice as many fighters, headed towards Dover, where it was tackled by some twenty Spitfires and Hurricanes, who failed to get through to the bombers before they dropped sixty bombs on Ramsgate airport and a further one hundred and fifty on the town, where there was extensive damage.

Once again there was no distinct gap between the end of one attack and the beginning of another, and shortly after noon some twenty Junkers 88s, escorted by fighters, and flanked by diversionary fighter sweeps, flew unimpeded to Manston, where nine Defiants just managed to get off before the 88s dived down and badly damaged the airfield and its installations. The bombers, however, spent too long over the airfield, and on their withdrawal across the Channel the Defiants, supported by a Hurricane squadron, caught up with them and shot down five and two escorting 109s.

During the early afternoon the Germans maintained strong patrols over the Straits, and occasionally their fighters penetrated a few miles inland, so that Fighter Command scrambled half a dozen squadrons, who were refuelling on the ground when the real attacks came shortly before tea-time. These consisted of another attack on Manston and two almost simultaneous medium-altitude attacks against the sector stations at Hornchurch and North Weald. During the long penetrations to these targets five defending squadrons intercepted, but could only destroy one bomber, thanks to vigorous fighting by the escorting Messerschmitts. At Hornchurch, however, the bombers were so harried by the London guns that only six bombs fell on the target. Thin cloud obscured North Weald from the bomber leader, who skilfully led his formation below the overcast, and from 13,000 feet saw his force plant two hundred bombs on the target.

By this time the escorting 109s had been flying for more than one hour and could remain airborne for about another thirty minutes. If they stayed with the bombers they would have the choice of either force-landing in England or ditching in the Channel, so their leaders called their squadrons together and set course for France, leaving the long-range 110s to bring the bombers home. As the bombers retired more defending squadrons came into action and, unhampered by the attentions of the lively 109s, evaded the 110s and shot down four bombers and damaged several more.

As the last German bombers disappeared from the sky over

Kent and the Thames Estuary, more Heinkels, escorted and flanked by nearly one hundred fighters, skirted the Isle of Wight and headed for Portsmouth. The opposition was light, a squadron of Spitfires seen below the bombers was easily driven off, the bomber leader was able to concentrate on his bombing-run, and Portsmouth town and dockyard were badly damaged. On the withdrawal across the Channel more R.A.F. fighters tried to get at the bombers, but were driven off by the 109s.

So ended a day of heavy and sustained attacks largely directed against sector stations and fighter airfields in the south-east. Reconnaissance photographs showed the Germans that Manston's days were numbered and North Weald had been badly hit, although its fighters were still there. Hornchurch had escaped lightly, but the sudden switch to the left flank, Portsmouth, would remind the defenders that the three *Luft-flotten* could mount a variety of attacks from their many and widespread bases. During the various engagements twenty-two Hurricanes and Spitfires had been destroyed, while German losses, from more than one thousand sorties, were less than four per cent, and this attrition rate could be sustained, if need be, for a long time.

The *Kommodore*, meeting at *Jagdführer* headquarters, were satisfied with the results of the fighting. Göring had told them that Fighter Command must be worn down by a series of air battles and, so far, the results were encouraging. Despite their Dunkirk losses, and some subsequent severe casualties, it was amazing that the English still operated the clumsy Defiants over the Channel. Over England the 109s usually had the height advantage and they were able to bounce Spitfires and Hurricanes below. On equal terms they were happy about the outcome of a straight fight with a Hurricane. The Spitfire, it seemed, could turn on a *Reichsmark*, and this was a most useful quality to throw off an attacker, but tight turns were more of a defensive than an offensive tactic and did not win air battles.

From the German angle a satisfactory feature of the day's fighting was the low proportion of R.A.F. fighters which inter-cepted before the bombing. On the other hand, more bombers were shot down on the withdrawal because the 109s, short of fuel, had to return straight to their bases instead of weaving round the slower bombers. Targets such as Hornchurch and North Weald, north of the Thames, could just be reached by 109 escorts if the bombers made rendezvous on time, did not hang about over France before setting course, and navigated accurately over England. But if timing and navigation were not perfect, then the bombers would have to manage with 110 escorts until they were met, over the Channel, by the reception escorts.

The bomber crews, however, were far from happy about their casualties; they foresaw heavier losses as the air battles moved farther inland, and their fears were justified when, on 26th August, nineteen bombers failed to return from raids against Folkestone, the sector stations at Hornchurch, Debden, and North Weald and, once more, Portsmouth town and dockyard. Further, many bombers returning to France were well shot-up and several contained badly injured crews. Thus the recent ugly dispute about escort tactics again flared up, the bomber commanders alleging that the fighter pilots were failing in their clear and first duty to protect the bombers.

Göring supported the bomber commanders, and had some harsh and unfair things to say about the fighting qualities and morale of his fighter arm. He had already decided to switch the bombers of *Luftflotte 3* from day to night operations, and the fighters of this air fleet would assist those of *Luftflotte 2*. In future, Göring ordered, the bombers would have close, high, and top fighter escorts; there would be three fighters for every bomber.

During the last few days of August the Luftwaffe hammered at a target system which, except for a heavy raid against Luton town and airport, was aimed at securing the invasion route from the Kent coast to the capital. Eleven of fifteen attacks were against the sector stations and airfields of 11 Group: one was against Warmwell, the most easterly airfield in 10 Group; and three were against Eastchurch and Detling, belonging to Coastal Command.

Since the R.A.F. usually intercepted in small packets, rarely more than a squadron strong, life was not too hard for the escorting fighter pilots. A raid against Biggin Hill, although opposed by a Spitfire squadron at Dungeness, a Hurricane squadron and a Spitfire squadron over Maidstone, and a further Spitfire squadron near Westerham, reached its goal in such good fighting order that one hundred accurate bombs hit and set fire to the operations block, destroyed hangars and other buildings, cratered the landing area, and shattered vital communications. Likewise, an onslaught against Hornchurch was challenged by four Hurricane squadrons, who were held off by the 109s and, while the opposing fighters clashed, the bombers flew on to aim one hundred bombs at the sector station. But four defending squadrons intercepting before the bombs fell was unusual, and the average was about two squadrons on the penetration and slightly less on the withdrawal.

Only on two occasions during August were low-level raids carried out against targets well inland, and one of these, against Kenley, has already been described. The second, against Biggin Hill, took place during the early evening, when a small force of some nine Junkers 88s, escorted by a dozen 109s, detached itself from other formations milling about the Straits and lost height over the Channel to get below a layer of cloud at 5,000 feet, where visibility was excellent. The leader made a landfall near Dover, flew across Kent to the Isle of Sheppey, where he swung left, lost more height, and made a fast, low run to the airfield on the hill. While the 109s strafed, each bomber dropped two weapons so that eighteen bombs wrecked workshops, the M.T. yard, the armoury, the meteorological office, and the N.A.A.F.I. The Sergeants' Mess, the W.A.A.F. quarters, and the airmen's barracks were made uninhabitable. Most of the transport, carefully dispersed, was badly damaged: two Spitfires were burnt out, all electricity, water, and gas mains were cut, most telephone communications were out, and thirty-nine personnel were killed. Six Spitfires fell in with the Junkers as they retired, and a Spitfire squadron engaged near the coast. Four Spitfires were brought down, while the cost to the Germans of the most successful attack yet carried out against a Fighter Command station was one Messerschmitt 109.

As the Junkers landed from this devastating foray the night bombers were preparing to take off. With more bombers available from *Luftflotte 3*, the night effort was increased and, apart from the harassing attacks and dislocation raids against widely separated places, the Germans began to concentrate against the Mersey ports and other cities. During the last four nights of August an average of nearly one hundred and sixty bombers attacked Liverpool and Birkenhead, and the last attack started many fires in the centre of Liverpool; a considerable tonnage of bombs hit Portland, Portsmouth, Bristol, Manchester, South Wales, the Tyne, and Hartlepool. On one night single bombers attacked six airfields in the western half of the country with only moderate success. The cost to the Germans of these night attacks was very small, for the opposing defences were ineffective. Although R.A.F. night fighters were occasionally seen, they did not perturb the bomber crews, whose main concern was with the anti-aircraft fire, which sometimes forced them to fly higher and hampered their aim on the bombing-run.

At the beginning of September there were three hours less daylight than at the beginning of July; three hours was sufficient time to mount and recover a major attack against Fighter Command, and Göring realised that time was running out and stepped-up his attacks on the sector stations vital to the defence of London. Biggin Hill was bombed for the fifth time in two days. Debden was heavily bombed for the third time, North Weald suffered its second big attack, Hornchurch escaped its third attack fairly lightly, while another raid against Kenley failed to find the target. Apart from the sector stations, the fighter airfields at Croydon, Gravesend, and Lympne were attacked; Detling was temporarily knocked out, while the big Coastal Command airfield at Eastchurch, twice heavily attacked on the same day, suffered great damage.

Göring's views about the increased fighter escorts were proving correct, for not only were the bombers getting through to their targets but their casualties were reduced, and air battles were being fought on terms favourable to the German fighters. Indeed, during the most intensive spell of air fighting Fighter Command lost one hundred and one aeroplanes in four days, while Luftwaffe casualties were almost identical, one hundred and six aeroplanes, of which only a small proportion

were bombers. The battle was being fought between the two
fighter forces.

At the beginning of September enemy bomber strength
showed an increase over the previous months; stocks of single-
engine fighters had very slightly decreased, by about three per
cent, and twin-engined fighters by seventeen per cent. There
was no shortage of trained crews and, although the twin-
engined fighter force required nursing, the bomber and single-
engined fighter forces could stand up to this rate of wastage for
weeks ahead. Could Fighter Command?

The German flyers could see they were pounding the sector
stations and airfields with great effect, and in early September
Mölders thought that the opposition slackened. Photographic
reconnaissance, properly interpreted, would have revealed the
front-line strength of Fighter Command, but it was the practice
at Kesselring's headquarters to write-off each R.A.F. squadron
whose airfield had been successfully bombed: thus the three
fighter squadrons operating from Biggin Hill were struck off the
order of battle, whereas one still flew from Biggin and two were
based at other airfields. It was hardly surprising, therefore, that
when Kesselring called a conference at the Hague there was
some doubt about the true strength of Fighter Command.
Kesselring thought it was finished: Sperrle ventured his opinion
that about one thousand fighters were left, while the expert,
the chief of Intelligence, said that during August the strength
had fallen to one hundred serviceable fighters but had recently
recovered to about three hundred and fifty. In point of fact on
1st September, 1940, Fighter Command had almost seven
hundred serviceable fighters.

Chapter 14

'THE HOLE'

THE 11 Group controller walked down a long flight of concrete steps to Park's battle headquarters, known to all who laboured there as 'the hole'. A short time ago he had commanded a fighter squadron, but he was wounded in a dogfight, and it would be some months before he could return to flying. So he had become a controller and admitted that controlling was the next best thing to flying. He and his fellow controllers, most of whom had flown operationally, knew the problems of fighting and flying; they spoke the same language as the fighter boys, and there was a good understanding between fighter leader and controller. They found that directing the fighter squadrons was a wonderful outlet for their energies, and their heavy responsibilities gave them a sense of power and achievement.

The controller entered a room which overlooked a lower and larger room where several W.A.A.F.s, wearing headsets, sat round a large map, known as 'the table', on which they plotted the movements of friendly and enemy aeroplanes. This underground building sometimes reminded him of a small, intimate theatre, for the controller and his assistants sat, as it were, in the sound-proofed, glass-partitioned dress circle, flanked by teams from the gunners and the Observer Corps, so that all could watch the drama below; sometimes when Park came down to follow the battle and sat in his special place it reminded him of the bridge of a great ship.

This building was the hub of a nerve system which had two distinct functions, reporting and controlling. The reporting of enemy raids came from the radars, and from thousands of field observers, who with glasses and telephone took over from radar once the Germans had crossed the coast. All this information was filtered before being plotted on the table, and this process took some time, but a controller could usually reckon on about fifteen minutes warning from the radars before a high-altitude formation crossed the coast. The other half of the system was used by the controller to get the fighter squadrons into the air to intercept.

The W.A.A.F.s placed small counters (red for attackers and black for defenders) on the table, and these gave the estimated height and number of an enemy raid. Each raid was given a number, and as the counters were moved to and fro across the table the group controller and the six sector controllers, who had similar presentations, could watch the build-up of big raids and follow their own defensive moves.

Opposite the control bridge was a huge board displaying, by a system of coloured lights, the squadrons' ever-changing order of battle—released, available (thirty or fifteen minutes), readiness (five minutes), and cockpit readiness (two minutes). Once they were scrambled more coloured lights indicated their progress, so that the controller could see at a glance the number of squadrons in the air, how many had sighted the enemy, what proportion were in action, those returning home, and what he had in reserve. This display was called 'the Tote'.

The nerve system stretched out across the land, over the Channel, over the North Sea, and into the air. It gave the group controller a minute-to-minute picture of an air battle fought a hundred miles away. But it was a complicated instrument of war, and because of this complexity some of its components—especially radar stations, surface operations rooms, and land-lines—were vulnerable to bombing.

The controller took a vacant seat, sized up the situation from the various displays, saw that two strong enemy formations were retiring across the Channel, noticed that the blonde team was on duty, and said to the staff officer, his deputy, 'What's the form?'

'Two raids came in at Dungeness about ten o'clock; about thirty bombers in each and the usual swarm of 109s. 501 Squadron intercepted one lot near Canterbury, but couldn't get at the bombers. Treble one* saw the others near Biggin and say they turned south-east when attacked, and a 12 Group squadron intercepted over Chatham.'

'Much damage?'

* 111 Squadron.

'Doesn't appear to be from the reports we've had so far. Scattered bombing at quite a few places, Westerham, Wilmington, Bromley, Bexley, and the main line between Charing Cross and the coast is cut. More damage from south-east London; the reports are still coming in.'

'Sixty bombers don't seem to have done much damage. But the haze probably stopped them finding Biggin or Kenley.'

The out-going controller, free for the moment, said, 'Good morning, old boy. Looks as if you'll have a busy time this afternoon. You'd better read the latest instruction from the old man; it's about reinforcements from 12 Group. And don't forget to sign as having read and understood!'

The controller picked up a secret file which contained several directives from Park to his group and sector controllers. These were his tactical orders to the men who directed the air battles; they represented what he had learned since the fighting began, and revealed his thinking as he constantly adjusted his tactics to counter the Luftwaffe.

When the fighting began Park instructed that the Spitfires were to tackle the high-flying Messerschmitts, leaving the Hurricanes to get at the bombers. These tactics had worked reasonably well until the Germans began to escort their bombers more closely, when Park had ordered his controllers to send both types of fighter against the bombers. The Luftwaffe replied, however, by providing even more escort fighters, and R.A.F. pilots were finding it increasingly difficult to break through the layers of Messerschmitts; and once they got through, the bombers, now well protected with armour plating, were hard to bring down from an astern attack. Machine guns were almost outdated for aerial combat, and R.A.F. fighter pilots wanted heavy calibre cannons—to smash and tear their way through engines and armour plate. However, there was but one squadron with cannon-firing Spitfires, and Park, at the beginning of September, reverted to his original instruction about putting the Hurricanes in against the bombers—since the four closely grouped machine guns on each wing of a Hurricane gave a denser bullet pattern than the staggered guns on a Spitfire.

Another instruction expressed Park's deep concern about the

number of bomber formations which reached their targets without hindrance from his fighters. Sometimes his complete force failed to intercept before the bombing because his squadrons were too high. When the group controller ordered a squadron to 16,000 feet the sector controller added on 2,000 feet for good measure, and the leader increased this in the vain hope that 109s would not be above him. The net result was that bomber formations slipped in unopposed at 15,000 feet, and were not intercepted until after the bombing.

Park knew there was a strong feeling among his fighting men that because of the great odds they faced everything should be done to put more aeroplanes into one fighting formation. Douglas Bader, commanding 242 Squadron in 12 Group, had read and reread the stories of the old air fighters, and followed their teachings about height, surprise, teamwork, and straight shooting. Aged thirty, he saw things differently from some of the younger leaders and, never afraid to speak his mind, he quoted Mannock and Richthofen, and argued for bigger wings of three, four, or five squadrons. His views were supported by his A.O.C., Leigh-Mallory.

Malan, Broadhurst, Tuck, and other leaders in 11 Group were all for bigger formations, even if they did not support the great gaggles envisaged by Bader. Park, who, when the shadows were lengthening, often climbed into his Hurricane, threaded his way through the balloons and landed on his battered airfields, discussed the size of fighting formations with his leaders. Although he was sympathetic to their views, he told them that since it was difficult enough to intercept with single squadrons before the target was bombed, how could a wing, which would take longer to take off, form-up, and climb, get there in time? He could intercept in wing strength after the bombing, but this would simply be playing into the enemy's hands.

Nevertheless Park was fully aware of the advantages of concentrating his fighters and, following some attacks against aeroplane factories, he revised his instructions to his controllers. In future, whenever big attacks threatened, the group controller would obtain two squadrons from 10 Group, one to patrol between Brooklands and Croydon, and the other between Brooklands and Windsor; these reinforcing squadrons would also protect airfields west and south-west of London and would be controlled by 11 Group. The main attack was to be met by as strong a defending force as possible between the coast and the sector stations and, if time permitted, squadrons should be put into the battle in pairs. Forward squadrons, at Hawkinge, Manston, or Rochford, were to rendezvous over Canterbury and form into a wing of two squadrons before engaging. Two squadrons were to guard Kenley, Croydon, and Biggin Hill; north of the Thames, Hornchurch, North Weald, and Debden were to be protected until 12 Group's squadrons flew south and immediately these arrived Park's squadrons were to join the main battle. Although 10 Group had already co-operated to the full, 12 Group unfortunately had not shown the same spirit, and on two occasions their squadrons had not been in the right place when Park's stations were heavily bombed. In future whenever 12 Group squadrons were required the 11 Group controller would put his request to the controller at Fighter Command, who would order the reinforcing squadrons to patrol a specific area; Park regretted that this process would take slightly longer than the previous direct link with 12 Group.

The controller sighed and closed the file. There was more in this than met the eye, for he knew that apart from the war against the Luftwaffe there was something of a private war within Fighter Command. Indeed, the 12 Group controller often rang up and asked when their squadrons were going to be let off the leash, pointing out that big enemy formations were building up over the Channel and that they had been at readiness a long time.

They, at 11 Group, knew all about the assembly of the big formations. Sometimes the table showed a maze of plots over the French coast for an hour or more, but the controller could not scramble the defending squadrons until the enemy began to move over the Channel. For if he scrambled, say, ten squadrons before the plots shifted from the French coast and the real attack came in an hour later, then the air defences of south-east England would be reduced by about fifty per cent when the ten defending squadrons were either returning home or were on the ground, refuelling.

If the bombers came straight across the Channel they would take fifteen minutes to reach the English coast at their usual height, 16,000 feet, and escorting 109s would be stacked above to 25,000 feet. Even if the Spitfires were sent off on receipt of the first radar warning, when the enemy were well over the Pas de Calais, they could not intercept the highest 109s over the English coast, because a Spitfire squadron took twenty minutes to climb to 25,000 feet. Unfortunately the arithmetic of controlling was further complicated because the radars were not entirely reliable, and enemy formations had often penetrated well over England without being plotted on the table. Accordingly, controllers could not obtain accurate information about the size and composition of enemy formations until these were seen or heard by the Observer Corps posts on the coast.

But if the controller waited until the enemy crossed the English coast before scrambling the majority of his squadrons they had barely enough time to reach the bombers before the bombs fell, and the shoals of escorting 109s would always be waiting above. On the other hand, if he committed his squadrons too soon the enemy could later roam virtually unopposed over southern England. He had to wait until the Germans were well on their way before he dared send off his second line of fighters, and he had to delay his final moves until he got more information from the Observer posts. This meant that some R.A.F. fighter pilots would never fight the 109 on equal terms, because they would always be underneath.

Sometimes controlling became a nightmare, especially when the table was laden with red counters and some were suddenly removed by the W.A.A.F.s—only to be replaced in different places; or when all the defending squadrons were committed and the communications system was stretched to the breaking-point. Controlling, like weather forecasting, was not yet an exact science. It called for a perfect sense of timing, plenty of common sense, and a bit of luck.

The controller studied the Tote, which showed that fourteen Hurricane and seven Spitfire squadrons still operated within the Group, the ill-fated Defiants having been taken out of the daylight battle some days ago. He thought of the hard-pressed squadrons flying from their cratered airfields and wondered if some would suffer Manston's fate and have to be evacuated. Fortunately, the landing areas were difficult to knock out for any length of time, because the craters could be quickly filled in. Similarly, although the destruction of hangars and barracks caused much inconvenience and some loss of life, it did not prevent the airfields from being used.

The Tote showed that some squadrons had been withdrawn from the forward airfields and that Biggin Hill and Kenley were operating at reduced garrison strength, but it did not show the extensive damage to six of the seven vital sector stations and to five forward fighter airfields. For this damage was not altogether measured in terms of loss of life, craters, and destroyed buildings, but in the time taken to get operational messages from group H.Q. to sector stations. Kenley's operations room was located in a disused butcher's shop at Caterham; Biggin was controlling from an estate office; all sector stations except Northolt had suffered some damage to their communications network. Radar and the Observer Corps were taking longer to report the movements of enemy formations, and executive orders from the group controller to the squadrons were taking longer to get through. The fighter squadrons, already hard pressed to meet the enemy well forward and at the right height, were thus further penalised. Fortunately the Germans had not sustained their attacks against the radar stations, although some occasionally reported what seemed to be deliberate jamming.

Unlike teleprinters and emergency operations buildings, Spitfires and Hurricanes could be replaced on the same day. Although the group had just suffered some of its heaviest casualties since July, the supply of fighters had not yet limited the scale of operations, and all squadrons had their quota. Reserves of aeroplanes were said to be sufficient. But this was not true of the men who flew them.

Ideally, a squadron should stay in the front line for about six weeks before moving to a quiet sector to rest the veterans and train the replacements. The fate of a squadron rested on the qualities of five people—the squadron commander, his two flight commanders, and their deputies. If these were wise and experienced leaders the squadron did its stuff. Some squadron commanders were far too old, and Fighter Command was relearning the R.F.C. lesson of long ago that the peacetime qualifications for promotion—age and seniority—do not apply in war. Park had asked that his squadron commanders should not be more than twenty-six years of age. This was being put into effect; but, meanwhile, the Command had paid a heavy price. The controller's old squadron, indifferently led, had been pulled out of the line after a few days, and there were similar instances when squadrons were cut to pieces owing to bad leadership. Replacement squadrons were available from outside 11 Group, but some were resting, others were inexperienced, and who could tell where the new blow would fall. On the other hand, some squadrons had been in the line too long and were reduced to two or three desperately tired leaders.

When, two months back, the Channel fighting had begun, the Command had been some two hundred pilots short of its establishment. Serious losses during mid-August had made it necessary to reduce the already dangerously low hours at the operational conversion units, and hastily to train volunteers from Bomber Command, Coastal Command, and Army Co-operation Squadrons. On paper these measures made good some of the deficiencies, but the newcomers lacked experience and were mere passengers on their first few missions. Moreover they were up against men with more air and combat experience, for German crews averaged between three and four years' service.

Towards the end of August the controller knew that the pilot position had worsened as a result of the bigger enemy fighter escorts. During the first three days of September ninety of the enemy had cost eighty-five fighters. The total wastage in fighter pilots was about one hundred and twenty a week and, since the output of the operational training units was some sixty-five inexperienced replacements a week, it was quite apparent that Fighter Command was fighting a battle of diminishing returns.

The Command was wasting away. If the Luftwaffe kept up the pressure against the sectors the delicate instrument of control and reporting would gradually disintegrate, and it would only be a question of time before the Germans dominated the air over southern England.

Was there a chance to hold the fort for another month? Until this shining summer gave way to the silver grey skies of autumn and prevented the daily assembly of the big gaggles? This would depend on the Germans. If they took out the radars and came low it could be over very quickly. If they continued against the sector stations it would be a close finish. The controller knew all about the striking increase in the number of barges between Ostend and Le Havre; and there could only be one reason why the Stukas had gathered together in the Pas de Calais. Thank goodness for the Channel . . .

> *Which serves it in the office of a wall,*
> *Or as a moat defensive to a house,*
> *Against the envy of less happier lands . . .*

Chapter 15

FALLING LEAVES

ON 7th September, following Hitler's declaration that London would suffer as reprisals for Bomber Command raids against Berlin, Göring switched his bombers from R.A.F. sector stations, and other airfields, to London and its sprawling docks. Towards five o'clock on that evening more than three hundred bombers, and many hundreds of fighters, rose from their airfields across the Channel, swarmed into a dozen formations and, without feint or decoy, crossed the Straits in two broad waves and headed for the capital. Because of their height, above 20,000 feet, and a stiff head wind, the bombers took a long time to reach London, but although R.A.F. controllers found it easier than usual to intercept, the enemy fighter escorts seemed bigger than ever. There were so many enemy fighters, layered up to 30,000 feet, that a Spitfire pilot said it was like looking up the escalator at Piccadilly Circus.

Near Cambridge the Duxford Wing of two Hurricane and one Spitfire squadrons had been at readiness all day and Bader, anxious to lead thirty-six fighters into action for the first time, had been agitating for hours about getting into the air. At last they were scrambled, and disobeying instructions to patrol North Weald at 10,000 feet, Bader climbed higher and sighted the enemy on their way home. 110s guarded the bombers, and higher still 109s darted to and fro. Tactically the Duxford Wing was poorly placed, but Bader led them in a steep climb towards the bombers, and they had some fleeting shots at the Dorniers before the 109s came down.

All but two of twenty-three defending squadrons were in action and they fought, except for the Duxford Wing, singly—and not in pairs as planned by Park. The balance to the defenders showed some improvement, forty-one destroyed for the loss of twenty-eight fighters, but the operation amounted to a success for the German bombers, who had reached and attacked London. As they returned to France many large fires raged at the Surrey Commercial, the East India and the Royal Albert Docks, at Woolwich, Barking, and the oil farms at the mouth of the Thames.

Before darkness fell another raid hit Hammersmith, Battersea, and Paddington; and as the night closed in a long orderly procession of more than two hundred bombers came over in single file, headed for the flames, which they stoked with loads of incendiaries and high explosive, and then withdrew—save one, which fell to the guns. Thus began the 'Blitz', which continued, unabated, for two months.

The fires of London served as beacons for the night crews, whose bomb aimers, like those of the day bombers, hitherto had to see a target before they could hit it. But now scientific aids were available to help the enemy bombers, and their *Knickebein* system, consisting of radio beams which intersected over or near a target, made it a simple matter for a pilot to guide his aeroplane along one beam and drop his bombs at the point of intersection, with an average error of about half a mile. Bad weather in the target area no longer prevented the bombing of urban areas.

For the first time in the Battle, enemy day and night operations seemed dovetailed into a common plan against London. But while the daylight clashes were largely waged between the opposing fighter forces, the night raids were fought by ground gunners and the civil defence services, for to counter the growing night threat Dowding had only a handful of decently equipped night fighters and a few inland radar stations. His Spitfires and Hurricanes were of little use on dark nights.

On 9th September the Luftwaffe repeated their tactics of the 7th, sending over two waves in quick succession, with fighter forces ranging ahead and on the flanks of the main formations. The Germans were after London and aeroplane factories at Brooklands, but had little success, for one raid was met, as Park intended, well forward, and the bombs were scattered through much cloud near Canterbury.

As usual Bader ventilated his feelings to his sector commander, Wing Commander Woodhall, about getting into the air; Woodhall pressed the 12 Group controller, who, in turn, inquired of his opposite number at 11 Group whether the

Duxford Wing was required. Eventually they were scrambled, and once radio contact was established between controller and wing leader, Woodhall said: 'Will you patrol between North Weald and Hornchurch, angels twenty?' Never one at the best of times for blind obedience to orders, Woodhall's 'will you' was not lost on Bader, and this intimacy between the two men was important, because it had wide repercussions on the authority of wing leaders.

Woodhall, affectionately known as 'Woodie', was a veteran of the Kaiser's War, and was one of the best and most trusted controllers in Fighter Command. His calm and measured tones seemed full of confidence and assurance, and he was fully aware of the limitations of radar, which, at this time, was often distorted by enemy jamming. Woodhall knew that his wing leader was in the best position to judge how and when to attack, and therefore his controlling technique was to advise rather than to instruct.

Bader, climbing hard to the south, figured that once again the Germans would come out of the evening sun, so he forgot about Hornchurch and the height and climbed high over Staines, thirty miles from Hornchurch and well within 11 Group's preserves. He was just in time to position his wing between the sun and two big shoals of bombers accompanied by the usual packs of 109s. Calling the Spitfire leader to cover their tails, he headed the two Hurricane squadrons at the bombers, hammered at the leading Dorniers, saw the bombers begin to break formation, watched sticks of bombs desperately jettisoned, and counted the burning bombers until the remnants of one bomber formation withdrew, still hotly pursued by some of his pilots.

Fortunately for Bader neither North Weald nor Hornchurch was attacked, otherwise Park might have lodged an official complaint with Dowding, who, however, would have taken into account the tremendous results of this engagement—twenty enemy aeroplanes destroyed before bombing, for the loss of four Hurricanes and two pilots. And Leigh-Mallory must have thought a bit of occasional poaching like this was well justified, for he was so delighted with the results that he offered Bader two more squadrons, making five in all, for the next show. So it was in 12 Group, if not in 11 Group, that a leader could interpret instructions from the ground as he thought fit.

Once again Park revised his fighting orders. The readiness (five minutes) squadrons were to be sent off in pairs, Spitfires to take on enemy fighters, and the Hurricanes to take on bombers. The available (fifteen minutes) squadrons were to be brought to readiness and sent to tackle the second wave, and similarly the thirty minute squadrons would repel the third wave. Wings should assemble over airfields, and the sector controller should nominate the wing leader. These arrangements were put to the test two days later when raids on Southampton and London cost the defenders twenty-nine fighters for twenty-five destroyed. Not encouraging arithmetic.

During the next few days unsettled weather with low cloud and rain curtailed the Luftwaffe's daylight activities; however, the night bombing, with casualties sometimes amounting to almost 2,000, caused great concern. The number of guns defending London was doubled, but little damage was inflicted on the raiders. Encouraged by the success of the night offensive, Hitler, meeting with his commanders-in-chief in Berlin, postponed the invasion for three days, blamed the weather for the lack of complete air supremacy, and forecast that only a few more days were required to finish Fighter Command, conveniently forgetting the previous estimates. Thus on the following day, 15th September, two hundred bombers attacked London, Portland, and Southampton.

On the morning of this day, which dashed all German hopes for the conquest of Britain in 1940, enemy fighters were active over the Straits. During the late morning two fighter sweeps came inland, but the 11 Group controller thought these were decoys and that the real threat came from big formations building up over Calais and plotted by the radars for an unusually long time. Thanks to this long interval between the first warning of attack and the enemy's advance, the controller had, for once, enough time to scramble ten squadrons and assemble them into wings and to bring in reinforcements from the adjacent groups before the first German bomber crossed the coast, when a further six defending squadrons were sent off.

The defensive arrangements, so carefully tended throughout

the long weeks of fighting by Keith Park, worked so well that the Biggin Hill Wing fought escorting 109s south of Canterbury, the Kenley Wing made a head-on attack near Maidstone, and two squadrons were in action over Gravesend. Nevertheless, the three German formations forged on and were met, over south London, by the North Weald Wing, who sorted out the bombers with surprisingly little interference from enemy fighters. The Duxford Wing, big even by Teutonic standards, were next in action, but Bader had to delay his attack until some friendly fighters had cleared away; then, as carefully rehearsed, the three Hurricane squadrons went for the bombers while the two Spitfire squadrons held off the 109s. Some bombs were dropped, but they did only little damage to property, an electricity station, and a bridge or two; an unexploded bomb lodged near Buckingham Palace. Thirty Germans were brought down at a cost of seven R.A.F. pilots. The arithmetic was improving.

After a two-hour break, which gave the defending squadrons ample time to rearm and refuel, the Luftwaffe put in its second big attack, again consisting of three heavily escorted bomber formations which crossed the coast on a twenty-mile front between Dover and Dungeness, within five minutes of each other. This time the radar warning was shorter, but nine wings and several independent squadrons came into action over south London, where there was some stiff fighting. Once again, the defenders had the best of the exchange. There were fewer 109s than usual, and these seemed less aggressive, so that some of the bombers were very roughly handled. Two formations were broken up near London—one retiring after a head-on attack by a lone Hurricane—and bombs were scattered over a wide area. The Germans were harried by more Spitfires and Hurricanes as they withdrew. During this action R.A.F. pilots claimed to have destroyed fifty-nine bombers and twenty-one fighters at a cost of eleven.

The fighting over London was at its height when about twenty Heinkels bombed Portland harbour. Only one squadron succeeded in intercepting, and that after the bombing. The final daylight operation was an attempt by twenty bombers to hit the Supermarine Works near Southampton, but the anti-aircraft gunners put up a heavy barrage and the factory was not damaged. At dark the bombers returned to London and continued their work throughout the night.

On this day the pilots of Fighter Command claimed one hundred and seventy-four enemy aeroplanes destroyed and the gunners a further eleven, making one hundred and eighty-five in all, for the loss of thirteen pilots. This claim was of course subsequently reduced to sixty on the evidence of the official German figures made available after the war. There can be no doubt that during the intricate and confused air fighting many claims were duplicated several times. Throughout the Battle R.A.F. fighter pilots claimed about three aeroplanes for every two brought down, while the Germans claimed more than three victories for every one they brought down. A few pilots tended, like the man who can never find all the birds he has shot, to over-claim persistently, but these were soon exposed by the rest of the squadron and either mended their ways or were posted.

Most of the sixty enemy aeroplanes brought down were bombers, and more struggled back to France on one engine, badly shot-up and with many crew members dead or injured. At the debriefings the bomber captains complained bitterly of the incessant Hurricane and Spitfire attacks from squadrons that had long since ceased to exist, if they were to believe their own Intelligence and the Berlin radio. Once again the old argument about fighter tactics flared up.

To try to get above London's anti-aircraft defences the bombers flew very high, sometimes above 22,000 feet, which was really too high for their power and bomb load. Consequently they were very slow, and this gave Fighter Command more time to react. Moreover the speedy 109s had to 'weave' continually to stay with the bombers and, like a terrier running around its master on a country walk, they covered a lot of ground.

Each outward weave carried a *Schwärme* of four 109s some distance away from the bombers, and made the crews more nervous and more insistent in their demands that the close escort remain very close. The fighter *Kommodore* pointed out that if their 109s flew straight and level at the same speed as the bombers they would lose their ability to move quickly and get at the Spitfires. On the other hand, if only the bombers would rendezvous on time and fly in a decent formation, unlike some recent straggling packs thirty kilometres long and quite impossible to protect, it would make things a lot easier for the fighter pilots. There were the usual reproaches and recriminations from both sides and Kesselring, fully aware of his master's strong views about fighting tactics, told Göring, who then instructed that close fighter escorts would cease weaving and would fly straight and level close to the bombers; moreover the high and top cover escorts would not leave the bombers, even when they could see Spitfires some distance away preparing to attack.

Göring's strict orders incensed able fighter leaders, such as Galland and Mölders, who realised that their men could never give a good account of themselves while they were hamstrung by such stupid instructions. But since they were good officers, they tried their utmost to obey Göring's orders, and Galland analysed all his escort missions and personally investigated the loss of every bomber for which he bore some responsibility. Some of his difficulties can be well imagined. From one escort mission he lost twelve 109s, not through enemy action, but because the bombers wandered all over the place and grossly exceeded their planned time over England. Seven of his pilots ditched their aeroplanes in the Channel, four others crash-landed on the French coast and Galland himself, bringing up the rear, thought he would have to land at Manston and surrender because he was so desperately short of fuel. But he flew on and just managed to get down in one piece on the beach at Gris Nez.

Aged twenty-eight, a brilliant leader, victor of some thirty combats, holder of the third Knight's Cross in the whole of the German Fighter Arm, Adolf Galland, *Kommodore* of *J.G.26*, had gained a powerful reputation. At a Channel coast conference Galland thought Göring was unduly influenced by the bombers' complaints. Göring had nothing but reproaches for his fighter pilots, and took them to task about the importance of getting the bombers on to the target. If only they would show a better fighting spirit fewer bombers would be lost. Galland, however, challenged Göring's theories about air fighting by pointing out that his large fighter escorts, strictly tied to the bombers, contradicted the basic purpose of the fighter aeroplane, which is to use its speed and height to find and destroy the enemy. To get the best results, went on Galland, fighters should as far as possible be used offensively; and in any case the escorts should have freedom to manoeuvre and attack, especially as the Spitfire was better at close fighting than the 109.

Göring was not pleased by this criticism from a young officer, and rejecting Galland's opinions, he again demanded close and rigid protection from the fighters. There were more strong words, but before his departure he turned on his not inconsiderable charm and asked about the future requirements of their units. Mölders wanted bigger engines, others better guns. Turning to Galland, the *Reichsmarschall* demanded 'And you?' 'I should like an outfit of Spitfires!' retorted the fighter pilot. This remark soon became a legend in Luftwaffe circles, but, in fact, the Spitfire would have fared little better than the 109 had it been so restricted in its tactics.

But there was not much time left for the Germans to experiment with fighter tactics, for the summer, and its opportunities, had gone. Autumn gales swept the Channel and much cloud prevented a steady rhythm and pressure of enemy daylight operations. The *Führer* ordered an indefinite postponement of the invasion, but the night blitz continued in all its fury.

While Dowding pondered the thorny problems of night defence, Park carried out a searching examination of his defensive moves on the 15th, from which he concluded that his squadrons must assemble into wings far quicker if they were to intercept before the bombing. He thought that the enemy's wing of about thirty aeroplanes was ideal for offensive operations, when timing was not too important and two or three minutes did not make the difference between success and failure. Critical about the size of the Duxford Wing and the discipline of its leader, he was nevertheless so impressed by their results that he arranged for his outlying units to fight in wings of three squadrons whenever there was time to assemble and climb. But he was careful to point out to his sector and squadron commanders that the bigger the wing, the longer it took to reach its fighting height and that, unlike the Duxford Wing, his pilots often climbed under the guns of enemy fighters and had no opportunities for training in the calm skies of Cambridgeshire. Therefore, apart from those occasions when the warning period gave time to assemble the larger wings, his squadrons would continue to fight in pairs.

The last two weeks of September saw daylight attacks so strongly escorted by fighters that they outnumbered the bombers by five to one. Targets varied from oil farms at the mouth of the Thames to greater London, while damaging attacks on the Bristol Aeroplane Company's factory at Filton and the Supermarine factory near Southampton emphasised the danger of heavy attacks in quiet and widespread areas. R.A.F. casualties were reduced by one-third to about eighty a week, and the production of fighters was higher than the wastage. For Fighter Command the crisis was passing.

At the beginning of October the daylight bomber attacks ceased, and it was left to enemy fighters and fighter-bombers to tie down Fighter Command. The day battle became a straight fight between the opposing fighter forces, with some advantage to the Luftwaffe because the 109s not only outnumbered the Spitfires and Hurricanes but also had better fighting qualities above 25,000 feet. Without the restricting responsibility of escort duties the 109s began to come over very high and fast, and since the high radar cover was incomplete, the warning period was much reduced. Sometimes only eighteen minutes elapsed between the first radar plot and bombs falling on London. Moreover, owing to much cloud and the heights at which the 109s flew, the Observer Corps had great difficulty in tracking enemy formations once they were over England.

The numbers of enemy fighter-bombers varied between four and about thirty. They rarely came over without an escort of clean 109s, and other fighters often swept well ahead. They were exceedingly difficult to intercept, and after many long and fruitless chases Park tried to shadow these elusive intruders with improved Spitfires, Mark 2s, from a special reconnaissance unit, 421 Flight, which in early October began to operate from Gravesend. These 'Jim Crows', as they were called, were to shadow enemy formations and report by radio to the 11

Group operations room; they were to avoid combat—easier said than done.

Even with the Jim Crows there was not time for the defending squadrons to reach 25,000 feet before the 109s were over south London, and Park had to resort to the wasteful system of standing patrols. At first these were restricted to one Spitfire squadron which patrolled Biggin Hill–Maidstone–Gravesend, but sectors were told to keep continuous wing patrols whenever the weather was suitable. Yet the interception rate was far from satisfactory—three out of thirty squadrons on one day; six from twenty-four on another; and the best result, ten from thirty-four. Hence the introduction of fast, high-flying, fighter-bombers countered some of the air defence economies introduced by radar.

As winter drew on the fighter-bomber sweeps petered out, and November saw a return to sporadic enemy attacks against coastal towns and shipping. One day the leader of a Hurricane squadron, trying to intercept bandits over the Thames Estuary, was astonished to see some strange bombers escorted by biplane fighters. This was the *Regia Aeronautica* (Italian Air Force), and the Italian fighter pilots put on a brave show in their Fiat fighters; but the bombers were soon split up and twelve enemy aeroplanes were shot down without loss. Soon after they got similar treatment when they were rash enough to return, and one wonders what the tough veterans of the Luftwaffe thought when they watched their untried Allies taking off from France in their obsolete aeroplanes.

With the coastal attacks the wheel had come full circle since the previous July. The daylight battle was won, but much night bombing had to be endured. For the two victorious commanders it was an opportune time for stocktaking, and to prepare for a bigger daylight offensive from the Luftwaffe which the spring would surely bring. The Battle had cost Fighter Command four hundred and fourteen pilots and slightly more aeroplanes, but the Germans had lost 1,733 aeroplanes and their crews.

There was time for Park to study all the tactical and combat reports, to meet with his junior commanders and discuss the radical changes in air fighting, and to think about the best means of stopping the enemy before, as the New Zealander put it, he again bombed the capital of the Empire. Wing fighting was obviously here to stay, but Park had noticed from his Hurricane that some of his squadrons still flew in tight, rigid, unseeing vics of three, while overhead loose Messerschmitt formations dived to attack, zoomed back to regain the precious height advantage, and then attacked again. He had also observed that the squadrons who had 'unofficially' adopted the open, line-astern pattern fared far better against the higher 109s. Accordingly, the deplorable vic of three was banished from 11 Group when the A.O.C. resolved that his squadrons should fly in three sections, each of four aeroplanes, in a loose weaving formation to prevent surprise from above; likewise, wing formations should be loose and manoeuvrable, with squadrons spaced well apart. Whenever squadrons were split up pilots should work in pairs, because the solitary air fighter could not guard his own tail, and sooner or later would be shot down.

Tactically, because the enemy abreast formation was better than the astern pattern, Fighter Command lagged behind the German Fighter Arm. It was not until the following spring that Douglas Bader copied the *Schwärme*, which he called the 'finger-four' because the relative positions of the fighters are similar to a plan view of one's outstretched finger-tips. Bader's pilots were immediately impressed with their finger-fours, for, unlike the line astern pattern, all pilots were always covered, and all stood an equal chance of survival. Soon all fighter squadrons followed Bader's lead. It had taken a long time to relearn the doctrine of Oswald Boelcke.

Chapter 16

FIGHTING TALK

THROUGHOUT the Battle many high-ranking members of the Air Staff, senior civil servants, and politicians had visited the fighter stations, and some had encouraged the flight, squadron, and station commanders to talk freely about their problems. Visitors to Leigh-Mallory's airfields heard that since September the big Duxford Wing had not been given a chance because they never got enough early warning from 11 Group, but when the same people arrived at Park's airfields they were told that the slow, clumsily conspicuous Duxford Wing could never get to 30,000 feet in time to take on the fighter-bombers. Unfortunately these discussions were not confined to healthy, frank arguments about fighting tactics, and there were some ugly accusations about poaching and morale. Upon their return to Whitehall some eminent men, who should have known better than to listen to junior officers denouncing their seniors, put pen to paper, and both Dowding and Park were called to the Air Ministry to discuss the size of fighter wings. The meeting was chaired by Air Vice-Marshal Sholto Douglas, Deputy Chief of the Air Staff, whose exploits during the First War have been mentioned.

The Air Staff had already decided that fighter operations in the south had not been well co-ordinated, and that squadrons had fought independently and ineffectively. They were anxious that R.A.F. fighters should meet the Messerschmitts on equal terms, and thought that wings should consist of three squadrons, and that whenever possible two wings should join together into a 'Balbo'* to tackle the massed raids. The squadrons of each wing should be based on the same airfield or on nearby airfields, and there should be opportunities for discussions and training together. They appreciated the problem of controlling

---

* Marshal Italo Balbo, who led large formations of Italian aeroplanes before the war.

large numbers of fighters on a single radio frequency, but thought better radio sets would help.

The agenda stated that the object of the meeting at the Air Ministry was to get the tactics right should the Luftwaffe make more determined, better organised, and heavier attacks with massed bomber formations strongly escorted by fighters; it outlined the problems of repelling massed raids, described Park's tactics, and related how the Duxford Wing had on five patrols destroyed one hundred and five enemy aeroplanes for the loss of fourteen fighters, with only six pilots missing or killed.

After the usual preliminaries the chairman, Sholto Douglas, outlined his views and asked for comments. Park said that the amount of warning from the radars often made it quite impossible for three squadrons to rendezvous, join together, climb, and fight before the bombing; also, whenever there was a lot of cloud, pilots had to fly carefully on their instruments, which increased the time to intercept. He was fully aware of the splendid results obtained by the Duxford Wing, but they usually arrived after the bombing, when his own squadrons had already been in action and when the bombers were sometimes separated from their escorting 109s. He thought a wing of two squadrons was the right size for his group, and his present policy against massed raids was to put these small yet manageable wings at different heights against the top fighter screen, the close escort, and the bombers. He had also arranged for some outlying units to fight in wings of three squadrons whenever there was time.

Leigh-Mallory said he would welcome more opportunities to help 11 Group with the big wing from Duxford, and could have five squadrons at 20,000 feet over Hornchurch in twenty-five minutes. He knew about the timing problem, but if Bader intercepted only once in ten times the effort would be worth while.

Squadron Leader Bader, who had been brought along by his A.O.C., listened carefully and thought the meeting was going against Park, who looked desperately tired. Bader thought there was a strong case for both big and small wings. He, Bader, thought that three or four Balbos, from the outlying sector stations—Middle Wallop, Tangmere, Duxford, and Debden—

should take off immediately the radars detected an enemy build-up and try to intercept well forward of London. These Balbos should be controlled by Fighter Command and should be followed, when the Germans were moving over the Channel, by the smaller wings and independent squadrons from 11 Group. Some people thought it would be an easy matter for the Germans to decoy the Balbos over the Channel, but he had never found the slightest evidence of such spoofing; all he knew was that whenever Woodhall told him the Germans were assembling over France they soon crossed the Channel and bombed London.

At thirty Bader was older than most of his contemporaries and therefore thought differently. Sometimes he got very angry because he had seen pathetically small clusters of Hurricanes and Spitfires badly chopped by the higher 109s. He had watched his friends fly south with their squadrons, only to be pulled out of the line soon afterwards because they had been shot to ribbons. He felt very badly about this, and often told Leigh-Mallory that if only the fighters were properly co-ordinated and, to some extent, controlled by Fighter Command, and not 11 Group, they would get better results. More squadrons ought to be fighting, not merely the twenty or so based in 11 Group. After all, this was the Battle of Britain, and not the battle of Kent or Surrey! 'L.-M.', he knew, supported him and had told the commander-in-chief, but Dowding seemed loathe to interfere with the present arrangement, under which Park, the tactical commander, fought the daylight battle and called upon Fighter Command for reinforcements.

It was a delicate business, and a mere squadron leader could not cast any reflections upon his commander-in-chief, for whom he had the greatest respect. The proper channels existed for such things, and he had complained many, many times to 'L.-M.', who had told him, on this occasion, to hold his peace about the high-level control arrangements and to speak only about his own experiences as leader of the Duxford Wing. When the chairman called for his views about the big formations he spoke very carefully about what his audience remembered from their own fighting days in the Kaiser's War—height, the use of the sun, good shooting from close range, the advantages of meeting strength with strength, and how the wing leader, not the controller, ought to decide how, when, and where to attack.

The meeting dragged on. There was some discussion as to whether or not wings should be permanent units, and about the value of Jim Crows. Bader was surprised to hear that some of the south coast radar stations were not back to full efficiency after the August bombing. He left the meeting feeling that little definite had been decided, but some days later when he received the minutes he read that whenever conditions were suitable three-squadron wings should be used against massed enemy formations and that two wings should form a Balbo and fight together. In addition, the Air Staff had ruled that the wing leader could dispense with sector control and would be responsible for engaging the enemy as he thought fit. Bader was delighted, but the commander-in-chief, in acknowledging receipt of the minutes, did not comment on the Balbo philosophy except to say that he thought 'Balbo' was quite a horrible term.

Despite the meeting at the Air Ministry, the commander-in-chief was not fully convinced about the value of Balbos because of the vital time factor. Leigh-Mallory had claimed that he could have his Balbo over Hornchurch in twenty-five minutes; but the Duxford Wing had recently taken seventeen minutes to leave the ground and a further twenty minutes before it set course from base. Also, because it absorbed five squadrons from a relatively weak group, it left some highly important targets in the Midlands short of fighter cover at a time when there seemed a growing tendency for the Luftwaffe to increase its attacks in that area. Dowding felt that Park had been slow to take full advantage of the possibilities of the Duxford Wing when they were first proposed by Leigh-Mallory, but thought it was not economical or effective against the high-flying fighter-bombers. Meanwhile, he informed Sholto Douglas, he would take counsel with his group commanders.

Park's counsel, after five and a half months of strenuous fighting in all kinds of weather against an enemy who, contrary to expectations, had employed an infinite variety of tactics, was that the vagaries of the warning system and the locations of his airfields made it imperative that his squadrons should be trained, firstly, to fight alone, secondly, to fight in pairs, and lastly, to fight in three-squadron wings when conditions were suitable. The Balbo was valuable whenever there was ample warning. But his fighters had been attacked over Kent several times when the plotting tables were quite clear of enemy raids. His squadrons had to be prepared to fight offensively or defensively anywhere south of London.

Thus despite the pressure from the Air Staff, Dowding backed his first lieutenant and was reluctant to meddle with the arrangements made by his tactical commander, who had coped with the Stukas against shipping, with the lightly escorted attacks on coastal airfields, with the heavily escorted attacks against the sector airfields and London, and with fighter sweeps, fighter-bombers, and a variety of decoys and feints. As commander-in-chief the question of how the squadrons should fight was a domestic issue which he, and not the Air Staff, would resolve. The Air Staff, all of whom were much junior to him, had offered some advice, and whether or not he followed it was a matter for him. There the matter rested, but only for a short time; for after four and a half years at the helm, Dowding was replaced by Sholto Douglas, and Park, after a mere eight months, by Leigh-Mallory.

The advantage of hindsight makes it difficult to fault Keith Park's record. When, in the spring of 1940, he took command of 11 Group his pilots were seriously hampered by years of stupid peacetime training; but when, eight months later, he abruptly departed they were meeting the 109s almost on equal terms. Park always tried to get at the bombers before they dropped their loads, and although his critics held that, since his main object was to knock down enemy aeroplanes, it mattered little where he met the Luftwaffe, the sector stations would have been destroyed had Park followed their policy. Moreover, the tendency was for the Luftwaffe to develop more destructive bombs, and better means of delivery, and when they hit our cities those at the receiving end would have gained little comfort from knowing that the air battle was about to begin. Bombing, as we had seen in Europe, could hasten the surrender of a nation.

The size of the fighting unit in 11 Group was conditioned by the time to intercept before the bombing. It might well have been fatal had Park always tried to get his squadrons into Balbos, for not only would they have taken longer to get their height but sixty or seventy packed, climbing fighters could have been seen for miles and would have been sitting ducks for higher 109s. Also, nothing would have pleased Göring more than for his 109s to pounce upon large numbers of R.A.F. fighters. Indeed, Galland and Mölders often complained about the elusiveness of Fighter Command, and Park's brilliance was that by refusing to concentrate his force he preserved it throughout the Battle. This does not mean, as Bader pointed out at the time, that two or three Balbos from 10 and 12 Groups, gaining their height beyond the range of the 109s, would not have played a terrific part in the fighting. Park only had time to fight a defensive battle. The Balbos could have fought offensively. This was a matter for Fighter Command.

It would be untrue to say that Park never made a mistake; but he never made a serious mistake and, after more than two decades, those fighter leaders, controllers, and staff officers who had the honour of serving under him still remain full of admiration for their commander, who was so largely responsible for the victory.

Some critics have held that Dowding was sacked and unfairly treated; but in this country a commander-in-chief, however successful, rarely holds his appointment for more than three years, and as the daylight battles waned it was an opportune time for the physically and mentally tired Dowding to go. He had led his pilots to battle wonderfully well and had displayed great moral courage when he, and he alone, prevented the disastrous fighter wastage over France.

Göring, unlike Dowding, had not done his homework. Perhaps the key to his strange behaviour was that in addition to directing the Luftwaffe he was a powerful political figure. There was no one except Hitler to hold him back. But Hitler disliked and did not understand air warfare. In 1940 he was content to leave the Luftwaffe to his 'loyal Hermann', to Göring, the extrovert, who lived in the past and still fancied himself as an expert on fighter matters; and so, as Galland said after the war, instead of delegating some authority, especially about tactical matters, to better qualified subordinates, he had to be in the swim all the time and to make all the decisions himself. Apart from his high-level conferences at Karinhall, he often flew down to the Channel coast to see how things were going, and to issue orders which contravened his previous instructions. His fighter pilots were dismayed and baffled by these ever-changing orders, and when some of the brighter spirits complained he displayed the gangster methods which he and his cronies had used on their way to power and threatened to have them shot—a habit not conducive to the maintenance of good order and discipline in any military organisation, including that of a totalitarian state.

Germany had the aeroplanes, the aircrews, and the opportunity to win the Battle, but Göring went about it the wrong way. He should have put out the eyes of Fighter Command by destroying the nineteen radar stations between the Wash and the Isle of Wight, destroyed R.A.F. fighters by strafing, and their communications by bombing. Simultaneously with the radar attacks the six fighter airfields near the coast between Tangmere and the Thames, the five sector stations near London, and the headquarters of Fighter Command and 11 Group, at Bentley Priory and Uxbridge respectively, should have been struck. Small, compact formations should have attacked each of these thirty-two targets two or three times a day until reconnaissance showed that further blows were unnecessary. The enemy's night bombers should have been dovetailed into the same plan and directed against the sector stations and aeroplane factories.

Since the object of the daylight raids should have been to knock out Fighter Command in the south, and not merely indulge in a series of exciting yet inconclusive dog-fights, surprise was absolutely necessary, and the bombers and their escorts should have crossed the Channel below five hundred feet to avoid radar detection. Having crossed the coast, these forces, proceeding well inland, should have remained at tree-top height, navigating by visual reference and changing direction every thirty miles or so, to confuse the Observer Corps, until their goal was reached. The low-level raid on Biggin Hill, by nine Junkers 88s and twelve Messerschmitt 109s, was the most successful attack against a sector airfield, and this sort of surprise attack ought to have been carried out against the coastal airfields, the sector stations, and the two headquarters, all of which lay within the radius of action of the 109.

Two years after the Battle of Britain the Luftwaffe exploited the low-level approach when enemy fighter-bombers often crossed the Channel at about two hundred feet to bomb and strafe towns on Britain's south coast. Sometimes they penetrated well inland, achieved surprise, and were gone before any of the numerous defending squadrons could intercept. In 1943 I often led a few Spitfires at tree-top height over France in search of parked aeroplanes on enemy airfields. You wanted good visibility to navigate properly, and when the airfield lay a few miles ahead you got the sun at your back, eased up to a hundred feet, and took the pilots in. Usually the flak was appalling, and we did not linger after the first pass, but we wrecked many aeroplanes, and I once saw a dozen enemy fighters, assembled for take-off on a runway, completely ruined by two strafing Spitfires; and when the Americans began operating their fighters deep into Germany they often came home 'on the deck' and destroyed many hundreds of combat aeroplanes by low, front-gun attacks. As for low-level bombing, Mosquito light bombers later specialised in this role and carried out many successful daylight raids, sometimes without fighter escort, against such targets as the jail at Amiens (to release some hundreds of Resistance fighters), a five-storey building used by the Gestapo in the centre of The Hague, and another Gestapo headquarters in the middle of Copenhagen. Just after Hitler's War we carried out many trials to try to find the answer to the fast, low-level intruder, but there is no adequate defence, and it is significant that today both America and Britain are producing strike aeroplanes which can operate at low altitudes.

Dowding's airfields were not well protected by light or heavy guns. Anti-aircraft resources were so stretched that captured Stuka machine guns were used to defend Tangmere; and one obsolete brass-bound cannon was the only heavy weapon available to another sector station.

In early August a small force of Junkers 88s destroyed the buildings of the Ventnor radar station, which, two months later, was not back to full efficiency. Four years later a Canadian Spitfire squadron, each fighter carrying a 500-pound bomb, destroyed a *Würzburg* radar station on the French coast, and Typhoon squadrons enjoyed similar successes. But the Stuka was a more accurate dive-bomber than either the Spitfire or the Typhoon, could plant a bigger bomb within a few yards of the aiming point, and was the ideal aeroplane, providing it was operated properly, to take out the conspicuous radar stations. Flying in squadron strength of seven or eight Stukas and escorted by a similar number of 109s, the Stuka force was capable of mounting at least two daily strikes against the fourteen nearest radar sites. Like the twin-engined bombers, they should have flown as low as possible in order to avoid combat, and should have then climbed steeply to their bombing height of a few thousand feet while the 109s covered the attack. Follow-up attacks should have used the skip-bombing technique, with delayed-action bombs, so that the Stukas remained at a very low height throughout the mission. Because of the longer sea crossing the fast twin-engined Junkers 88s and Messerschmitt 110s should have been used against the eight more distant radar sites.

It would not have been possible, or desirable, to provide a fighter escort for every bombing formation, because surprise was essential, and big, clumsy formations were more easily detected than small, mobile raiding parties. Owing to their extreme vulnerability, the Stukas required a fighter escort; so did bombers flying into the London area. But the remainder of the daylight bomber force, attacking radars and coastal airfields, should have relied on fighter sweeps to provide general support and reception escorts to cover their withdrawal. Had the bomber and fighter forces been employed in this fashion, it should have been possible for the Luftwaffe to hit the radars, the sector stations, and the headquarters twice daily, and the coastal airfields three times daily and still have had night bombers to carry on against the sector stations and the aeroplane factories.

These attacks should have been well co-ordinated, because a bad planning error might have flushed R.A.F. fighters too soon. A good planner would have concentrated his initial strikes against the radars and coastal airfields, so easing the task of the aircrews who, say two days later, had to penetrate to the London area. Surprise would certainly have been achieved against the radar and forward airfields, and had the attacks been well delivered, the eyes of Fighter Command would have been put out after, at the very most, three or four strikes. Once the radars and forward airfields were out of the way, it only remained to concentrate against the sector airfields and the headquarters until the dispersed aeroplanes were written off and landline communications destroyed.

Working to such a plan, how long would the Luftwaffe have taken to achieve air domination over southern England? When I put this question to Park he replied: 'This was the one thing I dreaded, because had they come in very low we could not have intercepted from ground readiness, and I should have had to resort to standing patrols, which were no substitute. There were more airfields in the south not belonging to Fighter Command yet available to us, but they did not have good signals,* and without signals the only thing I commanded was my desk at Uxbridge!'

In my view the Luftwaffe could have won air domination over southern England within two weeks and would then have been ready for the next phase of their campaign—the isolation of the battlefield—by blasting cities, towns, railway centres, and harbours. Then, opposed only by a British Army still handicapped by the loss of much equipment at Dunkirk and by a Royal Navy fighting at a great disadvantage in the narrow confines of a Channel dominated by the Luftwaffe, the German airborne troops might easily have seized a suitable piece of Kent in which to establish and build-up an invading force.

* Communications.

Chapter 17

IN THE DARK

DURING the early evening of 14th November, 1940, a dozen Heinkel bombers crossed the south coast. By following a radio beam intersected at known intervals by two cross-beams the navigators made good their tracks, found the speed and direction of the wind, and calculated their ground speed; armed with this information, they knew the exact moment to drop their bombs over Coventry.

Shortly after eight o'clock, on that bright moonlight night, the incendiaries rained down and kindled fires to guide more than four hundred bombers, who, in steady streams from the east and south, pounded the target with high explosive, parachute mines, and more incendiaries until just before dawn. From the air the old place looked stricken beyond repair, and the wretched scene somehow fitted the word coined by the Germans to described the attack—'coventrated'.

During the ten-hour raid Fighter Command flew well over one hundred defensive sorties, but only seven German aeroplanes were seen. Two Blenheims opened fire without success. The anti-aircraft gunners claimed two destroyed.

Thus began the worst winter yet endured in Britain's long history. The Coventry raid marked the peak of the Luftwaffe's power to make devastating attacks against our cities, and also represented the nadir of the night defences. Attacks swiftly followed against London, Southampton, Birmingham, Bristol, Plymouth, Liverpool, Sheffield, Manchester, and Cardiff, until it seemed to the citizens of those cities that darkness and the enemy approached together to bring yet another night of fire and death.

Göring had found that the heavy losses of the daylight battles were reduced to practically nil when he operated his bombers at night. He had more than seven hundred serviceable aeroplanes, each carrying over a ton of bombs. Training in night bombing and navigation, started long before the war, enabled the bomber force to operate round the clock. The Luftwaffe already had *Knickebein*, and now a new and improved beam, used on the Coventry raid, was ready. The beams were not sufficiently accurate to enable a bomber to hit, say, a particular factory, but they made it possible, whatever the weather over the target, to hit a town or city, for their average bombing error was about half a mile. Further, dozens of radio beacons were available on the Continent, and enemy navigators could either 'home' to the beacons or fix their positions from them. In fact the Luftwaffe had developed a reliable airways system which allowed them to keep the pressure on Britain from their great string of airfields during the winter months. Their offensive was not confined to bombing, for some crews, in Junkers 88s, flew on 'intruder' operations—when they patrolled airfields in East Anglia and Yorkshire and attacked R.A.F. bombers as they returned from their raids.

After the victorious daylight battles of the previous months the man-in-the-street found it hard to comprehend why the Germans enjoyed such a free hand at night. In the simplest terms it was because neither fighters nor guns possessed a fraction of their daytime efficiency. One reason for this was largely the lack of inland radars. Once a bomber crossed the coast the Observer Corps were responsible for tracking its progress. But ground observers could not see through thick cloud at night, and the Prime Minister of the day aptly described the handover from radar to Observer Corps tracking as 'a transition from the middle of the twentieth century to the early Stone Age'.

The stealthy, scientific techniques of night fighting were vastly different from the rough and tumble of the daylight battles, and called for different skills and temperaments. Both called for good teamwork, but a day fighter team consisted of section, squadron, or wing, while the secret of night fighting lay within the individual crew. Moreover, the pilot of a night fighter worked more intimately with the ground controller than did his day contemporary, for the latter could see gaggles of 109s ten miles or more away and could make big changes in height and direction to intercept; but on dark nights a pilot could not see another aeroplane unless it was flying at about the same height, and depending on visibility, within a range of one hundred to about one thousand yards: nor could he throw his aeroplane about the sky to search for his quarry, otherwise he would soon lose control. Bomber pilots often made splendid night fighter pilots, for both tasks, to be successful, demanded good captaincy and sound crew co-operation. Indeed the valiant Guy Gibson fought at night, destroying three enemy aeroplanes before returning to Bomber Command to win his Victoria Cross leading his squadron on the epic raid against the Möhne and Eder dams.

The technique of night interception was to plot the tracks of enemy bombers at sector operations rooms, where the sector controller assigned particular raids to other controllers at new radar stations, known as ground controlled interception (G.C.I.) stations. Here, the specialist controller called in a night fighter from its patrol line and, by instructing the pilot to steer different headings, he juggled with the two 'returns', or 'blips', on his radar scope until the night fighter was about three miles astern of the bomber, when the radar operator in the fighter, could also see the enemy 'blip' on his radar display. By giving directions to his pilot the radar operator narrowed the gap between friend and foe, until the pilot saw the bomber looming up—like a lamp-post on a foggy night. Then the fighter pilot slowly eased into the ideal firing position, from behind and below, so that he stalked a dark object against the lighter background of the sky, and at the same time the enemy gunners in the bomber had to search against the difficult, black background of the land. Having got to a position some two hundred yards behind, but still below, the fighter pilot opened his throttles, climbed, watched the bomber sink slowly into his illuminated gun-sight, pressed the firing button and saw his cannon shells tear the bomber apart. Then, if trade was brisk, the G.C.I. controller sent him after another bandit, or handed him back to the sector controller for homing to his airfield. So much for the theory. What of the practice during the winter of 1940?

Twenty night fighter squadrons, supplied with good aeroplanes and trained crews, would not have stopped the night bombers dead in their tracks. They would, however, have made the Germans think again. But Fighter Command had less than a dozen squadrons. Of these, six were twin-engined Blenheims, which, carrying a belly pack of four Brownings, were transferred to night fighting not because the aeroplane was suitable, but because it could not exist by day. Fortunately, two of these squadrons were receiving the new Beaufighter, but it was not until the following spring that all were re-equipped. The Defiants, too, had been switched to night fighting for much the same reason as the Blenheims; three Hurricane squadrons completed the night force. Even on a bright, moonlight night the efficiency of these squadrons was not high.

Fully realising their tremendous responsibilities, the night fighters took appalling risks to try to stop some of the bombers. Weather forecasting was unreliable, and the crews were often caught out by rapid and unpredicted weather deteriorations which cut down visibility and made it impossible for them to grope their way back to their feebly illuminated airfields. Radios often failed, and the crews desperately required navigational and airfield approach aids that would get them back to their bases and help them to carry out a safe approach and landing. There were few runways at this time, and it was not an easy matter to land a ten-ton aeroplane safely on wet, slippery grass. During these early months of the winter the deadliest enemy was the weather, for more crews were lost to low cloud, fog, ice, and freezing rain than to enemy action.

Fighter Command's greatest crew was pilot John Cunningham and gunner Jimmy Rawnsley, both Auxiliaries and pre-war members of 604 (County of Middlesex) Squadron. Cunningham's shy and modest manner concealed his great forcefulness, and he was a calm and superb pilot, probably one of the finest in the Service; both he and his 'little man', for Rawnsley was small in body if not in heart, had what Sir Winston Churchill has called 'the canine virtues; vigilance, fidelity, courage, and love of the chase'. But even this splendid team could not get results with their Blenheim until the control and reporting system could give them more accurate and timely information about the heights and positions of the bombers. The method of plotting the position of the fighter by radio direction-finding was slow and faulty and led to delays in the passing of vital information to the pilot; the new G.C.I. radars would solve this problem, but the first of these would not be ready until the end of the year.

The highly secret fashion in which the radar sets, carried in the night fighters, were introduced to the aircrews was unfortunate. Apart from a handful of scientists, few people on the squadron knew what was afoot. The noses and wings of the Blenheims began to sprout short, stubby aerials. Black metal boxes, with many knobs and much interior plumbing, were fitted near the gunner's position, and soon a strange collection of volunteers began to arrive to work the new sets. Somewhere they had been told how to turn on the set, what they ought to see if it worked properly, and how to intercept another aeroplane. Most of them had but the faintest technical knowledge, and once they were with their squadrons they could only learn by practical experience, because there was no one to instruct them. Some did not know the front from the back of an aeroplane, but they took to the air, sitting on the floor beside the gunner, and tried their hand at daylight interceptions with another Blenheim. They were not happy about their black boxes, for those early radar sets were very temperamental and, when they did work, often produced a poor picture, like a blurred television screen, and only showed a very approximate indication of the target's position. When the radar set produced a fair picture the operator could not translate what he saw into practical instructions to his pilot because he lacked flying experience. The pilot could see the target Blenheim a mile or so ahead, but waited patiently for his radar operator to coax the set into life and to give him some indication of range and bearing. Those early training flights were often abortive, and how could the crews expect to fight at night when they could not make a practice interception on a sunny afternoon?

It was a frustrating and miserable time for the night fighters, and things were not helped by the newly arrived radar operators being denied the comfort and privileges of the sergeants' mess, for despite the fact that all other aircrew held at least the rank of sergeant, these unfortunates did not wear a flying badge and lived with the rank and file. When they were not flying they were fair game for any prowling N.C.O., and were thrust upon the usual menial tasks, sweeping, cleaning, and guarding.

Little wonder they were bewildered and unhappy both on the ground and in the air.

Gunners such as Rawnsley were apprehensive about the black boxes, and some unkind things were said about 'magic mirrors' and 'black magic'. They knew they could fight with guns, but some Blenheims were having the gunner's turrets removed to make them slightly faster. There would be little future for gunners in night fighters unless they mastered the mysterious black boxes. Consequently, certain of the more enterprising gunners seized every opportunity to talk with visiting 'boffins' and to stand-in for the radar operator if, for any reason, he was unable to fly. But once in the air it was not uncommon for the gunner to declare that the set was unserviceable, whereupon he would struggle forward to his pilot and help to search the sky with a pair of real eyes. After all, seeing was believing!

It was thought that the fast, sturdy Beaufighter, with an improved radar set, a better view for the pilot, better heating to help the crews on freezing nights, and the formidable armament of four 20-mm. Hispano cannon and six machine guns, would help to turn the tide, and in late November John Cunningham saw a concentration of searchlights on the clouds and decided to investigate. After some time his radar operator (not Rawnsley on this occasion) got a good, solid contact on his tubes and was able to bring them behind a Junkers 88, which John identified and destroyed. This was the first squadron victory with a radar night fighter and showed that a good team could make the radar work.

Cunningham's success was a big tonic, but it was still a wearying game of hunt-the-thimble. Searchlights had greatly assisted night fighters during the First War, by holding the slow, clumsy Zeppelins in their beams, but they could not cope with the speed and height of modern bombers. They still relied on the old-fashioned sound locators, which did not pick up the sound waves from a high-flying aeroplane until it was almost two miles farther on. And they could not illuminate a bomber much above 12,000 feet—a height the Germans rarely flew below. The searchlights were thus of little assistance except to point the way.

Like the searchlights, the anti-aircraft guns were woefully

inadequate to deal with the bombers. Their methods of fire control were much out of date. Although gun-laying radar sets were slowly becoming available to help the guns fire accurately at unseen targets, most still relied on sound locators. It was not surprising that the anti-aircraft gunners used many thousands of rounds to bring down an enemy aeroplane. Various methods of integrating fighters and guns were tried. Sometimes the close defence of London was attempted by a gun barrage while the fighters tried to intercept before the raiders hit the capital; sometimes the height at which the shells exploded was restricted so that the fighters could patrol above. But both anti-aircraft gunners and aircrews wanted better information, which only radar could supply. During December, 1940, only a minute fraction of bombers were brought down at night, ten by the guns and four by the night fighters. These casualties had little or no effect on the Luftwaffe, who received hundreds of bombers each month from the factories.

As the cities burned, the more experienced members of Spitfire and Hurricane squadrons patrolled over the target when it was known that the German beam was on a particular city. Separated by five hundred feet, the pilots flew a few thousand feet above the shell bursts and relied on the sector controller to keep the Beaufighters away. Flying in bright moonlight, a good day fighter pilot found little difficulty in taking-off, navigating, and landing; but occasionally they were sent off in foul weather and were profoundly thankful to get down in one piece. One or two determined and reckless types destroyed a few bombers by prowling among the heaviest gun-fire, but it only taught the remainder to appreciate the problems of fighting at night.

The last attack of 1940 was an incendiary classic by one hundred and thirty-six bombers against the City of London. Once again the pathfinders followed the beam and started the beacon fires. Then followed more incendiaries, high explosive bombs, and parachute mines, so that hundreds of fires raged about warehouses, docks, railway stations, and churches. Many water mains were burst and, to add to the difficulties of the fire-fighters, the Thames was at its lowest ebb when the attack reached its peak.

The mood of the country was reflected in the correspondence

columns of the newspapers, for all manner of fantastic schemes (and some not so fantastic) were proposed by many people from all walks of life. What about R.A.F. bombers flying above German aeroplanes and dropping sand in their engines? Had the authorities considered mounting anti-aircraft guns on balloons? Could not magnesium flares turn night into day so that Spitfire and Hurricane pilots could see to fight? And what of aerial minefields, or even poison gas?

The grave problems of night defence exercised some of the best brains in the country, and many schemes were pressed forward with great speed. Long aerial mines, consisting of a parachute suspending a small bomb, could be dropped to form a barrier ahead of the bombers; likewise, a curtain of bombs could be hung from drifting balloons, but both failed, simply because the bombers could approach the target from any direction. One night twenty-four R.A.F. bombers patrolled over Birmingham to try to get at the raiders, yet, despite many sightings, they were too slow and cumbersome to fire at the Germans. A lot of time and energy was spent in fitting searchlights on to twin-engined, radar-equipped aeroplanes that would patrol with a Hurricane in close formation on either side. This 'Turbinlite' aeroplane would operate like a Beaufighter, except that when it reached a good range the searchlight would be switched on and the Hurricanes would attack. The idea, however, suffered from the fact that once the searchlight was switched on it gave the game away; for surprise, the essence of fighting by day or night, was immediately lost. Other schemes of a more passive nature, including decoy fires and dummy airfields, attracted a small proportion of the enemy effort, and an increasing number of German crews were baffled by the jamming and the distortion of their radio beams.

So passed the old year with all its bitter disappointments for the night fighters. Fighter Command failed because it was not prepared for such a contest, and because it was no longer practicable to design an aeroplane for one job and expect it to be adequate for another simply by sticking on a few guns and a black box here and there. Only two years before, the night fighters had flown old biplanes; then it had sufficed if the fighter consisted of a sturdy airframe and a reliable engine. The

Beaufighter was not simply another aeroplane, but marked the beginning of the age in which all the major components— engines, airframes, armament, navigational equipment, and radar—had to be matched into an efficient weapons system. The Service was caught unawares, for not only had the weapons system to be produced in reasonable quantities but also crews had to be decently trained to fly and fight at night; and, equally important, a sound ground organisation with skilled technicians and adequate workshops had to be provided to maintain the different parts of the weapons system. All this took precious time.

Gradually, after months of perseverance and ingenuity, of heartbreak and despair, things began to improve. Beaufighters replaced Blenheims. More squadrons were formed. Runways with improved lighting were built, and night flying became less dangerous as better radios, beacons, blind approach, and landing aids made their appearance.

Specialist radar officers and civilian instructors arrived on stations to help both ground crews and aircrews. Training devices, to help radar operators study their art on the ground, became available. Enterprising squadron commanders cut through the red tape and induced suitable acquaintances to try their hands, and some flew with borrowed kit before they were properly signed on. Radar operators were given aircrew status, and some keen and intelligent men who had been washed out of flying schools thus found an outlet for their desire to fight. Ground controllers, who understood this intricate radio and radar war, teamed up with pilots. These men understood the mysteries of the cathode-ray tubes, made the radar work, learned to read the range from the green line on one tube, to gauge the difference in height from the other tube, and to give their pilots practical instructions. They learned how to ignore the clutter from ground returns, to make the best of a bad picture, to distinguish between approaching their quarry head-on and from behind, to tell their pilots how to make an easy, converging turn so that they finished behind the bomber and not well out on a flank.

G.C.I. stations came on the air, but, since each controller could only handle two interceptions simultaneously, the system could easily be saturated, especially if the bombers came in thick and fast. The number of Beaufighters that could be closely controlled was strictly limited at any one time, and this was a severe handicap against a concentrated raid; other Beaufighters free-lanced at the discretion of sector controllers and, at long last, both closely controlled and free-lancing night fighters got the contacts, and their mounting claims inspired the whole force.

The anti-aircraft gunners, too, were able to fire more accurately as radar sets reached both anti-aircraft and searchlight units, for they destroyed almost one hundred enemy aeroplanes in the first five months of 1941. Counter-measures, including jamming and rebroadcasting, against the German beams improved to the extent that the enemy no longer set up his beams the afternoon before the attack, except to fool the defence, but waited until the bombers were on their way. Fighter Command, not content to remain always on the defensive, copied the Luftwaffe and formed a special Blenheim intruder squadron to patrol over enemy airfields and attack bombers as they landed or took-off; these aeroplanes were not allowed to carry radar, lest a set should fall into German hands, and although the squadron did not immediately gain spectacular results, it laid important foundations for this highly specialised form of long-range air fighting.

10th May, 1941, six months after the Coventry raid, was another bright, moonlight night and saw the biggest enemy attack of the Second War, when more than five hundred sorties were flown against London. Day fighters defended the capital, and the total claims were twenty-eight, but, according to their records, the Luftwaffe lost only eight bombers, and of these one crashed on take-off. Such an attrition rate, of less than two per cent, would never deter the Luftwaffe and if, with the coming of the good spring weather, they were ready to begin intensive, round-the-clock attacks, Britain was in for a rough time.

The Luftwaffe was indeed ready to move into top gear, but Hitler was set upon the destruction of Soviet Russia, and the Panzers were already deploying between the Baltic and the Black Sea. *Blitzkrieg* in the East called for the usual reconnaissance, bombing, and close support, and almost two-thirds of the Luftwaffe's combat units were soon established in secret along the Russian front. From time to time the bombers would return, but the long ordeal was over.

Even with its beams, skilled pathfinders and ingenious tactics, the Luftwaffe was not capable of night precision bombing, and had resorted to indiscriminate bombing of cities to try to stop industrial production and to break the nation's spirit; had the enemy possessed more powerful bombs, the story might well have been different. The industrial war effort suffered, but not desperately, and the people's morale was far better than during the Zeppelin raids of the First War. The mass bombing caused much distress and suffering, but the man-in-the-street thought only of hitting back and, eventually, when Bomber Command got into its stride, his wish was fulfilled a thousandfold.

The Battle of Britain had ended in victory for the fighters and proved that by day the aeroplane could defend the country against other aeroplanes. The lesson of the Blitz was that without a prodigious number of night fighters, guns, and radar stations, the country was wide open to attack by night. Even had these been provided, a good proportion of the bombers would always get through, and there would be heavy raids when weather grounded the night fighter force. Obviously, both day fighters and night fighters were required to hold the enemy at bay and keep the country secure. But the real solution, advocated by Trenchard years before, lay in offensive action—in carrying the war to the enemy.

Chapter 18

FORTRESS MALTA

DURING early April, 1942, the pilots of 601 and 603 Squadrons had embarked in Glasgow on the United States aircraft carrier *Wasp*, destination unknown except to a select few. Rumour was rife, and embroidered by the perpetual optimism of the young fighter pilots. The West Indies, perhaps? Or even America! After all, the Germans had just begun to take an interest in the eastern seaboard of America. Privately, of course, they felt that no such luck would come their way. They had not been plucked from the front line in southern England to be sent to bask in the sunny Caribbean. So they were not unduly surprised when, after a day at sea, and safe from the consequences of a careless word, they were informed that their destination was Malta.

They knew that the sole military reason for Malta's existence was to provide a base for offensive operations by both submarines and aeroplanes, especially against Axis shipping carrying supplies from Italy to the *Afrika Korps* and the Italian armies in the desert. At the same time, the island was used by R.A.F. reconnaissance aeroplanes to keep an eye on shipping and on the movements of the Italian Fleet. The 'unsinkable aircraft carrier', as the Germans dubbed it, had long been a thorn in their side, and its neutralisation had become of paramount importance to them.

The Spitfire pilots were to be cast off, so to speak, in their Spitfires some six hundred miles short of the island. This gave them something to think about—no single member of either squadron had ever been aboard a carrier before, let alone flown off one! Moreover, they were all fully aware of the fate of a Hurricane squadron flown off the aircraft carrier *Argus* a few months previously. The twelve Hurricanes, led by two Fleet Air Arm aeroplanes, took-off at extreme range. Unfortunately, the flight was not carefully planned, and the R.A.F. pilots did not realise that R.N. officers always made their calculations in nautical miles, not the shorter statute miles used by the R.A.F. The mistake was elementary, and costly. Only four Hurricanes reached Malta. Their fuel tanks contained, respectively, twelve, four, three, and two gallons of petrol.

U.S.S. *Wasp* had disembarked all her aircraft except for one squadron of Grumman fighters, and these were spotted and picketed on the flight deck. The hangar deck was bulging with forty-eight Spitfire 5Cs, some strapped to the roof. Each aircraft was armed with four 20-mm. cannon and fitted with a ninety-gallon drop tank, which could be released when empty. The evening before the flight to Malta those pilots and ground crews who could get at their aeroplanes were making last-minute preparations. The remaining pilots would have to wait until the morning and the launching of a few Spitfires before there would be sufficient room on the hangar deck to lower their aircraft.

The fighter pilots had listened intently to the final briefing in the pilots' ready room. As well as the two squadron commanders, two wing commanders were also present. One was in overall command of the R.A.F. side of the operation, the other was the expert. He had already flown off H.M.S. *Eagle*, and he was known to all as 'the Confectioner', for to him everything was 'a piece of cake'. In addition, a U.S. Navy commander was there to explain procedures on the flight deck.

The trouble about this operation was that, with aeroplanes not designed for carrier operations and pilots untrained in the technique of carrier landings, the point of no-return was reached the moment the wheels began to roll down the flight deck on take-off. Good weather was essential both for the long flight and for the landing at Malta. The R.A.F. commander gave an assurance that they would not go unless the weather was good, both for the flight and the landing at the island.

The Confectioner then explained the technique for taking-off an overloaded Spitfire from a carrier. All that was necessary was to open up to maximum power on the brakes, operate the boost override to give the extra thrust and press on down the deck. There was nothing in it. *Wasp*'s deck was three hundred feet longer than *Eagle*'s. It was a piece of cake! The U.S. commander detailed the procedure for take-off.

The American squadron would take off to make room for the first twelve Spitfires; space would then be available on the hangar deck for the aeroplanes strapped to the roof. After the first twelve Spitfires had left the remainder would start engines in the hangar and pilots would take off immediately they arrived on the flight deck via the lift. The whole operation was complicated, and the instructions were necessarily minute and all-embracing. Above all, he implored the R.A.F. not to allow any ground crew on the deck while flying was in progress. Untrained men among whirring propellers could only lead to an accident.

The following day dawned fine. The Straits of Gibraltar had been navigated in darkness, and the attendant escort of capital ships had not yet entered the Mediterranean, so that the sea looked empty and menacing and the few escorting destroyers hardly adequate to protect a ship the size of *Wasp*. A last-minute briefing on the weather and the pilots 'manned their ships', as the American voice ordered over the broadcast.

The first man off was the Confectioner. The apprehensions of those waiting behind him were not lessened by the spectacular nature of his departure. He failed to correct the swing normally to be expected from a Spitfire at the beginning of its run, this time aggravated by the increased power, and he disappeared over the side about half-way down the deck accompanied by shouts from the naval gun crews as they jumped into the safety nets. Miraculously, he appeared again, having somehow gathered sufficient flying speed to climb sluggishly away from the clawing waves beneath him. Amidst the excitement, an R.A.F. technical sergeant who had allowed his laudable keenness to overcome his discipline and had disobeyed orders by being present on the flight deck, backed into a propeller and was cut to ribbons. The West Indian sergeant pilot in the cockpit was only allowed to stop his engine long enough to inspect the propeller for damage; he soon took off, but he was never quite the same man again.

The remaining Spitfires were launched successfully. Some had not acquired enough speed at the round-down, but the top of the flight deck was some sixty feet above the water, and by pushing the nose gently down the pilots were able to gain the few extra knots necessary for flying speed. The drawback to the Spitfire for such a short take-off was that the landing flaps had only two positions—up, or fully down at an angle of ninety degrees to the under surface of the wing. Later, a simple but ingenious system was devised to enable the pilot to set the flap to provide extra lift for take-off without increasing the drag too much; wooden wedges were inserted between the flap and the wing, so giving the required setting of fifteen degrees. After take-off the pilot would lower the flap to the full extent, the wedges would drop out and the flap would then be fully raised. The system was used with success on future reinforcement flights to Malta.

The flight to the island was accomplished, though not without incident. Despite the assurances of the weather forecasters, a layer of cloud obscured the North African coast and the just recognisable landmarks turned out to be the west coast of Sicily —they were well off course. The leader called Malta for a homing and was immediately answered by a bogus sounding voice which gave them a course for Italy. Fortunately the Spitfire leader recognised the ruse and changed his compass heading towards Malta. Fortunately, also, all available Luftwaffe fighters were occupied at the time in raiding Malta, and none remained to intercept the force of Spitfires so close to their new home. The German intelligence in the Mediterranean was always good. There is little doubt that the German fighters had hoped to arrive over Malta as the reinforcement Spitfires were on the ground refuelling, but they had miscalculated, though by only a little. All this, however, was unknown to 601 and 603 Squadrons, whose pilots, after a long and tiring flight, were anxious to put down at Malta without a fight.

Forty-seven Spitfires landed at Takali and Luqa under the hovering dust cloud sent up by the bombs of the raid. Rumour had it that the forty-eighth pilot had landed in French North Africa, where the prospects of internment were evidently more attractive than life on a beleaguered island. That evening the new arrivals assembled in the mess at M'dina, a village on the escarpment overlooking Takali airfield. Living accommodation on the airfield had long been rendered uninhabitable, and the mess was a large Maltese private house, which, with its stone-flagged floor, wooden grilles, high ceilings and profusion of pillars, could not have altered much since the days of the Knights of Saint John.

The Air Officer Commanding, Malta, Air Vice-Marshal Lloyd, addressed the newcomers in the billiards room. Life was hard in Malta; there was little food, few amenities, and no respite from bombing. They had been brought to the island with one object—to kill Germans. Fuel and ammunition could be brought to the island only by submarine until the Mediterranean could be made safe for a convoy of ships. Therefore every gallon of petrol, every cannon shell, had to be exploited to the full. Nothing was to be wasted.

While he had been talking the Luftwaffe started their evening raid, this time directed at the newly arrived fighters. Wave after wave of Stukas and Junkers 88s dived down until it was impossible to count them in the failing light. The newcomers had never seen anything like it. The bombs rained down on the airfield below the windows of the mess; the pilots' attention was distracted and they shifted uneasily. 'Get in close!' shouted the air marshal, above the cacophony of bursting bombs and rattling windows. 'So close that you can't miss! Don't shoot until you see the whites of their eyes! You must kill the Germans or they'll kill you!' At this moment they heard the tell-tale whistle of a bomb about to explode close, too close, and, in unison, the pilots dived under the billiard table. The bomb missed the mess and they all came to their feet once more, rather sheepishly. The air marshal was still standing, impassive, and he fixed the company with a cold look. 'You see what I mean,' he said, turned on his heel, and left the room.

Many Spitfires were not in a fit condition to fight, for several cannon had not been fired since they were installed in the aeroplanes. Other cannon had not been synchronised. Many radios were not working properly and could not be made to work for a day or two. The result was inevitable: most of the Spitfires met a sad end, destroyed on the ground by bombing and strafing.

For the next eighteen days the situation did not improve. The enemy attacked in strength never less than twice and usually three times a day. The pattern seldom varied: Stukas and Junkers 88s, escorted by yellow-nosed 109s, carrying out dive-bombing attacks on the airfields at Hal Far, Luqa and Takali, and on Grand Harbour. The number of attacking aircraft varied from forty to over a hundred, and they were seldom opposed by more than a handful of Spitfires. Often the very numbers of the opposition allowed the few Spitfires to enter the fray, fire a quick burst, and depart unnoticed.

Those pilots nominated for operations spent the whole day on readiness. At dawn they would be decanted alongside their fighters from a wheezy old saloon car, and there they would remain until collected again at dusk. Living accommodation was in houses and flats dotted round the island, and there was insufficient petrol to allow for transport to run a shift system. The Spitfires were dispersed in blast-proof pens along the highways and byways of the countryside surrounding the airfield. Food for the pilots was brought round once a day in an ancient and rickety bus. The pilots' fare never varied, and consisted of two slices of bully beef, tinned peas as hard as marbles, resting in their own pale-green water, iron biscuits, and tepid tea as thick as glue. Eaten off a chipped enamel plate, garnished with thick Maltese dust, and shared with the flies, this meal proved no more than just adequate to withstand the pangs of hunger until the evening.

Each fighter was serviced by a ground crew consisting of three airmen and two soldiers. Refuelling had to be done by hand from four gallon cans, since most of the petrol tankers had long since been destroyed and the few that remained were reserved for the bombers. It was a laborious process, but the Army men became very skilled, and soon showed as much proprietary interest in their aeroplane and pilot as the airmen.

The order to scramble was given by Very pistol. Usually, anything that could fly would take off, it being safer in the air than on the ground. Aeroplanes unfit to fight would disappear out to sea and remain out of sight until the battle was over. The remainder would join up over the airfield in finger-fours if possible, in twos or threes otherwise.

'Vector one, eight, zero and climb to angels twenty,' the quiet, reassuring voice of Woodie Woodhall would come over the air. He always tried to scramble the fighters in good time for them to gain a height advantage over the enemy formations.

This was usually possible because the southernmost part of Sicily came within Malta's radar cover, and most of the big German raids could be seen joining up over their airfield at Comiso.

Whenever possible an old hand would lead new arrivals on their first operational sortie over the island. On one occasion three members of 601 Squadron were ordered to join up with an experienced flight lieutenant called Lucas, who had come out with a previous batch of Spitfires off *Eagle*. They were not to discover until later that this was the 'Laddie' Lucas who had gained renown as a Walker Cup golfer and was probably the finest left-hander in the world. Unhappily, on the climb out, Lucas announced calmly that his engine had stopped and he would have to leave the company. The other three not very experienced pilots watched him glide down and wondered what to expect next. They were not left long in doubt. 'This is Gondar,' said Woodie. 'Forty plus approaching towards Grand Harbour. No height yet. Probably Stukas with escort. Continue climbing and vector two, seven, zero. I will tell you when to come in.' Good, thought the leader of the three Spitfires, the controller was going to bring them in from the sun. But forty plus! He had never seen so many enemy aeroplanes together before. He wondered how many of them were fighters.

'Vector zero, four, five. Come in now and come in fast,' ordered the controller, 'target looks like Grand Harbour.' The three Spitfires winged over and opened up to full throttle. As they approached the harbour, black smudges of anti-aircraft fire appeared in the sky over Valetta. The gunners were doing their best as usual, but each gun was limited to twelve rounds per day, and there was no question of putting up a barrage. But this very limitation had improved their aim, and already some enemy aeroplanes could be seen diving towards the ground pouring black smoke.

The Spitfires arrived as the Stukas were pulling out of their dives and should have been sitting ducks, but the fighters were moving too fast, and the closing speed was too great to allow more than a fleeting shot. As the Spitfire leader pulled away in a steep climbing turn the 109s pounced from what appeared to him to be every direction at once. But he could turn inside the

109s and just managed to keep his Spitfire intact until their low fuel states forced them to withdraw. He returned to Luqa slightly bemused, but sufficiently in command of himself to attend to the dangerous business of landing.

The enemy, savouring to the full the delight of a superiority in the air which amounted almost to complete supremacy, was devoted to the sport of catching the British with their pants down. He usually swept the island with a small force of fighters immediately following a raid, and he liked nothing better than to surprise a Spitfire on the circuit of one of the airfields with its wheels and flaps down and about to land, or to find one taxying on the runway. From the British point of view, therefore, landing could perhaps be the most dangerous part of a flight, and careful attention had to be paid to the whereabouts of the German fighters as announced by the controller. So that few fighters should be taxying together, landings were spaced carefully and only one aeroplane was allowed in the circuit. This led to an amusing incident when a young pilot, evidently very reluctant to expose himself to an attack from patrolling 109s, was being covered by his flight commander, a Canadian called 'Buck' McNair, who was rapidly becoming bored with his protégé's indecision. 'Red two,' shouted Buck, 'if you don't land off the next circuit and if that Hun doesn't get you, I will!'

At the end of April the situation on the island was becoming desperate. Food stocks were running dangerously low, and so was ammunition. The bombing seemed heavy and continuous. The Luftwaffe were so short of military targets that they thought it worthwhile to mount a raid to destroy a single aeroplane spotted by their reconnaissance. Although their offensive had cost them dear, the opposition from the island's defences had been whittled away almost to extinction.

For all that, some pilots, notably Ray Hesselyn the New Zealander and Goldsmith the Australian, had achieved respectable scores. Lone-wolf fighting went out before the Kaiser's War ended, but often the defending fighter pilots had to fight alone, and the individualist, the man who preferred to fight alone despite the great odds, was in his element. In later months 'Screwball' Beurling, the raw Canadian with the infallible eyes, was to prove this to the hilt. But when he later returned to the

European theatre, where success depended upon teamwork, he was able to do little to add to the lustre of his reputation.

As the number of Spitfires diminished, more and more pilots found themselves with time on their hands. From vantage points on the island they would watch the enemy air raids, criticising the enemy's or their own friend's performance from a strange, almost cynical point of view. A Spitfire on the Takali circuit waited for an opportunity to land. A 109 was behind him . . . 'Turn, you idiot! Look behind you! Turn or you're going to get it,' the watchers shouted in unison. 'Oh, you clot!' as the Spitfire, with an obviously dead pilot at the controls, rolled lazily over and dived into the ground. It was the law of the jungle, and no credit was given to the man who failed to obey the essential rules.

Every evening three or four or five Cant bombers of the *Regia Aeronautica* flew across the island in a tight vic escorted by Macci fighters. This was the time the defending pilots hoped to be aloft, for the Italian fighter pilots could be guaranteed to put on an expert display of aerobatics when attacked and to leave the bombers unprotected. A Cant, shot down by the squadron commander of 601, fell near Biggi hospital. One member of the crew baled out, but his parachute 'roman candled' and he came down like a shuttlecock. Later the squadron commander accompanied his officers to recover a souvenir from the crash. They found that the Italian crew member had just been removed from the upstretched arm of a statue upon which he had been impaled.

One day in May the population of the island was overjoyed to see some sixty Spitfires overhead. This time the arrangements were much better, for the Spitfires were serviceable before they left the carrier and, having arrived during the middle of the morning, could go into action once they were refuelled. As each fighter landed on one or other of the airfields, one of the resident pilots jumped on the wing and guided the new pilot to a dispersal pen. In less than fifteen minutes every Spitfire was ready to fly again.

Soon after, the Germans arrived and received the first of many shocks. For once they were opposed by almost equal numbers. The Spitfires jostled each other to get into the queue of diving Stukas: one Stuka, one Spitfire, and so on until the disappointed were forced to take on the escorting fighters. One Englishman, intent on shooting down the Stuka in his sights, was in turn shot down by the front gun of the following dive-bomber, an ignominy which he took a long time to live down.

At the end of the day the Luftwaffe had lost forty aircraft either destroyed or probably destroyed. It marked the end of the Stukas' freedom of action over the island; from then on the Germans were forced to rely almost exclusively on the far more formidable Junkers 88s.

For the next month the Luftwaffe undertook only sporadic raids, both by day and by night, and the Beaufighters began to score spectacular successes in the dark. Although honours were slightly in favour of the R.A.F., the main problem, how to re-stock the base with essential supplies, still remained. During June a concentrated effort was made to reach the island with convoys from two directions, Alexandria and Gibraltar. The former was turned back by the assault of enemy aeroplanes based in Crete and the threat of a formidable Italian naval force, in spite of almost suicidal attacks by torpedo-carrying Beaufighters based on Malta.

The convoy from Gibraltar, consisting originally of six merchant ships and the attendant escort, was met off the island of Pantelleria by Spitfires operating at their maximum range, but by this time four of the merchant ships had been sunk. The remainder of the convoy was under constant attack from aeroplanes based in Sicily, and also threatened by a force of Italian cruisers. A continuous air battle was fought throughout the whole of 15th June until the convoy reached Grand Harbour that night. The Germans lost over twenty aircraft in exchange for six Spitfires, and no more merchant ships were lost. The troops, whose cynicism knew no bounds, announced that one of the ships was loaded exclusively with tins of meat and vegetable stew, and that the other held nothing but blanco!

The last days of June, 1942, saw the departure of 601 Squadron to Egypt. Rommel had broken through the British lines at Gazala and had begun his last advance, which was to end at El Alamein. A temporary respite had been gained for Malta, and more Spitfires were needed in the Western Desert. Eight fighters took off on the long, tedious flight to Mersa Matruh, navigated and led across the water by a Beaufighter. That evening the pilots cut loose in the flesh pots of Alexandria.

The island had, indeed, proved 'unsinkable'. The air battle was not yet won, but a good beginning had been made. A small island, with relatively few aeroplanes, had tied down an immense enemy organisation with many more combat aeroplanes. Later, more fighters and fighter pilots arrived. Keith Park replaced Lloyd, and the former pushed the air fighting away from Malta by intercepting as far over the sea as possible. As in the Battle of Britain, Park wanted to get at the bombers before they dropped their weapons and his tactics were an instant success, for his pilots continued to destroy enemy aeroplanes and there was a most welcome decrease in the number of bombs falling on Malta.

Chapter 19

THE DESERT

THE war in North Africa was vastly different from the Malta air fighting, for it involved large ground forces which, with their supporting aeroplanes, were often on the move. It began in 1940 when Italy declared herself against Britain and from her North African colony of Cyrenaica struck eastwards into Egypt, only to be repulsed with heavy losses by British and Australian troops. Following another reverse in 1941, Mussolini appealed for assistance to his German master, and soon afterwards the formidable *Afrika Korps*, commanded by General Erwin Rommel and with supporting elements of the Luftwaffe, arrived on the scene and advanced to the Egyptian frontier, behind which lay the Delta, housing all the workshops, stores, and headquarters of our forces in the Middle East. At the end of 1941 a British offensive drove Rommel back, but in the following year the 'Desert Fox' returned to the offensive and, supported by some six hundred German and Italian aeroplanes, broke through the defences, captured Tobruk, and pushed his armour forward as far as El Alamein, well inside Egypt.

The *Afrika Korps* had raced across the desert at such a speed that the Luftwaffe had been unable to keep up. Rommel, however, did not mind this, for he did not have a high opinion of air support, was prone to criticise the Luftwaffe and was not on good terms with its commander in North Africa. Retreating along the coastal road, the vehicles of the Eighth Army were helplessly bunched together, nose-to-tail, for several days during the four-hundred-mile withdrawal, and had the enemy fighter-bombers been active the retreat could have been turned into a rout. During the three days when the congestion was at its height and the 109s were based a mere forty miles away only six British soldiers were killed by strafing.

Hurricane 2Ds, carrying a 40-mm. cannon under each wing, had taken part in the recent fighting. The pilots flew their 'tank-busters' very low, and learned to control the violent kick when they fired the cannon. The heavy shells penetrated armour-plating of great thickness, and the pilots soon accounted for many enemy tanks. Naturally they were soon known as the 'can-openers' or 'tin-openers', and they painted a flying can opener on their Hurricanes.

The Spitfire 5s of 601 Squadron, recently arrived from Malta, were greeted with mixed feelings by some of the older hands, who for a long time had flown fighters inferior to the Luftwaffe's Messerschmitt 109F. Somehow, in their old Hurricanes and American Tomahawks, they had not only succeeded in holding their own against the enemy but had provided also a more than useful amount of air support for the Eighth Army. Now their Tomahawks were being replaced by another American machine, the Kittyhawk, no match for the Spitfire in the air, but a first-class aeroplane for ground attack.

The old fighter-bomber pilots, who daily faced much heavy and light flak when they flew their close support missions, were suspicious of the newly arrived fighter pilots; they wanted to know how the Spitfires would fit into the desert war. After all, the Desert Air Force was supposed to support the Eighth Army, and what sort of support would the Spitfires provide when they flew at 20,000 feet? So far they had managed with fighter-bombers and could not see why pure fighters were wanted in the desert. Surely, the veterans explained, the Spitfire ought to carry a couple of 500-pound bombs so that it could lend a hand with the real business, and bombs could always be jettisoned if they had to fight the 109s.

The Spitfire pilots, fresh from their experiences of air fighting over France and Malta, firmly believed that height was all-important and thought little of flying lower down where they would surely be jumped by the speedy 109s. Small wonder, therefore, that when they began flying well above the fighter-bombers they were soon accused of failing to 'get stuck-in', and fighting a private war which had little effect on the real thing. Gradually both sides came to appreciate the other's view: the fighter-bomber that the presence of the high Spitfires was some insurance against the Messerschmitts; the fighter boys, that failing to come down meant that the battle was sometimes over

Two Spitfires dive-bombing.

before they could engage. Later the Spitfires carried bombs, and when things were quiet in the upper air they took an active part in strafing and bombing.

Ground strafing could be exciting; on one occasion two squadrons of Spitfires came across an obvious headquarters encamped very snugly in a wadi some miles behind the enemy lines. It was in the evening, and the occupants of the camp were busy about their ablutions. They were taken completely by surprise, the flak was unmanned, and a great massacre took place. On withdrawal, one of the pilots, whose father was the Shell manager in Cairo, reported an engine failure and that he was crash-landing not more than a mile or two from the wadi. Fortunately for him, an Australian named Terry had stayed with him, and he quickly appreciated that Llewelyn's chances of staying alive for long after capture were slim indeed. At great risk to himself, he landed his Spitfire in the desert and Llewelyn clambered on his knees. A Spitfire's cockpit is small enough to inconvenience a single large man, and Llewelyn was six feet tall, but somehow they managed to take off, Llewelyn operating the throttle and control column and Terry the rudder pedals, with the former's head protruding well into the slipstream! The whole incident did not occupy more than about five minutes; even so, the protagonists were only just airborne when a truck load of very irate and blood-thirsty Germans arrived on the scene. Their outlook had not been sweetened by another pilot who had stayed behind to fire off his last remaining rounds at the approaching lorry in an attempt to hold it at bay.

The two landed back shakily but successfully. Terry received the D.F.C. for this exploit, and long before the award was announced Llewelyn's father had had to dig deep in his pocket for the celebration in Cairo.

The German flak, as usual, was very good. In their finger-four sections R.A.F. pilots flew to and from their targets at about 8,000 feet, where they were out of range of the light flak, which they thought more dangerous than the heavy stuff—although the veterans always treated the German 88-mm. flak gun with great respect. All fighter pilots hated the flak, for a single bit of shrapnel hitting their single-seaters in a vulnerable spot could bring them down. A fighter pilot who was shot down by an enemy fighter had usually only himself or his leader to blame, but there was little he could do against flak except to get in and out of the target area as quickly as possible and hope for a little luck. At least they fared far better in their Hurricanes and Kittyhawks than the enemy's Stukas, who not only had to face British anti-aircraft fire but had also been massacred so many times by R.A.F. fighters that there was an abundance of stories about different 'Stuka Parties'.

Fortunately, R.A.F. leaders had stopped a determined attempt to make the Service adopt the dive-bomber as a primary weapon for close air support; the Navy and the Army had been so impressed by the Luftwaffe's pin-up weapon that they had fallen into the trap of believing that such an aeroplane was a battle winner itself. In reality, it was capable only of exploiting a battle that had already been won—the air battle. The legend of the Stuka was slow in dying, for the Germans used this dive-bomber in one way or another until almost the end of the Second War, but it was never successful in the face of strong fighter opposition.

The principles of air support were thrashed out, as I have related, during the First War, and only their application had changed with the improvements in aeroplanes, weapons, communications, and methods of control. It was known that the fighter-bomber (what Trenchard called a bomb-loaded fighter) was the only suitable type of aeroplane for bombing and strafing whenever enemy fighters were about. It was known that the battlefield must be isolated to stop the enemy from moving into, and within, the combat area. It was known that the fighting men on the ground wanted close air support at the right time and the right place, and that the whole thing depended upon confidence between airman and soldier. Unfortunately, that close, intimate contact between soldier and airman in the First War had been lost, and it was not found again until the Eighth Army and the Desert Air Force got together.

Slowly, by trial, error, and the foresight of gifted men, not only airmen, the pattern of air support for the soldiers again took shape. Fighters to grind down the enemy bomber and fighter forces; fighters which could then be armed with bombs to attack the enemy ground forces; fighters which, armed or not with bombs, were always capable of protecting themselves and providing protection for the bombers. A bomber force which was as capable of bombing enemy airfields and installations as of attacking troops on the ground. A reconnaissance force to be the eyes of both Army and Air Force commanders.

The conduct of indirect air support presented no great problems to the R.A.F.; at a distance varying from five to one hundred miles and more behind the front lines one target was much the same as another from the point of view of the attacking force. Planning of the operation took place with plenty of time in hand to brief aircrews thoroughly and few mistakes were likely to be made. Moreover, if the wrong target was attacked no damage was done and only the effect was wasted.

Immediate, or close air support, was another problem. In this type of attack the front-line troops called for attacks against enemy troop concentrations, artillery or armour threatening their position or preventing them from moving forward. Here speed was the essence and, to be effective, the fighter-bombers had to be over the target in a matter of minutes. This placed a premium on first-class communications between soldier and airmen, on the training of aircrews and, above all, on the closest co-operation and mutual confidence between the two Services.

Identification of targets was often the crux of the problem; many of them were less than a mile, often not more than a few hundred yards, from friendly troops. A mistaken attack on friendly forces, effective or otherwise, would do untold damage to morale and would destroy that mutual confidence so laboriously built up over the preceding months.

There is little doubt that in 1942, after suffering many vicissitudes mainly through lack of the most modern equipment, the Desert Air Force had become a well-knit, efficient organisation, which already had the measure of the opposing Luftwaffe and the *Regia Aeronautica*, and had confidence in its ability to cope with anything the enemy might throw against it. It had acquired the trust of the British Army with its ability to provide the type of support needed at the time and place stipulated. From the air defence point of view, the control and reporting organisation was rudimentary but adequate; from the air support aspect, a system of communications had been evolved which was manned by the Army and which enabled a request for air support to be passed direct to the squadron likely to provide it.

Although the Desert Air Force went into action on wings, it was in many ways dependent upon wheels, the wheels of its vehicles. It was always on the move, sometimes forward and sometimes backward, and the short range of its fighters dictated the need to operate from airfields as close to the front line as possible. Consequently, the whole of the supporting organisation was placed in vehicles and could move in a matter of hours. The Army was responsible for providing the airfields, often an easy problem in the desert, when it was often sufficient merely to outline a strip of hard sand with white stones or painted barrels; on other occasions the sand had to be graded. Squadrons were so organised that they could operate for a few days with only half the supporting men and equipment. Thus one half of a squadron would move to the new airfield and would organise itself in a short time to receive the squadron aircraft, which had been seen off by the rear party. The aeroplanes would carry out an operation and land with the advance party; in this way operations continued without interruption throughout a move. Indeed, there was no alternative, since during an advance or a retreat moves were likely to occur daily.

The desert was an ideal place to fight a war. There were few distractions, morale was high, and health almost universally good. The simplest pleasures were enjoyed to the full, whether fishing for mackerel in the Mediterranean with hand grenades or setting elaborate booby traps for brother officers. Officers dressed according to their own tastes, so that corduroy trousers, lurid scarves, and suede shoes were sported by many pilots. It was not surprising that the many 'characters' in the Desert Air Force gave full rein to their predilections.

One of the greatest characters in the Mediterranean, and the greatest reconnaissance pilot ever, was Adrian Warburton of the R.A.F., a tall, slender, fair-haired man. Incredibly youthful in looks, he had the outward appearance of a dandy. The Mediterranean was his oyster, and he was likely to turn up on any airfield at any time of the day or night on some special mission. Already by 1942 his exploits were legendary, whether flying in a Martin Maryland, Beaufighter, or his sky-blue, camera-laden Spitfire. On one sortie over Taranto harbour he flew so low over the ships of the main Italian Fleet that one of his photographs showed little more than washing hanging on the stern deck of the biggest battleship.

One morning he arrived on the airfield at Luqa to be informed by one of his ground crew that he could not approach his aircraft because an enemy delayed-action bomb lay near by. Unperturbed, he asked one of the airmen to provide him with tools so that he could defuse the bomb, although he probably knew next to nothing about bomb disposal. He was only prevented by the refusal of the airman, who stated that the tools were on his charge and he would have to pay for them if they were blown up!

Warburton's iron nerve never failed him to the end. At La Marsa on the North African coast he crashed on take-off in an American Lightning. The wreckage of the first aircraft was still burning as he took off to carry through his mission in another aircraft. In the end, he disappeared without trace over southern Europe.

Another character was Wing Commander 'Buck' Buchanan. At heart he was probably a fop. He took great pains over his personal appearance and toilet; in another age he would have been a buccaneer. In the desert, when he was commanding a Blenheim squadron, he was said to require two crews because one alone could not stand the pace at which he flew on operations. He used to say that all he required for complete happiness was a tin of bully beef, a packet of biscuits, and an operation a day. His squadron was understandably suspicious of his seemingly insatiable desire to bomb the enemy, but he was a leader, and they would follow him anywhere. On Christmas Day a sergeant pilot stood up in the mess and said, 'I have a special message from the C.O. He says that as it's Christmas Day we can have two tins of bully, two packets of biscuits, and two ops!'

Wing Commander Buchanan went on to command a Beaufighter squadron and caused great execution among the German transport aeroplanes operating into and out of Tunis. He eventually came down in the sea in the Eastern Mediterranean, not far from the shores of Turkey. Both he and his navigator successfully entered their dinghy, but it was several days before the coast could be reached, by which time Buchanan was dead —it is believed of pneumonia. He had spent the whole war fighting and had even walked out of the Staff College at Haifa, where he had been sent for an enforced rest.

In the autumn of 1942, not long before the Battle of Alamein, Wing Commander Jackie Darwin took over command of 244 Wing, composed of two squadrons of Spitfires and two of Hurricanes. Darwin was a regular officer who before the war had served on the North-West Frontier of India and was also a keen follower to hounds. By a tragic misfortune he was dancing with his beautiful wife in the Café de Paris in London the night it was bombed, and she was killed in his arms. He never recovered fully from this shock, and developed a great hatred for the Germans and a complete disregard for his own safety. His pilots did not think much of flying next to him, for he always led them through the thickest of the flak, and whereas for some time he bore a charmed life, his wingmen were not always so lucky.

At this time the wing had a mascot, a seedy, mongrel dog called Rommel, and during periods of leisure Rommel was used to hunt the desert fox. The procedure was simple, though completely ineffective; every available Jeep was pressed into service and was driven at great speed over the desert until a fox was sighted, or one was suspected to have been sighted! At this moment Rommel would be launched from a moving Jeep, turn several somersaults and start off in the opposite direction to that desired, and the next few minutes would be taken up in catching Rommel. For some reason best known to himself, Darwin had with him his hunting kit complete—boots, breeches, and pink coat—and on the day of this particular story he was wearing it. Just as the hound was running well the wing was brought to immediate readiness and ordered to strafe enemy aeroplanes on the airfield at Daba.

The wing commander had no time to change and took off in his Hurricane in hunting garb. Later, when flying very low over the desert to escape the flak, he caught his propeller on the ground, the engine stopped and he came to rest, surprised but unhurt, in no-man's land. Luckily, a patrolling armoured car from the 11th Hussars was able to rescue him and took him back to their position near the front lines. He was taken into the dug-out mess, where he was met by the C.O. of the Hussars squadron with the words, 'This is the first time I've seen an Air Force officer properly dressed!'

There is little doubt that Darwin, for obvious reasons, had little use for life and deliberately took great risks. As often happens on these occasions, death eluded him for some time until he was eventually killed in Italy. He had dropped two bombs on a gun emplacement, went in for a second attack on the same target—always a dangerous thing to do—and was shot down in flames by the flak.

By the beginning of October, 1942, a new sense of purpose began to penetrate the atmosphere in the desert. Since August, when Rommel had been repulsed in his attempt to break through to the Delta, equipment had poured in to the Army units, new R.A.F. squadrons had been formed and airfields alongside the Cairo–Alexandria road were choked with aeroplanes packed wing-tip to wing-tip. Here was evidence, if it was ever needed, of the benefits of air superiority amounting almost to supremacy. Except for desultory night raids, the Desert Air Force was immune from attack. The reason was not only the lack of sufficient aeroplanes on the part of the enemy but also lack of fuel. Maritime aeroplanes operating from Egypt and Malta, now restored to its full might, throttled the sea lanes between southern Europe and Tripoli, Benghazi, and Tobruk. Few, if any, tankers succeeded in running the gauntlet, and those that did were attacked in harbour by our Wellington bombers.

More evidence of this air superiority was seen daily by the pilots of the Desert Air Force when they flew over and beyond the enemy lines. Not only were few enemy aeroplanes seen but there was little movement on the ground below. In fact, the enemy vehicles did not move by day at all, and a pilot returning from a sortie was well aware when he had crossed into friendly territory, since the roads were alive with transport of all types, nose to tail.

In early November the enemy finally cracked and began to pull out of the line, and this was the time that the Desert Air Force came into its own, for, initially, only aeroplanes could keep up with the beaten and fast retreating Germans. It had been hoped to cut Rommel off before he reached the Egyptian frontier, but heavy rains bogged down the pursuing Seventh Armoured Division at Fuka, and he lived to fight on many other days.

Air Vice-Marshal Harry Broadhurst, a renowned fighter-pilot, took command of the Desert Air Force at about this time. He proved to be a most outstanding commander and leader, and he soon gained the full confidence of the leader of the Eighth Army, General Montgomery. Hitherto, fighter-bomber pilots had made most of their attacks whenever they saw opportunity targets during their flights over the battlefield. Broadhurst, however, thought his pilots could provide better support for the soldiers if they knew more about the ground battle and the whereabouts of enemy tanks and armour. In other words, he wanted more planned, set-piece attacks, and less strafing of fleeting, opportunity targets. There was achieved by R.A.F. controllers in armoured cars, situated with the forward troops, and in radio contact with fighter-bomber squadrons already in the air. Pilots and ground controllers used similar photographic maps, with a grid superimposed on it, and the controller gave targets to the waiting 'cab ranks' of fighter-bombers.

This 'Rover David' system, linking the fighter-bombers with the armoured cars, proved very successful. 'Rover' patrols were decided upon the day before, at a joint conference, and enemy targets, stationary or moving, were attacked within a few minutes of a request from those forward troops in contact with the enemy. Initially Broadhurst was disappointed with the results, since his pilots often failed to hit moving vehicles, but after intensive training their shooting improved.

The Germans were on the run, and Rommel's line of retreat was cut off by Operation *Torch*, the Allied landings in French North Africa. From time to time, however, the air war flared up. The enemy's radial-engined Fokker-Wulfe 190, having four 20-mm. cannon (two firing through the propeller) and two machine guns, was far superior to the Spitfire 5. The Spitfire 5s could still be used on short-range, close support missions, but Broadhurst wanted his fighters to be multi-purpose, so that they could be switched to strafing, bombing, escorting bombers, or air fighting, as the occasion demanded. His fighters had to be flexible, and to get this flexibility he 'clipped' the elliptical wings of some Spitfires to improve their rolling characteristics at low heights, and 'cropped' the superchargers of their Rolls-Royce engines so that the aeroplane's best speed developed at about 8,000 feet. These modified fighters soon acquired the un-

lovely name of 'clipped and cropped Spitfires', but their pilots fared better against the Fokker-Wulfe.

Despite the improved performance of his Spitfire 5s, Broadhurst was concerned about the superiority of the Fokker-Wulfe. He knew that some wings in Fighter Command had received improved Spitfires, Mark 9s, which had proved more than a match for the Fokker-Wulfe during recent air fights over France. The engine of the Spitfire 9 was bigger (1,600 h.p.) than that of the 5 and produced a top speed of more than 400 m.p.h. at 21,000 feet. But the engine was mounted in the same airframe, and its great tactical advantage was that, apart from its longer nose and more numerous exhaust stacks, it looked exactly like the inferior 5. From the usual combat range it was impossible for the Luftwaffe pilots to distinguish between the two types. This suited the handful of men who brought six Spitfire 9s to the Desert Air Force, for they had one or two old scores to settle.

These fighter pilots were very experienced and were simply aching to get at the 190s. For these men were Polish fighter pilots. They were led by the able and gallant Squadron Leader S. Skalski, who, apart from his Polish decorations, held the D.S.O. and the D.F.C., with two Bars. 'Skalski's Circus', as these brave Poles were soon called, was very successful and shot down many Fokker-Wulfes. They showed that good aeroplanes, flown by resolute pilots, were far more important than mere numbers.

The advancing Eighth Army was halted at the Mareth Line, which, years before, had been constructed by the French in the tradition of the Maginot line. German troops were well dug-in and there was some stiff ground fighting. Montgomery planned a set-piece attack for 20th March, 1943, and despite the poor weather forecast, which was likely to ground the Desert Air Force, he decided to go ahead with it. In the event the airmen were virtually grounded at a critical point in the battle, and for this and other reasons, the operation was called off. This important lesson was well understood by Montgomery, who never again went into a set-piece battle without the assured support of his airmen.

It was near Mareth, in Tunisia, that one of the forward airfields came under heavy artillery fire from well-concealed German guns in the nearby mountains. Fighter-bombers had tried to take out the guns, but most of them continued firing, and Broadhurst had to say that unless the Army silenced the guns, he would have no option but to withdraw his squadrons. The Ghurkas were chosen for the job, and one night the small brown men from Nepal, complete with their razor-sharp *kukri*, climbed into the mountains. There was no more trouble from the enemy gunners.

In the spring of 1943 the Eighth Army joined up with American troops and Allied aeroplanes could reach all enemy targets in Tunisia. The Luftwaffe tried to supply their beleaguered troops from the air and Broadhurst, having more or less ceased ground-attack operations, switched all his fighters back to their natural environment to try to destroy the transports. He knew that the entry point for the air transports was near Cape Bon, and his fighter squadrons were moved to adjacent airfields. At first the results were disappointing, since the enemy pilots flew very low, below radar detection, and Allied fighter pilots

flew too high—at about 5,000 feet. When Broadhurst ordered
his pilots to fly just above the sea they immediately found and
slaughtered the transports and their escorting fighters—thirty-
eight on one day, fifty-two for the loss of seven Allied fighters
on another—until the enemy wisely confined the Junkers 52s to
night operations.

Later the Desert Air Force took part in the invasion of Sicily
and Italy. Forged and tempered in the continuous air–ground
battles in North Africa, it developed into a sound force which
could concentrate much striking power at the right place and
at the right time. It had achieved magnificent flexibility. Its
organisation changed little throughout the remainder of the
Second War, and similar tactical air forces proved successful
both in Europe and the Far East. Under very able commanders,
who put first things first, the Desert Air Force concentrated on
the air battle from the outset and showed that tactical air power
could play a decisive part in the land battle. Perhaps its greatest
achievement was to gain the confidence of the Army for the first
time in the Second War, and if this suffered some set-backs in
the forthcoming battles it was never lost again.

Chapter 20

COVER OF DARKNESS

THE tide of war was turning against the Germans, for shortly after the British victory at El Alamein Field Marshal von Paulus surrendered at Stalingrad and Soviet forces struck back in the East. In Europe the persistent offensive of Bomber Command, supported by many squadrons of the United States Army Air Force, based in Britain, had succeeded in transferring the air battle from Britain to Germany. Bomber Command had tried attacking in daylight, but the R.A.F. lacked a long-range fighter, and the only way the Command could hit Germany and survive was at night. Thus the Germans gained much experience of night fighting. Their night fighter force became very powerful, and highly dangerous to the bombers. But before resuming the story of night fighting we must look briefly at the threat posed by Bomber Command.

To be a valid night force Bomber Command had not only to find and hit targets but had to keep the casualty rate down to about four per cent so that crews and aeroplanes could be replaced; if, over a long period, the casualties rose to seven per cent, experienced crews, including squadron and fight commanders, would stand a very slender chance of getting through their tour of thirty missions, and Britain's only offensive weapon would become increasingly blunted.

Before the war Göring had boasted that no foreign bomber could attack the Fatherland, but when Bomber Command began its long and valiant bout of night operations he soon realised that flak and searchlights would not stop the raiders, and he began to organise a night fighter force. The Germans applied themselves to this task with their usual vigour, and so began the long battle in which scientists of both sides played ever-increasing parts as they devised device and counter-device, to help or hinder offence or defence.

As early as 1940 an experimental unit of Messerschmitt 110s was formed at Dusseldorf, and a rudimentary system of night defence failed because the searchlights still relied on obsolete sound locators. When it dawned upon the Germans that Britain was not going to be defeated in the Battle of Britain they increased their night fighter force with more Messerschmitt 110s, and with a night fighter version of the versatile Junkers 88. Meanwhile the small, capable General Kammhuber, who was entrusted with the new force, extended the early warning system along the coasts of Denmark, Holland, Belgium, and France; and when *Würzburg* precision radars, suitable for close control from the ground, were sent to flak units, he managed to get hold of a few sets and, during the autumn of 1940, he set up three night fighter zones near the Zuider Zee, the mouth of the Rhine and the Ruhr approaches. The zones were linked by a master control room, but the systems could be easily swamped, for only three night fighters, one in each zone, could be controlled at the same time. Radar sets in the night fighters themselves had not yet been developed, but improved *Würzburg* sets could bring the night fighter within some four hundred yards of the bomber, and Kammhuber introduced his *Himmelbelt* ('fourposter bed') system, in which one radar followed the bomber and another plotted and vectored the fighter. The next step was to improve and extend the zones, and soon the defensive belt stretched from the Ruhr to the Danish border, with planned extensions to Paris and Norway.

Not content with defensive measures, Kammhuber organised intruder units to attack and harass Bomber Command airfields in England, and proposed to increase the size of this useful force; but when many Luftwaffe units were needed for the Russian front Hitler himself gave orders that intruder operations should stop. In Germany, however, Kammhuber had provided such a sound night fighter force that during late 1941 bomber losses rose to about five per cent and Britain's offensive was temporarily called off.

It was not only the casualties that halted the bombing of Germany but also the ugly fact that after two years of war Bomber Command could not find its way at night. As in Fighter Command, complex aeroplanes such as Wellingtons and Whitleys were introduced without the proper backing. To escape the flak and the searchlights the crews flew above the oxygen height without oxygen supplies. They flew in icing conditions without de-icing equipment. The fuel tanks were not self-sealing, and a solitary bullet could bring them down in flames. They did not have a decent navigational aid, and the navigators calculated their courses from forecast winds, which all too often proved wrong. Whenever they could see the ground they could determine the speed and direction of the wind; but they often flew in or above cloud and were blown off-course as feathers across a polished table.

But they flew on, blindly, for five or six hours, twisting to avoid the flak, fighting their way through what they called the Kammhuber Line, fighting the ice, the freezing cold, and the clouds, until the navigator told his captain to open the bomb doors and the bomb aimer pressed the tit and shouted 'bombs gone'. Then they could think about the long journey home across a hostile land, across the North Sea, seldom knowing which part of the East Coast they would hit, wondering if they would fly over a trigger-happy shipping convoy or stray over a gun-defended area, and so eventually to Norfolk or Lincolnshire, where the weather might have clamped or a German intruder might be circling near their airfield waiting to hit them when, exhausted after the long flight, they came in to land. And after all the endeavour and sacrifice no one quite knew where the bombs had gone until high-flying photographic Spitfires brought back the depressing evidence that over the Ruhr only one in ten crews claiming to have attacked had arrived within five miles of the target.

When my squadron was based in Lincolnshire we often rubbed shoulders with these bomber crews, in crowded pubs or on the rugger field. We were fairly well versed about life in the Service, but there was something different about these men who were so ill-equipped to carry the fight to Germany. They tried to hide their feelings under a forced gaiety, but sometimes their snatches of conversation . . . 'our third flight commander in three weeks' . . . 'The squadron grounded until we can train the new chaps' . . . revealed the strain. Sometimes when we visited their airfields and listened to their long briefings about the weather, enemy dispositions, navigation, communications, and armament, we could feel the pressure steadily mounting.

We had the greatest admiration for these bomber boys, whose job was infinitely more dangerous than our brief excursions into the air.

In the spring of 1942 the bomber crews began to get more help in finding their way over Europe. For example, a radar aid called *Gee* sent out signals from ground stations in Britain which assisted the navigators in determining the positions of their bombers. At its extreme range of some four hundred miles *Gee* had such an error that it could not be used for the blind bombing of small targets, but, as the German beams had in 1940, it helped to find great cities.

The old port of Lübeck, on the Baltic, was selected for the new treatment, and although the target was beyond the range of *Gee*, it made accurate navigation possible for most of the route, and in the bright moonlight the crews of the first wave easily found the target and marked it with flares. A further two waves followed, and the timing was such that almost two hundred bombers went through the target in two hours and left the town, with its medieval wooden buildings, completely ablaze. Nevertheless, the night fighters were very active, and the lesson of this and subsequent raids was that one must saturate the defences by getting the maximum number of bombers through the Kammhuber Line and the target as quickly as possible.

So it was that during May, 1942, more than one thousand bomber crews were briefed to attack Cologne, and only ninety minutes elapsed between the first and last bombs. Despite bleats about a *corps d'élite*, 'private armies', and 'creaming-off the best crews', the next logical step was taken when a Pathfinder Force was formed to find and mark the targets. And not a moment too soon, for the enemy was on to *Gee* and about to jam it. But British scientists had not been idle, and towards the end of the year two more radar devices, having the unlikely names of *Oboe* and *H2S*, were available to help the bomber crews.

Oboe was more accurate than *Gee*, and could be used for blind bombing within its range of some three hundred and fifty miles. *H2S* was a very important advance, in navigation and bombing, for all the equipment was carried in the aeroplanes. Thus *H2S* made the bombers independent of ground radar stations. Meanwhile, other improvements to the Command's striking ability included fast twin-engined Mosquitoes, rugged four-engined Lancasters, bigger bombs, jamming devices, and 'spoofing' gear which made one aeroplane look like seven or eight on the German radar screens.

With all these improvements Bomber Command, in the spring of 1943, was able to show that it was no longer lost in the dark; and the Essen raid, when three waves of bombers plastered and laid waste the Krupps works and much of the town in some thirty minutes, at a cost of fourteen bombers, was typical of its vastly increased striking power. Other towns in or near the Ruhr were attacked during the following months, but the enemy night fighters were seldom idle and gave the bombers some hard knocks. Happily for Bomber Command, its forceful leader, Harris, known affectionately as 'Butch' to the crews he seldom saw, had another card up his sleeve called *Window*, consisting of strips of tin foil which when dropped from the bomber stream fell like a shower of silver rain on enemy radar screens, interfering with radar sets and dislocating the radar control of flak and searchlights. *Window* had been available for some time, and although it was calculated that it would reduce the Command's losses by about one-third, saving hundreds of bomber crews, Harris was at first not allowed to employ it because some people feared enemy bombers might use the same device over Britain. Fortunately, and none too soon for Bomber Command, Harris was eventually allowed to use *Window*, and made his plans to strike at Hamburg, Germany's second city and her seagate to the world.

Shortly before one o'clock on Sunday morning, 25th July, 1943, the Pathfinders arrived over the city to mark the target for the main force. On their radar screens the great winding river and the lakes made distinct contrasts with the surrounding built-up areas. Most of the marker flares fell near the centre of the target and greatly assisted more than seven hundred bombers, who went through the target in less than fifty minutes. On the afternoon of the same day sixty-eight Flying Fortresses of the United States Eighth Army Air Force struck the nearby port of Wilhelmsburg, and a few Mosquitoes returned to Hamburg that evening. On Monday morning the Eighth attacked again, while more Mosquitoes later gave the wretched citizens little sleep. On Tuesday night Bomber Command was ready to resume the battle, and again more than seven hundred crews dropped their loads in about forty minutes. A handful of Mosquitoes attacked on Wednesday night, and on the following night another great force of bombers added to the appalling destruction. Then followed a lull of four nights before the Command returned in extremely bad weather to make its fourth and final attack.

In little more than a week the bombers devastated the city and port. The merciless rain of incendiaries, high explosive bombs, and land mines transformed the streets into raging fires, which were fed by more bombs and the wreckage of buildings until the numerous fires ate their way towards each other and the city seemed like one great lake of fire. This terrible conflagration heated the surrounding air to a great temperature and created a vast suction, so that gale-like firestorms swept up and down the narrow streets destroying and devouring all before them. Thousands were buried alive or suffocated, or were overcome by the searing heat. Some tried to escape by standing up to their shoulders in the lakes, but the firestorms tore over the surface of the water and even charred the wooden mooring posts. The Battle of Hamburg reduced the population by about one-third. It cost Bomber Command less than three per cent of the numbers involved.

Kammhuber was appointed to a new post similar to Galland's: Inspector of Night Fighters; but he disagreed with Hitler about the transfer of night fighters from Germany to Russia, pointing out that he could no longer guarantee the night defence of the Reich and, like many others who had the strength of character to state unsavoury facts, he was posted to a position of lesser importance. Luckily for Bomber Command, the enemy became so completely pre-occupied with defensive measures that he forgot that a few well-trained offensive intruder units would have accounted for hundreds of bombers on the packed airfields in Yorkshire, Lincolnshire, and East Anglia.

Fearing that other cities would soon be 'Hamburged', the Germans set about improving their night defences and Schmidt,

Kammhuber's successor, realised that the system of close controlled interceptions was useless because the zones had little depth and were swamped by the massive saturation tactics of Bomber Command. Schmidt aimed at a method of broadcast control which would give his free-lancing crews a running commentary about R.A.F. raids, and so help them get into the bomber stream, where their new *Lichtenstein* radar sets could pick up the radiation from the radars in British bombers. Instructions from the ground about individual bombers were no longer given, unles the latter were coned by searchlights. Also, like Fighter Command during the Blitz, *Wilde Sau* ('Wild Boar') single-engined fighters were directed to the cities and above the flak attempted their local defence, often with considerable success and especially in good weather. Sometimes the night fighters remained in the bomber stream when it recrossed the North Sea.

Single-engined and twin-engined night-fighter units, flak, communications, radars, and control and reporting centres were improved, multiplied and combined into various fighter divisions for different regions. Special monitoring posts were built to listen for all radio transmissions from R.A.F. bombers, and to provide additional information for the controller, whose job was to fit all the jig-saw pieces of evidence together before broadcasting his running commentary from powerful transmitters difficult to jam. This greatly improved night fighter force possessed that remarkable flexibility which was typical of the Luftwaffe, and which enabled fighter units from northern Denmark to be alerted and scrambled and then to intercept over southern Germany before landing at a nearby airfield to refuel and rearm for a second mission.

These additions and refinements to the German night defence system soon proved their worth, and once again the balance swung in favour of the Germans as bomber casualties rose to eight and nine per cent. The leader of the single squadron of Beaufighters which supported the bomber stream was Wing Commander Bob Braham, twenty-nine victories, and one of the greatest fighting airmen of the Second War. Braham was horrified by the numbers of bombers he saw shot down, but both the modest performance of his elderly Beaufighters and their electronic aids imposed serious limitations on his conflict with the enemy night fighters. He was forced to introduce the dangerous tactic of allowing them to approach from behind, when he broke into a tight turn and tried to out-manoeuvre his opponent. But for all the bravery of Braham and his crews, a handful of Beaufighters could make little impression on the strong defences, and Harris demanded a reasonable number of the latest Mosquito night fighters, which had a better radius of action than the Beaufighter and much improved searching aids. These were refused on the grounds that they were required for home defence and that the radars could not be risked over Germany lest they fell into enemy hands. 'Use the scouts offensively' thundered Trenchard a quarter of a century before. But Bomber Command did not get the fighter support it sorely needed, and Harris had to try to contain the opposing night fighters by 'spoof' raids, deception, and jamming.

So more jammers and counter-jammers were introduced to confuse enemy radars and radio broadcasts. Powerful transmitters were built in Britain to counter the German technique of broadcast control, and German-speaking controllers gave false orders from Britain to enemy night fighters, which sometimes created utter confusion in the night defence organisation. For instance, during a raid against Kassel the German controller warned his crews: 'Beware of another voice. . . . Don't be led astray by the enemy. . . . In the name of General Schmidt I order all aircraft to Kassel.' On another occasion, after much contradiction and cross talk by the R.A.F. 'controller', the German controller became violent and abusive, whereupon the R.A.F. officer said, 'The Englishman is now swearing!' The German rejoined, 'It is not the Englishman who is swearing, it is me!' On another night the Germans tried to counter the deception in the middle of a raid by using a woman controller, but the state of the art was such that the R.A.F. had a German-speaking W.A.A.F. officer ready and waiting.

Radar was becoming a double-edged weapon because, as I have said, the German night fighters could home on to the radar transmissions from bombers, and R.A.F. night fighters could track down Junkers 88s in the same fashion. When the numbers of R.A.F. night fighters supporting the bomber stream increased the German crews became very apprehensive about their radar transmissions, especially those used for identification purposes; but they were assured by their scientists that it was impossible for Mosquitoes to home on such transmissions. One of the scientists, however, was much impressed by the crews' reasoning and decided to carry out a small trial; he rigged up the radar gadget in his back garden, switched it on during a raid and was not surprised when soon afterwards a Mosquito night fighter appeared overhead.

Despite all R.A.F. measures to fool the defences, the loosely controlled night fighters not only succeeded in getting into the bomber stream but sometimes flew across the North Sea to meet it. Once in the stream, experienced and clever pilots such as Heinz Schnaufer, Werner Streib and Johann Krause flew to positions where there was plenty of jamming against their radar sets and then searched upwards so that the bombers were silhouetted against the lighter sky. Streib claimed sixty night victories at this time, and the form of attack he liked best was to fly a little ahead of his quarry, then to throttle back and climb until his sight ringed the bomber. Only about ten per cent of the many bombers he attacked saw his black fighter before he opened fire, and these went into the corkscrew—the famous twisting manoeuvre practised by all Bomber Command crews both to

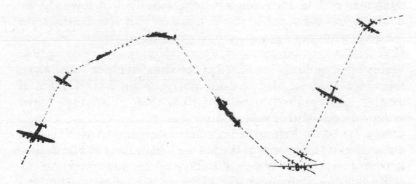

evade enemy night fighters and allow accurate fire from the rear gunners.

A corkscrewing bomber was difficult to hit at night because it was not only twisting and turning but also altering its speed, height, and course. Schnaufer, one hundred and twenty-one victories, taught his crews to stay with the bomber and to wait until it was changing direction at the top of the climb, when its wings would be level and they would have a non-deflection shot. If they did not get a flamer at this stage they broke away and found an easier target, for the violent corkscrews carried out by some Lancasters were amazing. Later, when their Junkers 88s were fitted with heavy calibre upward-firing cannon, enemy pilots used the same approach technique, but opened fire from about a hundred yards immediately below the bomber. There was plenty of trade for everyone, and a wise crew might see between half a dozen and twenty-five bombers according to moon conditions, cloud, and visibility. Schnaufer himself claimed that he had never lost a corkscrewing bomber, and at his peak he shot down nine bombers in twenty-four hours, two on an early morning raid and seven during the following evening.

Some night fighter crews dropped flares in the bomber stream, which guided other fighters, as did the blazing Lancasters and Halifaxes which so often fell from the sky. Sometimes lanes of very bright flares were dropped which turned night into day, so that a man in the blacked-out streets below could read a newspaper by them, and along these avenues of light many Wild Boar single-seaters barrelled-in towards the bombers and delivered head-on, quarter, and astern attacks.

In the winter of 1943–44 the German night fighter force was so powerful and dangerous that on sixteen major raids against Berlin bomber losses averaged more than five per cent. Even this defeat was eclipsed at Nuremberg, when from a force of nearly eight hundred bombers no less than ninety-four failed to return and another seventy-one were damaged.

In spite of all British radio counter-measures, which saved many aircraft and crews and paid a dividend out of all proportion to the capital invested, the cloak of darkness under whose cover Bomber Command had operated for years was fast becoming very tattered, and the only means of redressing the balance was to employ plenty of long-range night fighters to support the bomber streams. These were not forthcoming, and the only course open to Harris was to reduce the range of his attacks so that his crews would not have to penetrate the core of the enemy defences; and to take full advantage of bad weather so that the Wild Boar single-seaters, with their limited blind flying and navigational aids, could not oppose his bombers. In effect, the enemy night fighters had won this round of the fluctuating battle for air superiority over Germany.

Chapter 21

SEVEN LEAGUE BOOTS

SINCE Bomber Command had been forced to withdraw to fringe targets, the future of the war in the air depended on whether or not American daylight bombers could survive over Germany. This, in turn, rested upon the production of a fighter with the range of a bomber, a feat which both British and German Air Staffs thought technically impossible. And when the sturdy little Mustang first appeared over Hanover Göring refused to believe the reporting centre and censured its personnel; but when he was finally convinced he simply said, 'We have lost the war!'

In war the great thing is to select an aim and stick to it through thick and thin. At the beginning of the Second War one of the R.A.F. aims was the daylight bombing of Germany, but this had to be abandoned. I have already told how the Luftwaffe's failure to maintain their aim cost them the Battle of Britain. The American aim was to attack Germany by day, but when they brought their bombers to Britain R.A.F. leaders were firmly convinced there was little future in daylight bombing and tried hard to make the Americans think again. Much pressure was put upon them to change their policy, especially when their bombers suffered appalling losses, but they persevered until their aeroplanes not only roamed the length and breadth of Germany but also flew over it to land at bases in Russia and Italy. Their achievement is one of the finest extant examples of selecting an aim and sticking to it.

The British view about the folly of day bombing was brought about because the R.A.F. plan for daylight precision bombing against selected key targets had to be abandoned owing to the strength of German air defences. Although daylight bomber operations of deep penetration, and on a sustained scale, proved impossible, Bomber Command had provided, in 1941, a few bombers to provoke air battles over France. A dozen Blenheim bombers, heavily guarded by close escort, escort cover, high cover, and top cover fighter wings, attacked short-range targets in France, while other fighter wings provided diversionary, forward support, target support, withdrawal cover and flanking support for the bombers.

This daylight bombing had the desired effect, for it made the 109s come up and fight. Some of these *Circus* operations, as they were called, were bitterly opposed. R.A.F. fighter pilots would have fared better had fewer of them escorted the bombers, for when the 109s attacked, the many escorting fighters got in each other's way and the danger from collision was often greater than that from enemy fighters. The mass of fighters, twisting and turning round the bombers was called, appropriately, the 'beehive'. Like the Luftwaffe, Fighter Command fell into the trap of providing too many escorting fighters and too few supporting fighter sweeps.

These *Circus* operations were not a success, for basically Fighter Command was a defensive force. Its aeroplanes, tactics, and organisation were suited to the air defence of Britain. It was not capable of taking part in the bomber offensive over Germany. Let us see how the Americans produced a powerful, offensive fighter force.

During the summer of 1942 Spitfires began to escort the four-engined Flying Fortresses to targets whose selection was largely influenced by the fighter's meagre radius of action of about one hundred and seventy miles. The American bombers bristled with guns, and it was soon discovered that their gunners were very trigger-happy and blazed away at friend and foe alike—probably, it was said, because they got a medal for their first kill. The number of escorting wings was reduced to close escort and escort cover wings, while other wings flew diversionary and supporting missions. The escorting fighter pilots did not fly alongside, as they did with R.A.F. bombers, but held positions well out of gunshot and let the American gunners deal with those enemy fighters which slipped through the screen of fighters.

The handful of American volunteers who fought in the Battle of Britain had so increased that the R.A.F. had formed three Eagle Squadrons, which in 1942 were transferred to the United States Eighth Army Air Force and became the Fourth

Fighter Group. These pilots formed the hard core of fighter experience in the 'Eighth', and this was an excellent thing, for the only difference in tactics was that their squadrons put four sections into the air while R.A.F. squadrons—having fewer aeroplanes per unit—continued to fly in three sections.

One ex-Eagle pilot, tall, lean, vigorous Don Blakeslee, joined the Royal Canadian Air Force before his country was at war, and after a tour on Spitfires from Biggin Hill went to 133 (Eagle) Squadron and became its commander. Eventually Blakeslee became one of the best leaders ever to fight over Germany, but when he exchanged his blue uniform for khaki (and multiplied his pay four times) he wondered whether he had made a wise decision when he heard that he and his comrades were going to change their graceful Spitfire 9s for ungainly looking Thunderbolts, whose big cockpits seemed like old-fashioned bath tubs. Nor did Blakeslee and his contemporaries think highly of the Thunderbolt's six $\frac{1}{2}$-inch calibre machine guns. But the Thunderbolt had some good points, and her 2,000-h.p. Pratt and Whitney radial engine and rugged airframe could take a lot of punishment and still fly home. After his first flight Don told me the Thunderbolt seemed very reluctant to leave the ground and very anxious to get back on it. And when congratulated about its diving qualities, after destroying a Fokker-Wulfe 190 just above the tree-tops, he retorted, 'It ought to dive. It certainly won't climb!'

The Thunderbolt had much the same radius of action as the Spitfire, and wisely the few Luftwaffe squadrons in France and the Low Countries refused combat unless they had every advantage. But it was a different story when the Eighth began to enter Germany, for the enemy fighters waited until the escorting fighters turned back and then set about the bombers, who were sometimes badly mauled.

The American reply was to sling drop tanks under the wings of their Thunderbolts and Lightnings, which theoretically doubled their radius of action. But the Fokker-Wulfe leaders went for the fighters when they crossed the Dutch coast, and the tanks were dropped immediately, since they reduced manoeuvrability and were highly inflammable. Having lost much of their petrol, the fighters had to return early, and the bombers were again sitting ducks for the German fighters. But Galland was not happy about the air fighting and called the *Kommodore* together to talk about tactics and weapons.

He had arranged for long-endurance aeroplanes to shadow the bomber formations and to report on their course and height, on the strength of the fighter escort, on the weather, and the progress of attacks, and he thought this up-to-date information would result in more victories. He wanted to give his fighter pilots the chance to intercept the same raid twice, once on the penetration and again during the withdrawal, and he was linking some airfields in western Germany, Holland, Belgium and northern France with the control system. There would be ammunition, fuel, mechanics, operations rooms there, and once a few pilots had joined together on one of these airfields, the senior pilot would take charge, get them into the air, tune in to the running commentary and try to intercept before Allied fighters met the returning bombers.

Galland had inspected a captured Fortress and noted that its fire power was much greater at the back than at the front. Leaders should therefore try to fly parallel and to one side of the bombers, until they were about three miles ahead, when sections of four fighters should turn for head-on attacks. Pilots should aim at the cockpit, open fire at eight hundred yards, and get away by flying over the bombers; but he had noticed that few pilots seemed to have the courage to do this, and that most of them half-rolled ahead of their target and dived away. This habit was to be discouraged, because it reduced firing time and pilots could not attack again until they had wasted precious minutes in regaining height. On the other hand, those who carried out their orders properly usually hit the bombers and could soon attack again.

There would be many occasions when there would not be time to gain position ahead of the bombers, and fighters would have to carry out rear attacks by sections, in rapid succession, from slightly high or low, and would escape over the top of the bombers. The half-roll and dive was to be avoided at all costs, because this manoeuvre gave the rear gunners an easy deflection shot, and they should remember that a 'box' of twenty-seven Fortresses could defend their rear with a lot of cross-fire.

In addition the single cannon and two machine guns of the Messerschmitt 109F did not have enough hitting power to bring down the big, well-armoured bombers. Galland therefore explained his plans for *Sturm* (storm) squadrons, whose Fokker-Wulfe 190s would carry four heavy cannon, and would be fitted with plenty of armour plate. The storm pilots would make mass, astern attacks very close to the bombers, while the 109s held off the Mustangs. Galland wanted more powerful long-range cannon, so that fighter pilots would not have to run the gauntlet of the bombers' cross-fire. He had great hopes for the new rocket projectiles which would soon be fitted to the twin-engined fighters, and eventually to some of the single-engined aeroplanes.

During the summer of 1943 more fighter units were recalled from the Russian front, southern France, and the Mediterranean to cope with the American daylight raids, and German fighter production so increased that output was well in excess of the target figure of a thousand aeroplanes per month. So it was that on 17th August the Luftwaffe's reorganised fighter squadrons were ready for the double raid of three hundred and seventy-six Fortresses against Schweinfurt and Regensburg; and, assembling near Frankfurt after the Thunderbolts had turned back, they fell upon the bombers and destroyed sixty, approximately sixteen per cent of the bomber force.

This disaster forced the Eighth to nurse its strength for a few weeks and to operate within the range of fighter cover; but its leaders were determined to bomb Germany in daylight, and in early October they were ready to resume deep raids. The Luftwaffe, however, was also ready, and early warning radars saw the bombers climbing and assembling over East Anglia, while the listening service intercepted many radio messages from ground stations and formation leaders. Accordingly, the enemy controllers had ample time to make their various counter-moves and, once they had diagnosed the probable destination of the bombers, were able to scramble fighters from areas not directly threatened. Unlike the situation that obtained in the Battle of Britain, when there was no time to assemble large defensive formations, the American bombers were over hostile land for a long time, and this enabled the Germans to organise a concentrated fighter defence. Sometimes the bomber penetrations were so deep that keen German staff officers left their desks, flew light communications aeroplanes to the nearest fighter airfield, transferred to Fokker-Wulfe 190s and joined the party. On 14th October the Luftwaffe flew well over five hundred sorties against two hundred and ninety-one bombers again raiding Schweinfurt and, fully exploiting their new weapons and tactics, shot down sixty bombers—more than twenty per cent.

On this day, soon to be known as 'Black Thursday' in the annals of air fighting, the news filtered down to R.A.F. airfields in Britain that the Americans were in a bad way, and it would be a good thing if we could get off a little earlier than planned and meet them farther over the Continent. It was a clear afternoon, and we first saw their contrails many miles away, as well as the thinner darting contrails of enemy fighters above and on either flank. As we closed the gap we could see that they had taken a terrible mauling, for there were gaping holes in their precise formations. Some Fortresses were gradually losing height, and a few stragglers, lagging well behind, were struggling to get home on three engines.

We swept well behind the stragglers and drove off a few 109s and 110s, but the great air battle was over, and what a fight it must have been, because more than half the bombers we nursed across the North Sea were shot-up. One or two ditched in the sea, and many others, carrying dead and badly injured crew members, had to make crash-landings. How we longed for more drop tanks, so that some of the many hundreds of Spitfires based in Britain could play their part in the great battles over Germany, instead of being confined to unprofitable sweeps over the familiar and now barren hunting grounds where a man could complete a tour of operations and never fire his guns in anger. We regretted this lack of vision about long-range fighting, for the Spitfire was the best close-in fighter of the lot, and specially equipped Spitfires had flown the Atlantic. With a little foresight Spitfires could have fought well inside Germany and could have helped the Eighth in their great venture; but it was not to be, and for lack of long-range fighters the Eighth, like Bomber Command, had to retreat to less distant targets and the Luftwaffe had won another victory.

With the Eighth Air Force shaken from these disasters, and the night fighter having got the better of the night bomber, the outlook for round-the-clock bombing looked bleak, especially as the enemy's Fighter Committee, charged with expanding fighter production, was getting astonishing results after a drastic pruning of the many different types, and sub-types, of aeroplanes in production, and after obtaining Hitler's consent to the production of more fighters at the expense of bombers. We desperately needed long-range fighters.

Fortunately for the Allies, some three years earlier the R.A.F. had bought some Mustang fighters; but because of their disappointing high-altitude performance these aircraft had been used only for reconnaissance and close support. Later, when the Americans were seeking a long-range fighter, the Packard-built 1,520-h.p. Rolls-Royce engine gave the P-51B Mustang a much improved performance at height, with a top speed of 440 m.p.h. at 35,000 feet. Clever engineering gave her a tremendous amount of fuel, including some carried in two large drop tanks, one under each wing, and a belly tank which could be jettisoned. More than 2,000 P-51B Mustangs were ordered for the U.S.A.A.F. They were capable of accompanying daylight bomber formations to their targets, and could still meet enemy fighters on equal terms after jettisoning their external fuel tanks. The Eighth's first Mustang escort mission was flown to Kiel in December 1943, and a few weeks later Mustangs

accompanied bombers on the 1,100-mile round trip to Berlin. The Mustangs had seven league boots. They imposed a severe problem on the enemy's defence system, and added tremendous impetus to the daylight offensive.

There was great competition among American fighter pilots to get their hands on the Mustang, and Don Blakeslee pleaded with his general to exchange their old Thunderbolts for them. But a great daylight offensive was planned, the Normandy invasion would take place within three months, and so the general answered that he did not see how Blakeslee's group could become non-operational for several weeks while they retrained on to the new fighter. 'That's O.K., General, sir,' replied Don. 'We can learn to fly them on the way to the target!'

Blakeslee's remark was not made out of sheer bravado, but because he and many others like him had fought from Britain for a long time and knew something of the odds which their countrymen faced in Fortresses and Liberators on their ten-hour flights. There was something very inspiring in the sight of a thousand bombers joining up over East Anglia; sorting themselves into great trains of aeroplanes, and setting a steady course across the North Sea for Germany. To the escorting fighter pilots the bombers looked serene, unflinching, and eminently worthy of the great country whose star they bore.

At this time I was a staff officer at 11 Group Headquarters, and worked very closely with the American staff officers who planned the fighter cover and support for their bombers; and they were very keen to learn from our long experience of fighter affairs. Moreover, we had one wing of the latest Mustangs, whose operations had to be integrated with those of the Eighth. We provided fighter support for the daylight activities of our own medium bombers (Bostons, Mitchells, and Mosquitoes) and also worked intimately with the staff planners of the United States Ninth Army Air Force, whose hundreds of twin-engined bombers (Marauders and Havocs), accompanied and supported by both British and American fighters, attacked short-range targets in Europe. Naturally, we timed the missions of the medium bombers to suit those of the Eighth, hoping that some enemy fighters would be diverted from attacking the heavies; but so few enemy squadrons were now based outside Germany that the medium-bomber crews rarely saw a 109.

These American planners were high-calibre officers who saw air fighting on a big canvas. They were determined not to repeat Göring's mistake in the Battle of Britain by failing to exploit the offensive qualities of their fighters. They did not therefore restrict their escorting fighters by keeping them near the bombers. They devised a shuttle escort service where the fighters escorted the bombers only for part of their route, so that, when relieved of these duties by other fighters, they had plenty of fuel left to roam and hunt as their leaders thought best. Realising also that there is no such thing as absolute air superiority, and that it was impossible to seal the air space round the bombers, they used more fighters on sweeps than on escort duties, and hoped by so doing that their pilots would get opportunities to attack climbing and assembling enemy fighters.

The Americans also remembered Göring's failure to take advantage of the radar gap at low heights, and encouraged their fighter leaders to make their way home very low, not only because small formations were safer at this height but also because it afforded splendid opportunities for strafing the many airfields which lay in their path on the long return journey.

Blakeslee got his Mustangs and always led his group on the big shows, when some eight hundred Mustangs and Thunderbolts sometimes supported 1,300 bombers to Berlin and back. From his still expanding fighter force Göring could defend with about nine hundred interceptors, and the numbers of aeroplanes taking part in these air battles far exceeded those involved in the Battle of Britain.

There was little subterfuge about these great contests fought over Germany in 1944, for the Americans did not want their bombers to spend more time over hostile territory than was absolutely necessary, and usually routed them straight to the target, except when they detoured to avoid heavy flak concentrations. There was, of course, some jamming and 'spoofing'; but it was difficult, to say the least, to disguise the straight approach of some 2,000 aeroplanes, and the Germans had ample time to reinforce the threatened area with plenty of fighters. The Americans were fully aware of the enemy's ability to switch squadrons from one area to another, and countered by routing their sweeps hundreds of miles ahead and on the flanks of the bombers. German fighters, especially the twins, tried to avoid Mustangs and Thunderbolts so that they could make concentrated attacks against the bombers, while American fighters were out to break up the German formations before they got to the bombers. With such numbers of attacking and defending aeroplanes, with such tactics, and with such deep penetrations, the stage was set for the biggest air battles of all time.

Blakeslee led his group in much the same manner as wing leaders in Fighter Command, except that he controlled forty-eight Mustangs while R.A.F. wings rarely exceeded thirty-six Spitfires. On one mission over Berlin he was authorised to direct the activities of all the supporting fighters, but it was impossible for one man, cramped in a narrow cockpit, to watch and assess the development of the air fighting round a bomber train twenty miles long, apart from all the skirmishes on the flanks many miles away. The idea of an airborne controller was sound enough, but at this time the right tools were not available for the job. (After the Second War the U.S. Navy developed the idea by fitting radars and means of communications into large, four-engined aeroplanes, and so provided an airborne command post for the flying controller and his staff.)

Blakeslee normally got some information about the build-up of enemy fighters from Fighter Command's control and reporting system, but once he crossed the Dutch coast he soon passed beyond its range and had to rely on eyesight, and on any information available from the bombers, or from other fighter leaders. His group had to be sufficiently wieldy and compact for him to hold them together. The Americans found that three squadrons was the greatest number of aeroplanes one man could hold together in this sort of offensive fighting. Personally, I preferred to lead two Spitfire squadrons rather than three on our supporting sweeps over the Low Countries, because whenever I fought with the larger formation I found we got in each other's way in a fight, and only the leaders were able to bring their guns to bear. I also found that a single, common radio frequency made it difficult to control the activities of more than four or five sections, especially in a fight. But we must remember that the American fighter pilots were meeting far more opposition than our fighter sweeps, and had I been required to lead Mustangs over Berlin I would have infinitely preferred to be at the apex of forty-eight fighters rather than twenty-four.

While three squadrons of fighters proved to be the most one man could lead and control on offensive operations, this does not mean that bigger formations were never effective. Douglas Bader successfully led sixty fighters on defensive operations during the Battle of Britain, because he insisted on having enough fighters to break up the massed bombers. Now that Galland had a similar yet even bigger problem than Bader's, he reacted in the same manner, and his pilots often fought in a *Geschwader* of about ninety aeroplanes.

For fighter pilots this was the toughest air fighting of the Second War. In their small aircraft, which could be brought down by a bullet from a machine gun, they had twice to cross the North Sea. They flew over heavily defended areas, and if they ventured over the Ruhr it meant crossing the greatest concentration of flak in the world. Moreover, German civilians now began to maltreat and sometimes kill Allied airmen who crashed or baled-out. Sometimes their own fighter pilots who were brought down suffered from angry mobs who mistook them for Americans. After the war Galland told us about a German pilot who was hanging from a tree in his parachute, and shouted to a man with a shot-gun, 'Help me down, you fool.' But the man raised his gun, saying, 'So! The pig even speaks German!'

American fighter pilots were encouraged to follow evading enemy aeroplanes down to the ground and to fight above the tree-tops. The R.A.F. discouraged its pilots from similar tactics, because German fighters could out-dive Spitfires, and too many British pilots were last seen half-rolling after a 109. But once she had jettisoned her drop tanks, the lively Mustang could out-dive and out-turn both the Messerschmitt 109 and the Fokker-Wulfe 190, and the Americans were not slow to exploit this superiority in performance. Thus, for the first time in the Second War German fighter pilots could no longer get out of trouble by the famed half-roll and dive tactic. The Americans dived after the Germans and fought them just above the ground. When the Germans did not come up to oppose the bombers the Americans went down and strafed their airfields. When the weather was too bad for the bombers the Mustangs and Thunderbolts went out on low-level attacks, called *Rhubarbs*, and destroyed hundreds of enemy aeroplanes. American fighter pilots seemed to be everywhere. The Germans tried to intercept these low-flying strikes, but they were too low for their radars, and the enemy's other method of reporting hostile aeroplanes, by ground observers, took too much time.

Flying near the ground, the Americans found the German light flak as accurate as ever, and they suffered heavy losses from enemy ground gunners. On one occasion a Mustang pilot rescued his squadron commander, Major McKennon, when he was hit by flak while strafing Prenzlau airfield, near Berlin. McKennon baled out some six miles from the airfield, and his wingman, Lieutenant George Green, watched the Mustang explode in a field near his leader's parachute. Circling lower for a better look, Green decided there was a sporting chance of getting down safely and picking up his C.O. Then he saw several soldiers running towards McKennon, so calling on the other Mustangs to strafe, he put his undercarriage and flaps down and landed in the meadow. Green stood on the wing, threw off his parachute and watched McKennon run towards him. There was no argument about who should fly the aeroplane, for the squadron commander was over six feet tall. He heaved himself into the cockpit, and the smaller Green struggled on to his lap to handle the controls. There was only a take-off run of some three hundred yards, instead of the usual eight hundred yards, and there was a copse at the edge of the field, but somehow they staggered into the air, and two and a half hours later Green called the control tower at Debden:

'Clear the runway.'

'Is this an emergency?' asked the controller.

'I guess so,' replied Green. 'We've got two pilots in this ship.'

The Americans stressed fighter teamwork above all else, and Blakeslee's group produced the best pair ever to fight over Germany; these were Captain Don S. Gentile, twenty-three victories and seven aeroplanes destroyed on the ground, and

Captain John T. Godfrey, eighteen victories and another eighteen aeroplanes destroyed by strafing. When they began to fight together Gentile, known to his brother officers as 'Gentle', usually led the pair of Mustangs; but later Godfrey, unlike the normal number two or wingman, alternated with Gentile as leader, and they were happy taking turns to shoot down enemy aeroplanes and protect each other. They developed team fighting to perfection, and often pretended not to see an enemy fighter overtaking them until they broke violently into climbing turns in opposite directions and came barrelling down to attack. Such was their fame that Göring is alleged to have said that he would gladly give two of his best squadrons for their capture, while Winston Churchill called them the Damon and Pythias of the twentieth century.

One day Gentile, for once without Godfrey, shot down a 190 and followed another to the ground in order to destroy it. He was climbing back to rejoin his squadron when another pilot saw a 190 sitting on his tail and screamed, 'Break, Gentle, break! Break, Gentle, you damn fool!' Meanwhile some miles away the commanding officer of the Eighth's fighters, Major General Kepner, was cruising serenely in his Thunderbolt listening to the combat on his radio when he heard the warning shout, which sounded like, 'Break, general, you damn fool!' It was, to say the least, unusual for a general to be addressed in this fashion, but Kepner put his fighter into a tight turn to clear his tail.

These long-range fighters pioneered well beyond Germany's eastern borders. On one famous occasion Don Blakeslee's group, increased to sixty-eight fighters for this special occasion, picked up four combat groups of Fortresses south of Berlin, while more than one thousand bombers attacked the German capital, and, near Warsaw, shot down five 109s for the loss of one Mustang. Blakeslee's fighters then parted company with the Fortresses and made for their destination. At 7.15 p.m., after close on eight hours in the air, the leader studied the last of his sixteen maps and glanced apprehensively at his watch and the flight plan strapped to his leg, for his pre-flight calculations told him that this epic 1,600-mile flight should finish in about twenty minutes.

Blakeslee found their Russian airfield, put his pilots into tight formation, peeled them off and put his Mustang down exactly at his estimated time of arrival, although one of his section leaders—a precise man—claimed he was one minute late. After being presented with a large bouquet of flowers Blakeslee was hurried to Moscow to make a broadcast to America, while the rest of his pilots were entertained by their admiring hosts. Unfortunately, a Heinkel had shadowed the Americans, and shortly after midnight the Luftwaffe showed their ability to strike telling blows by mounting a highly successful strafing and bombing operation against the American bombers parked on the ground. Five days later the Mustangs took the remaining Fortresses to bomb an oil refinery in Poland and flew on without meeting any opposition to land in Italy. From Italy, Blakeslee's fighters escorted some bombers to Budapest, and lost a pilot during a stiff fight with some fifty 109s. They flew another escort mission into Rumania and finally returned to Debden after bringing bombers from the Mediterranean to attack railway yards in France. These historic missions by Blakeslee's Mustangs showed how well-trained, well-disciplined, and well-led teams of fighters gained air domination of vast areas in 1944.

There were fifteen fighter groups in the Eighth Air Force, and Blakeslee's outfit claimed the most victories, with 1,006½ enemy aeroplanes destroyed for the loss of two hundred and forty-one pilots; but the 56th Fighter Group, led by another outstanding and fearless leader, Colonel Hub Zemke, were beaten into second place only by the narrow margin of half an aeroplane. Blakeslee, fifteen victories, was not an outstanding shot, but his greatness lay in his brilliant leadership of his group. He fought from Britain without respite for more than three years, and so stayed on continuous operations longer than any of his American contemporaries. He and his comrades of the Eighth won a great victory, second only in importance to the Battle of Britain, for they wrested command of the daylight skies from the Luftwaffe and exposed the heart of Germany to bombing.

Chapter 22

THE EASTERN FRONT

So far I have said little about the Soviet Air Force and the part it played in the evolution of air fighting. During the Russo-Finnish war of 1939–40 Russian pilots made a very poor showing, losing hundreds of aeroplanes to obsolete fighters and guns. In the Spanish Civil War the main task of Russian pilots was support of the ground forces, and in 1941 the Soviet Air Force still remained the handmaiden of the Army. The tactical unit was the air regiment, which consisted of three squadrons, each containing ten aeroplanes. The control of the air regiments was vested in local Army commanders. The Russians had no strategic concept of air power.

The Soviet Air Force at this date was inferior, both in pilot training and the quality of its aeroplanes, to that portion of the Luftwaffe, numbering some 3,000 aeroplanes, which in the summer of 1941 was deployed on airfields behind an immense front stretching from the Baltic to the Black Sea. When the German Army began to advance through Poland into White Russia the usual and hitherto successful pattern of *Blitzkrieg* was seen. The Luftwaffe, too, played its traditional part— concentrated attacks in close support of the ground columns, and the bombing and strafing of Russian airfields.

The Luftwaffe took the Soviet Air Force completely by surprise and delivered some paralysing blows. Russian anti-aircraft fire was meagre and poor. The Messerschmitt 109Fs, escorting the Stukas, went down with the dive-bombers and strafed aeroplanes on the ground. Few Russian fighters were seen in the air, but hundreds were destroyed on the ground, where many, according to a German pilot, 'were closely parked, wing-tip to wing-tip, as if on parade'. By the end of October the Germans claimed to have destroyed some 20,000 Russian aeroplanes; even if this figure is suspect, there can be no denying that in a few months German fighters, fighter-bombers, and dive-bombers gained command of the air within their striking range.

The Rata was still the standard fighter of the Soviet Air Force. It was 60 m.p.h. slower than the 109F, some of its equipment was primitive, and its open cockpit was obsolete. The best Russian fighter was the single-seater I-18 monoplane, but it was inferior to the 109F. Russian fighter pilots flew in tight vics of three aeroplanes, but some squadrons soon copied the enemy *Schwärme* and began to fly eight fighters in two loose sections of four. They did not have radars to help them find enemy formations. Few fighters carried radio telephones, and the leader had to control the rest of his pilots by visual signals. They lacked gunnery training and opened fire too far from their enemies. When separated from their companions they seemed to lack confidence and initiative; they fought better together. Here and there an aggressive Russian fighter pilot was encountered, but the rank and file seemed reluctant closely to engage German bombers and broke off their attacks too soon. They failed to stop the Stukas. When attacked by German fighters they went into the defensive circling manoeuvre learned in the Spanish Civil War, and tried to escape at low level.

The best Russian close-support, or ground-attack, aeroplane was the single-seater IL-2, the famous Ilyushin 'Stormovik', which had a speed of about 210 m.p.h., carried cannon, machine guns, and bombs, and had plenty of armour plate to protect the pilot. Russian ground-attack pilots were more courageous and aggressive than their fighter pilots, but their lack of both training and tactical lore cost them many pilots. For example, when strafing or bombing ground targets a good leader always tried to attack out of the sun so that he gained surprise and so that the anti-aircraft gunners could not see his formation. But on one rare occasion when Russian ground-attack pilots attacked a German airfield the Russian pilots, instead of approaching from the direction of the sun, flew round the perimeter of the airfield at 3,000 feet, alerted all the enemy flak, and were all downed.

Exploiting the vast depth of their country, the Russians withdrew, and by so doing gained vital time to refurbish and train their squadrons. Since Russian losses had been largely confined to aeroplanes destroyed on the ground, many pilots had survived the first onslaught and, in the winter of 1941, were ready to fight again. Also, the early arrival of an exceptionally severe winter gave the Russians a further breathing space, for they were better accustomed than their enemies to operate in such arctic conditions. The Germans found it difficult to maintain their aeroplanes, and some squadrons could only get about one-third of their fighters into the air. Here and there along the front the initiative passed from the Luftwaffe to the Soviet Air Force, and Colonel Rudel, a brilliant Stuka pilot (he was eventually credited with no less than five hundred Russian tanks), met fighter opposition and formidable anti-aircraft fire. The Soviet Air Force had begun to recover.

A Russian counter-attack drove back enemy troops from Moscow, and this success heartened all Soviet pilots. Fighter pilots and ground-attack pilots began to lose their feeling of inferiority, and their squadrons, according to the Russian concept of air power, were given more priority than bomber and reconnaissance units. They began to show more aggression and more initiative in the air. They paid more attention than before to the planning and co-ordination of fighter and ground-attack missions. Their tactics improved, due, in some measure, to the assistance received from Britain and America. The R.A.F. sent two squadrons of Hurricanes under Wing Commander Ramsbottom-Isherwood, who explained and demonstrated modern fighter tactics to his hosts. Before handing over their Hurricanes the British pilots destroyed a few German aeroplanes; they were also much impressed by some Russian pilots who insisted on flying the Hurricanes in the most appalling weather.

The Battle of Stalingrad gave further proof of the recovery of the Soviet Air Force. The German ground offensive, against Stalingrad, was supported by some 1,000 aeroplanes, of all types, but the city was held, and when the Russians counter-attacked their advance deprived the Germans of their forward airfields. Thus, German single-engined fighters could no longer reach Stalingrad. The Russians concentrated their fighters and soon gained air superiority over the encircled German troops. The Luftwaffe tried to supply the isolated German garrison from the air with Junkers 52 transports and some bombers—

hastily converted to transports—but many were shot down by Russian fighters. Other Russian fighters harassed German airfields and destroyed the transports just after they had taken off or were about to land. More transports were destroyed on their airfields by the Stormoviks. The Luftwaffe had to resort to air supply at night. When, in 1943, the Germans were defeated at Stalingrad it was estimated that the Luftwaffe had lost nearly five hundred aeroplanes in the attempt to save their troops.

The Germans had to think about a better-balanced Air Force in Russia; a force more equally divided between offensive and defensive functions. Von Richthofen, promoted to the command of *Luftflotte 4*, raised special squadrons whose defensive task was to try to destroy Russian tanks that had broken through the German lines. Other squadrons, equipped with heavily armed Junkers 88s, tried to isolate the battlefield to prevent the movement of Russian supplies and reinforcements, by destroying road and rail bridges. Bomber units tried to make night attacks against Russian troop concentrations. These measures, however, could not be effectively developed owing to the growing Russian strength.

Blitzkrieg, which had won Germany her great military successes, was failing. There remained one final and classic example of Lightning War when many Luftwaffe squadrons, under the able von Richthofen, blasted the way for German ground columns to recapture Kharkov. This temporary success, however, was soon overshadowed by a great Russian ground offensive, and as the Germans fell back their leaders realised that the *Blitzkrieg* policy of close support would not prevail against the Russians. They would have preferred a more strategic concept of air warfare, so that the bomber force, once released from its Army support duties, could attack Russian industry and prevent the Soviet Air Force and Army from gaining further strength. Eventually the decision was made for the Luftwaffe's bomber force to make strategic attacks, but it was too late, for the Germans had retreated so far as to place Russian industry well beyond the range of the bombers. The Germans were suffering from a *Blitzkrieg* of their own making, but in reverse.

Russian fighters, now fitted with radio telephones, were far superior to their earlier models. Their Yak-9 had a top speed of 370 m.p.h. and could, in 1943, hold its own against the best enemy fighters. Later, the Yak-3 and the La-7 (2,000-h.p. engine) were faster, more manoeuvrable and could out-climb the best Messerschmitt and Fokker-Wulfe fighters; their cannon, however, had a slow rate of fire and were inferior to German cannon. Russian aeroplane production was reinforced by thousands of machines from the Western Allies, including Hurricanes, Spitfires, Tomahawks, Kittyhawks, Airacobras, and Lightnings. All these fighters were flown by Russian pilots.

The Soviet Air Force's numerical superiority over the Luftwaffe was further emphasised, in the autumn of 1943, when many German squadrons were withdrawn from the Eastern Front to strengthen the air defence of the Reich against Anglo-American bombing. These deficiencies were never made good. Another clear indication that the Eastern Front was, in German eyes, losing its priority was the transfer of von Richthofen to the Mediterranean theatre.

Throughout the war the Russians regarded their ground-attack squadrons as more important than any of their other air arms—fighter, bomber, reconnaissance, and transport. For ground-attack purposes the Russians continued to rely upon their sturdy IL-2, but the IL-3, a two-seater, gradually replaced the single-seater. Like its predecessor, the IL-3 was well protected; its welded steel plates and bullet-proof glass shielded the crew and all the vital parts of the aeroplane. It could not, of course, withstand heavy anti-aircraft fire, but German pilots found the IL-3 could take a lot of punishment and one said, ruefully, that it was far easier to destroy a tank than a Stormovik.

The Russians, learning from the Stalingrad fighting, concentrated their fighter and ground-attack units near the fiercest ground fighting. They were able to do this by their ability to construct temporary airfields within twenty-four hours. Such airfields were made in forest clearings and on the plains, and if they were far below Western standards, their very simplicity was an advantage in this campaign, where the contestants were so often on the move.

Before a Russian ground offensive these airfields filled with their squadrons and, here and there, they wrested local air superiority from the Luftwaffe. Fighters were employed as fighter-bombers, and the Russians began to fly over the battle-field to a greater depth, seeking enemy airfields, railroad installations, and the like. German commanders, however, were amazed that the Stormoviks did not operate deeper into their territory, especially when they, the Germans, were retreating and the roads were choked with vehicles.

As the war progressed the Soviet Air Force made more and more set-piece attacks against enemy targets. Air strikes were integrated into the fire plan of the Soviet artillery. The number of attacking aeroplanes was determined by the importance of the target. The ground-attack pilots usually operated in regiment strength of about thirty aeroplanes, but against important targets two regiments flew together and were escorted by three fighter regiments. Against priority targets three ground-attack regiments, two fighter-bomber regiments and three bomber regiments, all protected by strong fighter escorts, hammered at the enemy. The bombers went in first and dropped their bombs from about 10,000 feet. The ground-attack units followed the bombers, and the fighter-bombers were the last to attack.

The ground-attack pilots flew, at about 5,000 feet, in a loose weaving formation to try to confuse the enemy gunners; their fighter escort remained some 2,000 feet higher and slightly astern. When attacked by German fighters they stubbornly flew on towards their target, relying on their own fighters and their robust Stormoviks to see them through. Sometimes they amazed their enemies by their seemingly fanatical disregard for their own safety. Whenever the Germans succeeded in breaking up a ground-attack formation the Russian pilots no longer resorted to their defensive circling, but tried to escape in a snake-like weaving dive.

When the ground-attack formation approached the front trained ground observers gave directions, by radio telephone, about the exact whereabouts of the target, and had it marked with coloured smoke by the Russian artillery. Before attacking the pilots assumed a staggered formation, echeloned either to the right or the left, so that the leader attacked first; inexperienced pilots followed him, and the last man, in an echelon of four Stormoviks, was another veteran.

They began their attacks at about 4,000 feet, and during the dive fired their machine guns, cannon, and rocket projectiles; their bombs were the last to go. When the pilots climbed away their observers continued firing at the target. The pilots regained their original height and attacked again and again, until all their weapons and ammunition were gone. Sometimes sixty Stormoviks attacked enemy positions for almost one hour.

The Russians showed some ingenuity when their ground-attack pilots set fire to large areas of dry, steppe grass, forcing German troops to change their positions, when they lost much equipment. They often laid smoke screens to hide their approach from enemy gunners. They often surprised their enemies by flying in foul weather conditions, when the cloud base was only a few hundred feet above the ground and the visibility about a quarter of a mile. They seldom flew at night.

Although ground-attack pilots were the hard core of the Soviet Air Force, fighter pilots were the *élite*. Many units were honoured with the title of 'Guards Fighters', and most 'Heroes of the Soviet Union' were fighter pilots. Fighter squadrons sometimes contained a number of women, who were employed as mechanics and, exceptionally, as pilots. Fighting a Yak-9, Major Meyer, an experienced German pilot, jettisoned his cockpit canopy when his fighter began to burn. The canopy was blown into the Yak's propeller and it crashed. Meyer had to make an emergency landing near his dead foe, who proved to be a woman without rank badges, without means of identification, and without a parachute.

The Russian control and reporting system, non-existent when the war began, was built upon radio control stations, ground observers, and acoustic devices. It was a rudimentary scheme, but it served to direct some Russian fighters to enemy bombers and forced the Germans to provide more escort fighters. Later the Russians produced many radars, copied from those supplied by Britain, but their control and warning system did not compare with those in Britain and Germany.

At the beginning of the war the Russians knew little about

night fighting, and did not develop a night fighter force until German bombers attacked at night. Some day squadrons were switched to night fighting, and during the short summer nights, when visibility was usually good, the pilots accounted for a few bombers. They experimented with flares, and some night fighters carried searchlights to illuminate enemy bombers. Radar sets were not carried in night fighters, and on dark nights the Russians did not have the technical capabilities to find and destroy enemy bombers. Towards the end of the war the Soviet Air Force attempted some night intruding in twin-engined Bostons, supplied by America, but these missions, requiring high skills, produced only modest results.

Day fighter operations were always planned within the framework of Army operations, and the fighters, like the ground-attack squadrons, were concentrated at the main points of enemy ground resistance. Some units still flew too close together, but the best squadrons patrolled over the battlefield, at 16,000 feet or so, in a good, extended *Schwärme* pattern. Russian fighter pilots became more aggressive, and not only accepted more German challenges than before, but sought for them. They showed more initiative against enemy bombers, but were still inclined to open fire too far away. They were ruthless with the dive-bombers, whom they had come to hate. Experienced German fighter pilots still considered themselves superior in combat; and despite the large number of fighter regiments in existence, very few Russian air aces became well known.

By 1944 the steadily improving qualities of Russian fighter pilots and their crushing numerical superiority, had gained them command of the air over the whole front. Their massive ground-attack arm had so well supported ground operations that the last of the German gains in the East, so easily won three years before, were recaptured. In the West the Allies had landed in Normandy.

Chapter 23

DECLINE AND FALL

DURING the high summer of 1944 the Allied landings in Normandy were followed, a few days later, by another great Russian offensive. The Soviet and Allied Air Forces were far more powerful than the Luftwaffe, which had to divide its attention between the 1,500-mile Russian front, the Mediterranean, bombing Britain, the Atlantic shipping routes, and the defence of Germany. The Luftwaffe had always been very flexible, and squadrons were moved thousands of miles to reinforce a threatened position. Dive-bombers were flown from Estonia to Finland. Day fighters departed from Germany for airfields in Poland. Fokker-Wulfe 190s were taken from the already depleted Italian front to operate against the advancing Russian columns; other German fighters followed from Normandy, and more were sent from the Balkans.

Allied fighter pilots patrolling over the Normandy beachhead saw few enemy fighters. Later, however, when the Germans switched hundreds of fighters and fighter-bombers from Germany to France they carried out low-flying attacks against Allied forward troops and armour. The enemy flew in smaller numbers than before, in squadron rather than wing strength, for two reasons: firstly, he wanted to keep down the number of his aeroplanes flying from any one airfield; secondly, the greater speeds and altitudes of his latest fighters meant wider turning circles and less manoeuvrability. Large formations to punch holes in massed daylight raids were still wanted for defensive purposes, but the close and swift skirmishes over Normandy made it impossible for a leader to handle more than a dozen fighters. The R.A.F., too, found that wing fighting was on the way out.

Spitfire 9s were fitted with the latest gyroscopic gunsights, which, unlike the predecessors, automatically computed the amount of deflection one should allow when attacking an enemy aeroplane. A fighter pilot simply aimed the guns by

flying his Spitfire so that the cross bisected the target, and the
range was ideal when the surrounding 'diamonds' embraced the
silhouette of his opponent. Some pilots obtained remarkable

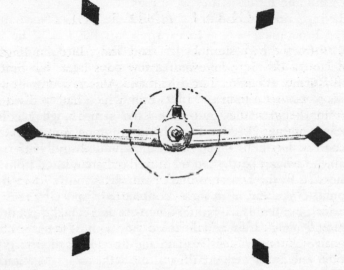

results with this device, but I found that I spent too long with
my head in the office, as it were, peering into the sight and not
paying enough attention to my tail, and I preferred the old
reflector sight, which I kept installed in my personal Spitfire
until the shooting was over.

The low-flying and small German formations often escaped
radar detection, but their radio discipline was sometimes so
poor that they were heard by a 'listening' organisation, and
R.A.F. fighter pilots were told where the Fokker-Wulfes could
be found. So they were brought to battle, where, except for a
leader here and there, they seemed a poor lot who bore little
resemblance to those fierce and highly trained pilots who had
fought so well over Britain.

The enemy fighters were so outnumbered and outclassed
that they could not survive over the battlefield and, in a vain
attempt to take the pressure off their sorely tried troops, they
tried to bomb and strafe Allied front-line positions at night.
But the enemy could not afford to wait for the full moon, and
when he tried to attack ground targets on dark nights he soon

found that this form of combat flying demands high skills and much training. Hence his attempt to turn fighters into night intruders over the rolling country of Normandy was far from successful and his casualties were high.

Having gained undisputed control of the air over Normandy, Harry Broadhurst was able to apply all the lessons he had learned from the Western Desert and Italy. Broadhurst commanded 83 Group, whose squadrons supported the Second British Army. Broadhurst had his headquarters alongside that of his opposite number, Miles Dempsey. General and air marshal thought alike and spoke the same language. This happy state was to be found at all levels of the air–ground team. Trained Army liaison officers kept the squadrons fully informed about the ground battle and what the soldiers wanted from the airmen. As in the Desert, R.A.F. controllers rode in armoured cars and tanks, and from these 'contact cars' spoke by radio to the waiting cab ranks of fighter-bombers and called them down to blast enemy tanks and fortified positions. Tactical reconnaissance pilots flew well beyond the front line, reporting not only on enemy movements but also on the exact positions of British armour and troops so that Dempsey had up-to-date and detailed knowledge about the ebb and flow of the land battle.

When things were quiet in the air Spitfire pilots sometimes carried 500-pound bombs, but if they saw a few 109s before they reached their target they jettisoned the bombs and got on with the real business of fighting. The lack of enthusiasm of the average fighter pilot for beating up ground targets was illustrated by a radio conversation overheard between two Canadians:

'Red one from red four. Trucks at four o'clock below.'

'What's that, red four? Say again.'

'I say again, trucks at four o'clock below. Near that wood. At three o'clock now.'

'Okay, red four. I don't see any damned trucks at three o'clock, either above or below!'

Broadhurst, however, took more than a keen interest in his pilots' ground-attack missions, studied their ciné films and had some harsh things to say whenever they failed to get a decent

bag of enemy vehicles, or even worse, failed to find them. He
kept them at it, exploiting to the full the dual ability of his
fighter-bombers, and it was Spitfire pilots of 602 Squadron
(City of Glasgow) who strafed and overturned the staff car of
that splendid German general, Erwin Rommel; 'The Desert
Fox' was flung into the ditch, fractured his skull, and survived
only to kill himself before standing trial for high treason, the
charge being complicity in the recent attempt on Hitler's life.

Yet despite this massive superiority in the air, the German
troops held their ground in the face of terrible poundings by
thousands of Allied aeroplanes, including the heavy bombers.
In Normandy, and especially at Caen, these steadfast and
resolute troops showed that all the might of Allied air power
could not break them and that, if the best material and psycho-
logical results were to be obtained from heavy carpet bombing,
the joint plans would have to include ample fire and movement from Allied ground forces soon after the last bomb had
fallen. The planners had to overcome many problems, for
heavy bomber crews were not trained for this type of pinpoint
attack, and sometimes the countless bomb craters hindered the
follow-up ground offensive. But when the heavy air bombard-
ments were co-ordinated to dovetail into the ground attack the
Germans began to give ground; and once they gave ground
and exposed themselves from their dug-in and fortified positions the fighter-bombers caught the German Seventh Army at
Falaise, and within a few days turned the retreat into a rout,
and a rout into a slaughter by writing off two panzer and eight
infantry divisions.

After Falaise the Germans were forced into a rapid withdrawal across the Seine, Paris was liberated and the headlong
retreat continued into Belgium. On the ground the situation
was not unlike that four years previously when Dowding
fought against sending more fighters across the Channel to
operate from a crumbling France. Dowding won the day for
Britain, but now Hitler lost it for Germany when he again
ordered hundreds of fighters from Germany to try to stop the
rot. Some units landed on airfields already over-run by Allied
armour, while others found their troops had 'borrowed' vehicles
and fuel to make good their escape. Many fighters were burnt

by Luftwaffe personnel before they left, and others were destroyed by Allied strafing. Very few were flown in combat. As enemy airfields and radar sites were captured, the enemy's powerful night fighter force, so long a menace to Bomber Command, began to collapse. Advancing across France with his wing of Hawker Typhoon fighter-bombers, Group Captain Tim Morice found himself based at Douai, and made quite certain that his Typhoon was parked on the very spot from which the Baron took off to fight him twenty-seven years before.

As the advance continued towards Germany the fighter-bombers were able to attack the flying bomb (V.1) and ballistic rocket (V.2) sites, which during the past few months had made life uncomfortable in southern England. The pilotless, jet-propelled flying bombs were set to fly, by means of simple auto-pilots, at a height between 1,000 and 4,000 feet, and their speed steadily increased from 200 m.p.h., just after the launch, to about 400 m.p.h. They carried a warhead of nearly 2,000 pounds of high explosive. They had a wing-span of less than eighteen feet, and presented small radar targets which did not always show up well on the radar screens. Their maximum speed equalled that of the fastest R.A.F. fighters. They could be launched in any kind of weather. Their engines were stopped at calculated times, when an automatic device depressed the elevators and the bombs dived steeply into the ground.

Since the flying bombs flew in a straight line, it was not difficult for Fighter Command to organise a defensive system of balloons, anti-aircraft guns, and fighter patrols—for the bombs were too fast to be intercepted from ground readiness. Fighters patrolled as far to the south, across the Channel, as the radars could detect the missiles. Behind the patrolling fighters lay the guns, and behind the guns a thousand balloons formed the last defence of south-east London.

By mid-July, 1944, some 3,000 flying bombs had entered Fighter Command's defence zone. About 1,200 reached London, while twenty-five fell on Portsmouth and Southampton. R.A.F. fighter pilots, flying Spitfire 14s (2,050-h.p. Rolls-Royce engine), Hawker Tempest 5s, Mustang 3s, and twin-engined de Havilland Mosquitoes, destroyed about one-third of these 'doodle bugs', and would have done better had their aeroplanes been a little faster. For a flying bomb could be over-hauled in a stern-chase only if the attacking pilot started well above the bomb and could increase his speed by diving. Having overhauled the bombs, it was not easy to shoot them down. The fighter pilots had to close to three hundred yards, or less, to be sure of hitting such a small target; at two hundred yards range the blast from the exploding warhead could harm the fighter.

Some successful day pilots flew ahead of and roughly parallel to approaching bombs, allowed them to catch up, and fired as they passed. One pilot destroyed a bomb by flying alongside, getting a wing under the bomb's wing, then lifting his wing so that the bomb turned on to its back and fell out of control. At night the bomb's fiery tail was easy to see and helped the pilots, who, however, were sometimes temporarily blinded by the flash of the exploding missile.

Later, the guns obtained better results, and four bombs from every five entering the defence zone were destroyed. The R.A.F.'s most successful pilot against the flying bombs was Squadron Leader Berry, of 501 Squadron, who, in his Tempest, destroyed more than sixty bombs. Just as it seemed that defensive and offensive measures had won this contest, the first V.2 rocket fell on Chiswick.

From the defence viewpoint the rocket was a very different kind of weapon from the flying bomb. From launching sites in Holland it had a range of about two hundred miles, and its ton of high explosive could fall upon London and other British cities. The method of launching was simple. The rocket, standing on its four fins, was fired from a slab of concrete. It was radio-controlled for the first part of its flight, accelerated to a speed of 3,600 m.p.h., rose sixty miles into the sky and fell upon London within a few minutes of being launched. Defensive fighters, guns, and balloons could do nothing about it. Fighter Command tried to give warning of the firings, but this was not successful. The only solution lay in bombing attacks on the launching sites, and components of the system, and, ultimately, in the capture of the sites by Allied ground forces already in Holland. The V.2s heralded the space age. They gave ample warning that the era of the defensive fighter was ending.

Further ingenuity of the German race was shown by their jet aeroplanes. They had thought about jet aeroplanes before the war, and their first had flown in 1941. Now, with the approach of the war's fifth winter, two twin-engined jets were coming into operational service, the Arado 234, which was developed as a bomber-reconnaissance aeroplane, and the Messerschmitt 262 (each Junkers Jumo turbojet giving 1,980 pounds of thrust), which was developed both as a bomber and a fighter because everyone wanted this outstanding machine. The bomber protagonists wanted it because the 262's speed of well over 500 m.p.h. and the great altitudes at which it could fly would make it ideal for attacking Britain's crowded airfields, while the fighter advocates wanted it to stop the daylight raids. But when Hitler saw the jet he called it 'the blitz bomber', and there the matter rested—for the moment.

Naturally Galland fought hard for the jet, and somehow got a few 262s together to prove them in combat, for he thought that if they were very successful the *Führer* might change his mind. Soon the jets, with their four 30-mm. cannon, began destroying the high-flying Mosquito bombers which had long roamed free over Germany; and whenever Allied fighter pilots came across a 262 they could not catch it because of its remarkable speed and climb. Suddenly, piston-engined fighters were outmoded.

One day Hitler asked about the 262 programme and how many could carry bombs. Göring told him that the jet was being produced as a fighter, whereupon the *Führer* foamed with rage and accused Göring of disobedience. The *Reichsmarschall* subsequently ordered all 262s to be converted to bombers, and never again was it to be called a fighter! But later Hitler changed his mind and allowed the 262s to be shared equally between bomber and fighter units.

The first 262 wing was given to a proved leader, Walter Nowotny, two hundred and fifty-eight victories, and formed near Osnabrück and within the range of Tempests and Mustangs now encamped on the west side of the Rhine. Broadhurst, realising that his piston-engined fighters could not tackle the jets once they were in the air, ordered frequent strafing attacks to smash them on the ground; but these were costly, because the thick and accurate flak brought down many Tempests, so he kept standing patrols near the airfield to hit them taking-off or approaching to land. Nowotny countered with standing patrols of 109s, and some fierce little air battles were fought over the airfield, during which Nowotny was shot down in his jet and killed. In this way Broadhurst was able to prevent the small numbers of 262s from becoming dangerous; meanwhile Allied bombers struck at jet factories.

More revolutionary interceptors were based deep in Germany, including the rocket-propelled Messerschmitt 163 whose engine produced 3,750 pounds of thrust and whose amazing

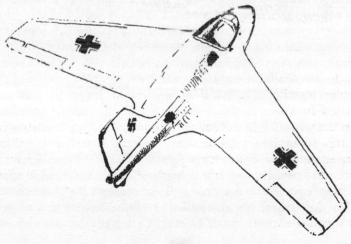

rate of climb, to 40,000 feet in less than three minutes, made it suitable for the local defence of important factories and the like, but its range was so limited that the enemy's Fighter Committee dropped it from their programme in favour of the Heinkel 162, the 'People's Fighter', which had an astonishing history, for its 'lead' time from drawing board to production was only four months; but the 162 was aerodynamically un-sound, and its accident rate was such that pilots called it 'the cheap and nasty'. A few 162s were seen by American fighter pilots, but the Messerschmitt 262 and the Arado 234 were the only proved and satisfactory non-piston-engined aeroplanes used by the Luftwaffe. These were well ahead of any Allied aeroplane, including the few Meteor 3s based near Brussels, whose poor climb and modest range made them unsuitable for combat; eventually, after more powerful engines were fitted, the Meteors carried out some strafing, but they never destroyed an enemy aeroplane in the air over Europe.

The Allied failure at Arnhem to secure a bridge-head on the far side of the Rhine meant that the final assault would have to wait until the following spring, and this breathing space en-abled the Luftwaffe so far to recover that about 2,000 fighters, including some jets, were available. With this powerful force the Germans planned the biggest fighter operation of all time, *Der Grosse Schlag* (The Big Blow), when eleven large formations, each consisting of a strong core of Fokker-Wulfe 'storm' fighters protected by many 109s, would be thrown against the American bombers, while night fighters patrolled the German frontiers to deal with any crippled bombers heading for neutral coun-tries. Every available fighter would fly a second sortie, and the Germans hoped to destroy between four hundred and five hundred bombers, and so convince the Americans, once and for all, that daylight bombing was not on. The Inspector of Fighters supervised some of the training, but The Big Blow never came off, because many fighter units were transferred to the West to support von Rundstedt's offensive when, in Decem-ber 1944, he tried to push his armour through the Ardennes to the North Sea to delay any Allied ground offensive and to gain time for the development of Germany's secret weapons and jets.

These squadrons now came under the command of *General-major* Dietrich Peltz, a young, pugnacious, and distinguished officer who would not be content to restrict his fighters to a defensive role, for he knew all about the low-level approach and his fighter-bombers had often achieved complete surprise when, in 1943, they came in low and attacked Canterbury, Ramsgate, and other places on our south coast. Peltz had also successfully used these tactics in the Mediterranean.

True to form, Peltz sent his fighters across the Rhine to beat-up the vulnerable Allied airfields; but why did he wait until New Year's Day, sixteen days after von Rundstedt began his offensive, when he knew full well that he must take out the tactical air forces opposing him before the panzers began to roll? After all, this was the very essence of *Blitzkrieg*, and although Peltz briefed his subordinate commanders on the eve of von Rundstedt's attack, it was not until New Year's Eve that the pilots were told that the meticulously planned attacks against the Allies' congested airfields would take place on the morrow. The enemy records state that the prospect of fine weather on 1st January, 1945, gave Peltz his long-awaited opportunity to mount this operation and, although bad weather had sometimes grounded the aeroplanes of both sides, Peltz was able to fly almost 1,000 close support sorties during the first two days of the ground offensive. One can only assume that since the Luftwaffe was invariably subordinate to the German Army the fighter-bombers were ordered to provide close support, instead of trying to get air superiority by strafing Allied airfields.

Von Rundstedt made some progress during the first few days and continued his advance when thick fog grounded Allied squadrons. But once the fog lifted all the might of Allied air power, both strategic and tactical, was brought to bear against the German offensive. Allied fighters clashed with enemy fighters over the battlefield; fighter-bombers strafed tanks and armour; light and medium bombers attacked road and rail networks, while the heavies blasted enemy airfields. Soon von Rundstedt's forward elements began to flag, and Allied ground commanders could think about turning from defensive to offensive fighting and resuming their march to the Rhine.

Belatedly, when von Rundstedt had reverted to the defensive, Peltz sent some eight hundred fighters and fighter-bombers across the Rhine. They flew very low in four great waves, led and navigated by Junkers 88s who turned back near the Rhine. The raiders achieved complete tactical surprise, for their cannons were already sounding over several airfields when the group controller ordered the defending fighters into the air.

In all thirteen British and four American airfields were attacked, and in each case some squadrons were caught bunched together on runways and about to take-off. The Americans and British admitted to the loss of one hundred and fifty-five aeroplanes, and a similar number badly damaged, but for various reasons those shot-up aeroplanes considered repairable by their units were not reported. On the other hand, the Germans lost nearly two hundred fighters and cannot have considered it a profitable venture. It was a bold stroke, in keeping with Peltz's character, but it failed in the tactical sense because his pilots were not well enough trained and their shooting was poor. Also, they spent too long over their targets, so that when they withdrew they had to face an alerted defence, fighters from secure airfields and anti-aircraft guns. Operation *Hermann* was the last significant Luftwaffe operation of the Second War, for their losses during the Ardennes campaign came close to a thousand fighters and from this set-back they never recovered. The Luftwaffe's final decline had set in.

Adolf Galland's life during these last weeks of the war in Europe reads like a thriller. He still held the allegiance of most fighter pilots, but he had made powerful enemies, and now his telephones were tapped, he was spied upon, and his political activities were investigated. Once more he was summoned to Karinhall, where Göring accused him of disloyalty, of setting up a private empire, and of introducing unsound tactics. He made no defence, and simply asked to be sent back to the front as a jet pilot.

The news of Galland's dismissal soon spread and created much unrest within the fighter arm, for the *Kommodore* thought that with his going there would be no one to speak for them; consequently Göring called a meeting of all *Kommodore*, turned on his charm and invited them to speak frankly. Soon the old arguments about the 262 waxed fast and furious, Galland's sacking was criticised and Göring called them mutinous dogs, threatened to have some of the rebels arrested and shot, and adjourned the meeting. Later Galland was placed under house arrest and was told that charges of disloyalty, gambling, and the misuse of official cars would be made against him. Disillusioned and dispirited, the young general decided to end it all by taking his own life, but Hitler, who always had high regard for this brilliant pilot, heard of his downfall and the charges were dropped. Instead, Galland was told that his *Führer* wished him to organise and lead a combat unit of Messerschmitt 262s.

And so in this disintegrating Germany of divided counsels, of plot and counter-plot, *Generalleutnant* Adolf Galland, late Inspector of Fighters, holder of Germany's highest decorations, with two brothers already killed in air combat, left his high office to end the war as he began—a leader of a few fighters. Some of his old friends, including ten holders of the Knight's Cross, joined him, and sometimes they managed to scrape together twenty jets and get them into the air. Exploiting the great speed of their aircraft, they were able to avoid the fighters and concentrate against the bombers, where their racks of 50-mm. cannon, slung under each wing and supplementary to the standard armament, were very useful, for a single properly aimed round could destroy a bomber. They scored some victories, but, moving from airfield to airfield as the Allied net tightened, the chain of command gone, short of fuel and with Allied fighters always above, their task was hopeless, as was that of the Fokker-Wulfe pilots of a special ramming unit, *Sonderkommando Elbe*, who on 7th April, encouraged by patriotic music and other suitable exhortations, tried to ram some of the 1,300 bombers of the Eighth over Germany.

Towards the end of April, 1945, American and Russian troops linked up. The remaining Luftwaffe units were compressed into a relatively small area in Central Germany. It was no longer possible to differentiate between enemy airfields containing units employed against the Russians or the Western Allies. Broadhurst's fighter wings were based deep in

Germany, and one day I led my Spitfires over the smoking rubble that was Berlin and met a collection of Russian Yak fighters. Göring, 'the loyal Hermann', was sacked, but would live to outwit his captors at Nuremburg. Galland was shot down and wounded. Bomber Command and the Eighth Air Force ceased operations because of lack of worthwhile targets. The aeroplanes of the once mighty Luftwaffe burned on the ground. And in his bunker, below the ruined city, Hitler prepared to take his life.

Chapter 24

OVER THE YALU

TOWARDS the close of the Second War the R.A.F. formed the Central Fighter Establishment to study air fighting and train fighter leaders. Once a year fighter leaders from the R.A.F., the Commonwealth Air Forces, and the United States Air Force assembled at the Central Fighter Establishment to discuss fighter tactics. At one of these happy and successful gatherings someone gave a lecture about in-flight refuelling, for all were keenly interested in Sir Alan Cobham's invention, and the R.A.F. had modified a few Meteor interceptors to receive fuel from a Lancaster tanker. The owner of the Meteors said that slipping the probe of the Meteor into the Lancaster's drogue called for such precise flying that the average fighter pilot could not cope, but if anyone wanted a go he was welcome! Several pilots tried to receive fuel from the Lancaster with varying degrees of success, but Colonel David C. Schilling, U.S.A.F., fared better than most.

While Britain, because of geography, still concentrated on defensive fighting, the Americans, because of the size of their country and their overseas responsibilities, thought increasingly about offensive fighting, and Schilling saw at once that if enough tankers were available swarms of fighters could be sent from the United States to any part of the world at short notice. It was true, of course, that fighters could be sent to most parts of the world along the ferry routes, but they were often delayed by bad weather, and during the winter the route from America to Europe—staging through Newfoundland, Labrador, Greenland, Iceland, and Britain—was often impassable. But if fighters were refuelled above the overcast they would beat the weather. Also, in-flight refuelling would extend the range of fighters and, if enough tankers were not available, Schilling thought one fighter could refuel another; eventually, such a system, called the 'buddy-buddy' technique, was introduced.

Schilling lost no time in approaching the head of his Service,

General Hoyt S. Vandenberg, and soon a few Republic F-84s (Thunderjets) were flown to England to be modified for the job. In September, 1950, Schilling and his wingman, Bill Ritchie, took off from Manston in their two Thunderjets to make a non-stop flight to New York. Head winds dogged them. They lost almost an hour looking for a tanker over Iceland. Over Labrador Schilling had only three minutes fuel remaining when he locked-on to the tanker. But Ritchie found he had a defective probe and could not receive any fuel. Ritchie told Schilling to get on with the mission and stretched his glide towards the coast; he baled out thirteen miles short of the great airfield at Goose and was picked up by helicopter. At New York the weather had closed in and Schilling went to Maine and landed safely after flying 3,300 miles in ten hours. As a result of their endeavours, more fighters with refuelling equipment and more tankers were ordered into production, and today a great number of American combat aeroplanes have this important capability.

I saw a lot of Schilling, for after a year at the Royal Canadian Air Force's Staff College at Toronto I was sent, as an Exchange Officer, to the Tactical Air Command, in Virginia, where I worked for a human dynamo, Lieutenant General 'Pete' Quesada, and organised all air displays and demonstrations within his large parish. I had to deal with a lot of people who for various reasons wanted a few jet fighters to fly over their towns, and these civilians upon telephoning our headquarters and asking for the chap in charge of air shows found it bewildering when they were put through to an Englishman. There were a lot of involved explanations until I acquired a southern accent and called myself 'Colonel Johnson'!

All went well until the Mayor of Yorktown, Virginia, phoned and said he would like a squadron of jets to fly over the town on 13th October; the Marines would be there, a destroyer would be alongside the quay, and a jet fly-past would complete the programme. I said I was sure General Quesada would agree, but would he tell me what occasion they were celebrating? Was some politician visiting, or was it a county fair or even the centenary of the town? There was an astonished silence, broken only when he shouted, 'Hell, Colonel, we're celebrating the hundred and seventy-second anniversary of the defeat of the godamn British!'

I did plenty of flying from Langley Field, Virginia, and when the fighter group there got the finest interceptor of those times, the F-86A made by North American Aviation Inc., I lost no opportunity in checking out in this splendid aeroplane. The Sabre handled as beautifully as the Spitfire; at height, its 5,000 pounds of thrust pushed it along at a top speed approaching that of sound, it was supersonic in a very steep dive, and had a good radius of action. And it was just as well I was in good flying practice, for shortly after the Communist troops of North Korea crossed the border on 25th June, 1950, and began the long, bitter struggle in that mountainous country, I found myself reporting to the Headquarters of the United States Far East Air Forces, in Tokyo, for another spell of active service.

At the beginning of the Korean War the Far East Air Forces were in poor shape to stop the enemy's advance, because for years its main responsibility had been the air defence of Japan, and there was little know-how, material, and communications for air–ground operations. Fortunately for the Americans, the few obsolete Yak fighters of the North Korean Air Force were poorly flown and were soon driven from the sky by the far superior F-80s (Shooting Stars), who then tried to help the U.S. 24th Division, which had moved to Korea from Japan.

During these highly critical days when the North Koreans advanced south with the intention of driving the Americans into the sea, two Shooting Stars were sent from airfields in Japan every fifteen minutes, but their long flight meant that they could spend only a short time over the battlefield. Sometimes they landed at one of the few airfields remaining to the Americans, but the best of these, Taegu, had to be evacuated twice because of nearby enemy troops. Fighter pilots were rarely briefed over the battlefield because of the absence of air–ground communications, and even when the tactical reconnaissance pilots reported important enemy targets, the ground situation often changed before the information filtered to the fighter squadrons. Consequently little could be done from the air to stop the Communists, and the 24th Division, together with some South Korean troops, found themselves driven towards the bottom of the peninsula, where they set up a defensive perimeter based on the port of Pusan. But they were still in grave danger of being pushed into the sea.

By this time, however, the Americans had formed an elementary joint operations centre, consisting of some communications and radio-equipped jeeps called tactical air control parties—their equivalent of our contact cars. These jeeps patrolled the perimeter calling down fighter-bombers flying from Korea and Japan, but the high mountains gravely reduced the range of the radio sets, and so the Americans filled this dangerous gap with light aeroplanes, called 'Mosquitoes', whose pilots could talk both to the operations centre and the fighter-bombers. These 'Mosquito' crews did a great job searching for and finding the enemy, and co-pilots often helped the circling fighter-bombers by throwing smoke grenades from the rear cockpit. Sometimes when the fighter-bombers were absent they took matters into their own hands and, in the fashion of the old timers, hurled hand grenades at the enemy—sometimes with fatal consequences to themselves. Later the U.S. Army commander told me that without the fighter-bombers his men would have been driven into the sea. But the situation was still highly dangerous, so dangerous that strategic bombers had to take part in the land battle. The first the controller in the operations centre knew of this was when the bomber leader asked for target information; the controller, thinking they were fighter-bombers, asked for details of their armament and was amazed to hear that each aeroplane was carrying forty-eight bombs!

Meanwhile the Americans had got into their stride, and such was the flow of men and material into Pusan that in early August the situation was under control. More tactical air-control parties and 'Mosquito' aeroplanes were on hand. Communications were improved and radars moved in. Thunderjet fighter-bombers were on their way from the States. A great airlift over the Pacific was established. Fighter reinforcements flew from Okinawa and the Philippines and, most important of all, General Vandenberg sent an experienced and outstanding commander, Major General O. P. Weyland (known to one and all as 'Opee'), to direct the operations of the Far East Air Forces. The Americans were now ready to strike back, and during September they broke out of the perimeter, mounted an amphibious assault near Seoul in the MacArthur tradition, and advanced to the capital. From here, after some regrouping, they marched to the north, joined forces with airborne troops and began to bed down before the tight fist of winter closed over the terrain—which was to see almost another three years of bloody combat before an uneasy truce ended the struggle.

There being no air opposition, I flew the reconnaissance version of the sturdy, twin-engined B-26, and took some day and night photographs of enemy concentrations. It seemed odd to fly over those inhospitable hills, over a land stripped of all softness, as far north as the Yalu River and not see another aeroplane once we had left the vicinity of the ground fighting. But, for the present, the sky was empty of enemy aeroplanes, and except for a little flak there was no opposition. I took full advantage of this strange state of affairs and, apart from getting the feel of things, the B-26's long endurance helped me to watch the lively fighter-bombers at work.

Despite the introduction of jets, fighter-bomber tactics had barely changed since the Second War. Finger-four sections of Shooting Stars and Thunderjets arrived over the front line at regular intervals, having already clocked in at the joint operations centre, which directed them to one of the many tactical air control parties working with the troops who, in turn, passed them on to a forward controller on the ground, or to a 'Mosquito'. Whenever possible the forward controller marked the target with coloured smoke and the 'Mosquito' pilot fired small smoke rockets at his objective. The jets peeled off, bored in, and attacked with high-explosive bombs, rockets, machine guns, and Napalm fire-bombs—so called because the extremely unpleasant mixture contained napthenic acid. Napalm was the deadliest weapon used by the fighter-bombers, for while a rocket or an ordinary bomb had to score a direct hit to be successful, dropping a Napalm bomb was rather like throwing a bucket of water over the floor—the liquid spread along the line of throw and sometimes destroyed Russian-built T-34 tanks within thirty yards of the impact. It was most useful against dug-in troops, for the wicked liquid flowed over the hard ground and poured into depressions, such as slit trenches, with disastrous results for the occupants. One could understand why the North Koreans loathed the combination of jet and fire-bomb.

Sometimes, during the advance from Pusan, the U.S.A.F. flew almost seven hundred fighter-bomber sorties daily, while Naval and Marine aeroplanes flying from carriers on the surrounding seas raised the total to about 1,000 sorties. Jets and piston-engined aeroplanes waited in the queue to blast any moving thing and 77 Squadron, a notable outfit from the Royal Australian Air Force, won everyone's admiration for the zest and accuracy of their attacks in their somewhat ancient Mustangs. Pilots preferred to fly jets, since, having fewer moving parts than the Mustangs, they could withstand more flak damage and, not having a propeller, they gave pilots a better view forwards and downwards; also, the cockpit of a Shooting Star was far quieter than that of a Mustang, which made the jet less fatiguing to fly.

Having to face such an onslaught from the air, the enemy wisely kept his head well down during daylight and moved at night. To keep the Communists pinned down the Americans flew B-26 intruder missions at night, and since the R.A.F. had much experience of these highly specialised operations, one of our greatest experts, Wing Commander Peter Wykeham, flew to Korea to help. Wykeham knew that this sort of flying between the mountains called for high skill and he thought that the best crews were usually ex-flying instructors who had plenty of hours and who kept their heads in tricky circumstances.

Novice crews liked the moonlight, because it helped the navigator, and the pilot could see the ground; but the moon, especially when low and hazy, gave the mountains a deceptive look, so that the experts preferred clear, dark nights when they could find their targets, illuminate them with flares and attack. Wykeham stressed that the proper navigation of an intruder aeroplane was the most difficult type of navigation in the world. The navigator had few aids, his radar was of little help at low heights, and his aeroplane was often thrown about the sky when the pilot saw and attacked opportunity targets. Unless their navigation was always perfect, he said tersely, sooner or later they would find themselves draped round a mountain.

All United Nations pilots realised that the state of affairs in the air was most unreal. They roamed over Korea without seeing a hostile aeroplane and similarly the U.S. Navy operated their carriers without interference. Some people were apt to forget that one day the Communists might do something about these happy circumstances, and the armchair purists argued that the fighter-bombers had simply become flying artillery. But large numbers of fighter-bombers were available to spray all kinds of targets and, although some of these were not altogether profitable, they encouraged the troops below, who were having a stiff time.

Once or twice American pilots flying over the Yalu River had seen swept-back fighters taking off from airfields in Manchuria, on the far side of the river, but it was not until November 1950 that these Mig-15s first showed their paces, when the leader of four Shooting Stars spotted seven Migs well below. The Americans went after the Migs and there followed a long tail chase as the Migs headed back for Manchuria, over which U.N. pilots were forbidden to fly, and the American leader gave up the chase. The Migs, however, climbed into the sun, split into pairs, recrossed the river and bounced the Shooting Stars. Although no aeroplanes were damaged in this brief fight, the Americans soon found that the sleek, well-finished Migs were faster, could out-climb their F.80s and could stay with them in tight turns.

As winter approached, more Mig formations were seen at positions and heights which made it obvious that they were controlled by radar. It was thought that the Migs were probably scrambled whenever their early warning radars plotted the approach of American formations, lurked on their side of the Yalu until sent across by their controller, bounced the Shooting Stars and then streaked back for Manchuria to wait for another go. Every advantage lay with the Communist pilots, for the American radar cover did not extend to the Yalu. They were fighting over their own territory, while the Shooting Stars flew from airfields hundreds of miles south at Kimpo and

Taegu. Whenever a Mig pilot found himself in trouble he simply headed for the northern side of the river, where he was protected by the cloak of a bogus neutrality.

On my reconnaissance and fighter-bomber missions I never saw a Mig, but in the evenings, when the day's work was over and we had showered, changed, and supped well, the veterans got together and talked about the Migs. What bothered us most was not their high performance, but the people who flew them. Who were these chaps? They flew and fought too well to be North Koreans. So they had to be Chinese or Russians. And even if they were Russians they had come a long, long way in the last five years. For in their use of the sun, their finger-four pattern and their line-astern defensive manoeuvres they were strangely reminiscent of the Luftwaffe.

The Migs, it was later discovered, were flown by Russian pilots, and they enjoyed much success against the slower and inferior B-29s, B-26s, Shooting Stars, and British Meteor 8s, then flown by Australian pilots of 77 Squadron. No longer did U.N. pilots have unlimited access to the Korean sky, and Weyland realised that he had to fight for air superiority over and south of the Yalu. He had to get Sabres into Korea at once, and during December they began to fly from Kimpo airfield, near Seoul. Within two weeks the Sabres destroyed eight Migs for the loss of one F-86, and this ascendency was a feature of the subsequent air fighting.

The Kimpo airfield was about two hundred miles from the Yalu, and the problem was to get enough Sabres into this area at their best fighting height to tackle the Migs. Towards the close of Hitler's War the R.A.F. had found that fighting in wings of thirty-six fighters was on the way out, and had fought in squadron strength of twelve fighters, while the Americans had flown sixteen. But in Korea they did not have the fuel to assemble sixteen Sabres over Kimpo and then fight over the Yalu, and Schilling's techniques for in-flight refuelling had not reached the squadrons. And once over the Yalu a leader could not hold together sixteen Sabres at very high speeds, because everyone flew with high engine revolutions to keep the speed up, and a pilot did not have a sufficient margin of power to catch up once he fell behind in a combat manoeuvre.

Leaders flew near the speed of sound, for if they allowed their speeds to fall off they were sitting ducks for the Migs. Survival could no longer be found in tight turns and, at all costs, wingmen had to keep up, for the leader was still the gun and his

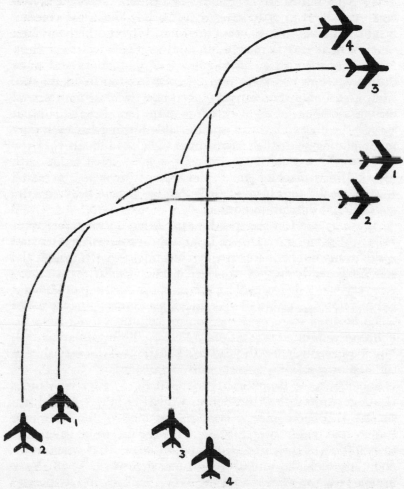

wingman the eye. Sabres flew, therefore, to the Yalu in finger-four sections and staggered their take-offs to arrive at five-minute intervals so that sections could support each other. Thus almost forty years after the beginning of air fighting the number of fighters flying together diminished further, and in 1951 the finger-four section was not unlike that introduced by Boelcke in 1916, except that the Sabre pilots held a wider spacing between aeroplanes.

Having reached the Yalu, the Sabres flew between 27,000 and 33,000 feet in order to stay just below the usual contrail height, and be able to see those made by the higher Migs. Once a fight was imminent, the Sabres threw off their drop tanks, increased their speed, and fought in fours and pairs until their low fuel state obliged them to return to Kimpo. They could only stay on patrol for some twenty minutes, and during a combat of eight or ten minutes found that the great speeds, the high stick forces and the wide turning circles usually made aiming with their gyroscopic sight so difficult that the average pilot managed only to get one good burst of fire with his six $\frac{1}{2}$-inch machine guns; and when their speed increased to 0·95 mach* and beyond their Sabres became heavy on the controls and difficult to handle.

Above 27,000 feet the speeds of the Mig and the Sabre were about the same, but at lower heights the American fighter had a slight advantage. Sometimes Sabre pilots went through the sound barrier when they exceeded 1 mach in a steep dive, and recovery was a delicate affair. Once, during these jet clashes, a Sabre pilot diving after a Mig had his controls 'freeze', and when he tried to recover the control column sprang from his hands to the full rear position. Somehow he regained control, but it says much for the Sabre's sturdy construction that it suffered only a few wrinkles on its metal skin.

Sometimes the Communists tried the decoy trick of sending two aeroplanes below the Sabres while the others waited up-sun for an opportunity to bounce, but most of the American leaders had fought over Europe and were not to be caught by this old dodge. Instead they waited until the Migs came down and then took the initiative by turning towards them. Very occasionally the Migs chased the Sabres halfway to Kimpo and the Americans thought they would be poorly placed if they were harried all the way back. Happily, the Russians seldom

* The mach number is an aeroplane's speed expressed as a proportion of the speed of sound at that height and temperature.

flew over territory held by the United Nations, probably because they wanted to avoid the risk of capture.

Sabre pilots were getting good results, but they were convinced they would destroy more Migs if they had powerful cannon, for the Mig could take a lot of punishment from their small-calibre machine guns. Unfortunately the new Sabre, the F.86E, still carried the standard fit of six machine guns; but

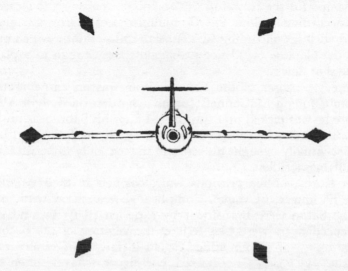

deflection shooting was made easier with its radar computing sight, and its increased thrust made it superior to the latest Mig-15B. Also the Americans, together with the handful of R.A.F. and R.C.A.F. fighter pilots flying with the United Nations, were better trained and had more experience than their opponents, for towards the end of 1951 Russian and Chinese jet pilots were assisted by the first North Korean Mig unit based at Uiju, near the Manchurian border.

The Uiju project was doomed from the start, for the Americans, ever seeking the offensive and able for the first time to get at an enemy jet base, attacked the Migs by day and by night. Superfortresses droned overhead in the darkness to plaster Uiju, and although radar-equipped Migs flown by Russians gave chase, they usually failed to intercept; by day, low-flying jets strafed the parked Migs, and after some six weeks of this treatment the North Koreans retired happily to Manchuria, whence they did not return until after the truce.

During the Korean War United Nations F-86 pilots claimed some eight hundred Migs for the loss of fifty-eight Sabres. American claims were most carefully checked, and an enemy fighter pilot, Senior Lieutenant Kum Sok No of the North Korean Air Force (who after the truce surrendered his Mig-15B at Kimpo for the tidy sum of $100,000), confirms the victory. For according to him the Communists lost more than eight hundred Migs, including two Russian units entirely wiped out, and the Chinese could not train pilots fast enough to replace those shot down.

The top scorer of the Korean War was an ex-navigator, Captain Joseph McConnell Junior, who destroyed eight Migs before he was picked up from the sea after his Sabre was hit by flak. Typically, he returned to the fray on the following day, and eventually brought his score to sixteen, only to perish later in a flying accident.

In Korea, unlike previous wars, colonels in their twenties were no longer the vogue. Complicated weapons systems such as the Sabre were best flown by experienced flyers, and experienced flyers were best led by the veterans of the Second War, many of whom added to their tally of German and Japanese victories. Grey haired, well decorated, and often the fathers of many children—one resolute colonel had eight—they were impressive not for their youth but for their age. They were dedicated men; their motto—*not the boldest, but the oldest!*

But it was not only better aeroplanes, better training, higher morale, and more experience that beat the Migs over the Yalu. Victory was only possible because 'Opee' Weyland never forgot Trenchard's dictum about using scouts offensively. Nor was he likely to forget, for he had fought over Europe and knew what a magnificent contribution long-range fighting had made to victory. Weyland did not wait for the Migs to come to him, but pushed his aggressive Sabre pilots as far north as they were allowed to go, to the Yalu River. He fought the enemy hundreds of miles from his airfields, and so contained the far larger Communist jet fighter force.

Chapter 25

HINDSIGHT

THE story of air fighting began in 1914, when four R.F.C. squadrons flew to France and scouted for the British Expeditionary Force. The slow two-seater machines were unarmed, but pilots and observers usually carried rifles or revolvers to defend themselves should they be forced down. Sometimes they saw German aeroplanes also making reconnaissances, and there began a crude form of duelling in the air when speeds did not exceed seventy miles an hour and heights not more than 4,000 feet. In these early clashes there was a sense of sharing the same sport, which made a man hesitate to shoot down a crippled opponent; but later this affinity between opposing airmen disappeared.

The next step was to arm the two-seaters with machine guns, but as the air fighting intensified it was apparent that fast, single-seat scouts were required to carry out fighting patrols and so obtain 'elbow room', later called air superiority, for the bombing and reconnaissance two-seaters. The French were first in this field with a scout whose propeller carried steel wedges to deflect striking bullets, but it was Anthony Fokker who gave Germany a tremendous lead with his flying gun. Although France produced some experimental scouts armed with cannon, the machine gun was the standard armament on all fighting aeroplanes throughout that war.

It was Oswald Boelcke who evolved the preliminary tactics for the first flying gun, and who helped win for Germany her first period of supremacy in the air. To counter the Fokker superiority Trenchard introduced formation flying and formed special fighting squadrons. Later, on the Somme, the *Jadgstaffeln* won another phase of the air struggle and showed that good machines were more important than mere numbers.

So the air fighters began to fly and fight together. For defensive purposes we thought a pair of scouts to be the ideal tactical unit, but when flying over enemy territory we required more strength, and flight commanders led small formations of between three and six machines. The vulnerable two-seaters had to be protected, and scouts provided the close escort and the above guard so that Trenchard could maintain his offensive. Later, offensive patrols were flown in squadron strength of about a dozen machines. Eventually squadrons were built into wings to counter Manfred von Richthofen's Circus, when sometimes fifty highly painted scouts flew together. Except for a few individuals, such as Ball and Bishop, team fighting replaced lone-wolf tactics. As air fighting speeded-up aerobatics became less important; for slow speeds, near the stall, made aeroplanes easy targets. Duelling in the air vanished, and as the combats became less personal a pilot could not pause to consider the plight of his adversary, because in doing so he might himself be shot down. Courtesy and good manners vanished when pilots shot to kill.

The Zeppelin and the Gotha raids showed that Britain was open to bombing, especially at night, and drew attention to the need for a proper system of air defence, including specialised aeroplanes; for the single-seat scout was gravely handicapped at night. Thanks to Trenchard, it was not lost upon us that the only proper defence is offence.

Scout pilots were the defenders of the people, and their exploits were widely followed, not only for their dramatic quality but also because they took peoples' minds from the horror on the ground. When Georges Guynemer, fifty-four victories, failed to return from a patrol the children of France made him immortal when they said he flew so high he could not come down again.

During the Kaiser's War the soldiers soon found that the airmen could help them by bombing and strafing enemy targets, and Army commanders asked for the bombing of bridges, viaducts, and towns to isolate the battlefield and to stop the enemy from reinforcing it. There were so many requests for close air-support and harassing operations that the Germans formed their *Schlachtstaffeln*, while the R.F.C. fitted scouts with bomb racks and ordered a ground-attack aeroplane.

The soldiers always wanted plenty of reconnaissance, and when our scouts began to strafe and bomb the pilots were en-

couraged to report on enemy ground activities. Tactical reconnaissance by scouts increased that already supplied by the two-
seaters, and by the end of the First War the scout was used for
four main purposes—for day fighting (and occasionally for
night fighting), for bombing, for strafing, and for fighter
reconnaissance.

Who was the greatest air fighter of the First War? To answer
this I must say what I mean by 'great air fighter', and explain
that I think a man does not come into this category unless he is a
proved leader. A brilliant scout pilot did not always make a good
leader, and some outstanding individuals such as Albert Ball,
Billy Bishop, and Georges Guynemer simply did not possess the
temperament to lead. These men fought emotionally from the
heart, with impetuosity, never weighing the odds against them,
and depended on superlative skill and marksmanship to shoot
down their enemies. Usually they waited in the sky until a
formation appeared below and then, exploiting speed and surprise to the full, they dropped hawk-like on their opponents.
Such tactics could be used only by individuals, because even a
small formation of scouts could never stay together in such fast
manoeuvres, and they would have found their styles seriously
handicapped had they flown as patrol leaders. Because they
fought individually they never developed the qualities of
leadership in the air.

The greatest air fighter had a high sense of duty, was unselfish about his personal claims, and during the fight his pilots
knew he would watch over them and bring them home. He
studied the ever-changing developments in his craft and took
great pains to pass on his knowledge to others. If he was
allowed authority and freedom of action he made the most of it
to plan and lead his squadron or wing on offensive patrols, and
thus his character and ability influenced the pattern of air
fighting. Both by precept and example the great air fighter
inspired his pilots.

The R.A.F.'s two outstanding air fighters were James Mc-
Cudden and Mick Mannock. Mannock's score of seventy-three
victories was more than McCudden's fifty-seven, and there can
be little doubt that Mannock was the more gifted patrol leader
and teacher. Mannock's fine score was slightly bettered by a

great French air fighter, René Fonck, seventy-five victories, who fought for the last two years of the war and was only once hit by an enemy bullet. We must remember, however, that from the first Battle of the Somme, in 1916, the Germans realised that Britain and not France was the power they must defeat in the air, and for the remainder of that war their crack squadrons were deployed against their prime enemy, the Royal Air Force: so it was the squadrons of our Service who saw the most severe fighting. Richthofen's eighty victories were against British aviators. Therefore I consider Mannock a greater air fighter than René Fonck.

The first units of the American Air Service were not in action until the spring of 1918, although a great number of American volunteers had for long served with Allied squadrons, notably the famous *Escadrille Lafayette*. America did not possess a scout pilot whose record compared with those of Mannock or Fonck, and their top scorer was Captain Eddie Ricken- backer, who during the last eight months of the war shot down twenty-six aeroplanes.

The modest Oswald Boelcke was one of the greatest air fighters. He set a fine example, and his teachings were followed long after his death. Boelcke was killed, however, before the zenith of air fighting, and his achievements were eventually overshadowed by those of Richthofen.

Who was the greater air fighter: Richthofen, respected by his pilots, or Mannock, revered by his pilots? Their personal scores were separated by only a small margin. Both men were good scout pilots and proved leaders. Mannock's two tours in France lasted some thirteen months, while Richthofen fought first as an observer and then for more than two years as a pilot, with hardly a break, suffering a head wound from which he had not fully recovered when he was killed; for a long time Rich- thofen's Circus was the fighting spearhead of the German Air Force.

Mannock invariably patrolled over enemy territory, while Richthofen usually fought over his own ground. Here were two different air fighting roles, the one offensive, the other defen- sive. Mannock's tactics were to flush, stalk, and kill his oppo- nents, and since in his heyday the R.A.F. outnumbered the

German Air Service, the odds were that he would not be surprised continually by superior enemy forces. Patrolling and fighting offensively, he could exploit the inherent qualities of his scouts, speed and surprise, to the full; his disadvantage was that a single bullet in a vulnerable part of his machine meant, at the best, a prison camp until the end of the war.

Some of Richthofen's critics have asserted that since most of his victims fell on the German side of the lines, he was a cautious fighter and not in Mannock's class. We must remember, however, that for the greater part of the war on the Western Front the German Army was on the defensive, and those units of the German Air Service deployed behind that Army were employed in an ancillary and similar defensive role. Richthofen did not govern the strategy of the war; on the contrary, he was a junior officer whose duty, because of the very nature of the air war and the fact that the German Air Service was heavily outnumbered by the Allies, was to inflict the maximum number of casualties on the Allies with the minimum risk and losses to his own units, and in this he succeeded admirably.

Some writers have belittled Richthofen's deeds because he shot down a considerable number of our two-seaters when in their opinion it would have been far more sporting to attack the faster scouts. But Richthofen did not regard fighting in the air as a sport; it was a very serious affair, where a calculating leader tried to destroy the enemy's reconnaissance aeroplanes, which did far more damage than the scouts. There can be no doubt that the tactics fashioned by the wily and highly elusive Richthofen were perfectly suited to the conditions under which he fought. When a few weeks after his death another leader, Göring, adopted more aggressive tactics, *J.G.1* was fought to such destruction that it was temporarily withdrawn from the battle. In my opinion, Richthofen's great achievements over a long period of operational service rank him the greatest air fighter of the First War.

Between the wars both sides forgot a lot of tactical lore, but the Spanish Civil War served to remind the Luftwaffe of the old lessons, and German fighter pilots were far better prepared than their R.A.F. contemporaries for the 1939–45 contest, when our inept peacetime training cost us dear. The rigid Fighter

Attacks curbed initiative, and may be compared to the Royal Navy's equally foolish Fighting Instructions, which from Cromwell's time until almost the close of the eighteenth century severely restricted a commander's freedom of manoeuvre at sea. Just as Rodney's defeat of the French in the Caribbean in 1782 discredited the Fighting Instructions, so the defeat of the Luftwaffe in 1940 discredited the Fighter Attacks which, unlamented, have faded into oblivion.

In the Battle of Britain Bader's wing was not unlike Mannock's, except that the Hurricanes and Spitfires flew higher and faster than the S.E.s. Radar and good communications gave Keith Park centralised control over his squadrons, but this control was not applied too rigidly, and our fighter leaders were aided rather than controlled by the men on the ground. Without radar and radio the bravery of the fighter pilot would have been of little account.

Göring's faulty judgement materially helped us to win the Battle. The integrity of any commander is a precious thing, for men must know and respect their leaders. But the German airmen had little admiration for Göring, and were frequently dismayed and baffled by his ever-changing orders.

Apart from its military significance, the Battle of Britain provides the moral lesson that Providence is not always on the side of the big battalions, a lesson we might remember in this divided world of warring camps. We might also remember that during this ordeal not all fighter pilots were of our race. The Poles, many of whom still live with us, made up one-eighth of our numbers.

Having won the day battle, the Blitz was upon us, and we had to endure much bombing before Fighter Command could offer some protection at night. As in the previous war, single-seaters were of little use on dark nights. Also, we had arrived at the stage when it no longer sufficed to design an aeroplane for one job and expect it to cope with another by sticking on a few extra bits and pieces, for the era of the weapons system had arrived.

Germany's attack on Russia took the pressure off Fighter Command and our well-proved defensive fighters, Spitfires and Hurricanes, began to fight offensively over France. Thanks primarily to Douglas Bader and Sailor Malan, we had, at long last, got our fighting tactics right, and the finger-four formation, the Luftwaffe's *Schwärme*, was flown operationally for many years. Fortunately we were not beguiled by our defensive victory, and our bombers struck at Germany in ever-increasing numbers. Sometimes we escorted a few bombers on day missions over France, but, like the Luftwaffe during the previous year, we tied too many escorting fighters to the bombers and did not provide enough free-lancing fighter sweeps. This air fighting over France, in 1941, was often very strenuous, but it did not achieve much of military significance. Our losses were greater than the Luftwaffe's, and even after the majority of enemy fighters were transferred to the East, for the attack on Russia, a comparatively small number of 109s and excellent Fokker-Wulfe 190s reduced our penetrations over France and showed, once again, that good aeroplanes are more important than superiority in numbers.

Confident in her *Blitzkrieg* policy, Germany had paid but scant attention to her air defences, but soon after Bomber Command began its long, hard struggle, the Luftwaffe organised a rudimentary system for night fighting, which in the winter of 1943–44 became so formidable that, despite all the ingenuity of our electronic counter-measures, the Command had to seek less distant targets. Fortunately, and thanks to their steadfast views about daylight bombing and their weapons of production, the Americans defeated the Luftwaffe in the great daylight battles over Germany, and this victory helped our bombers at night. Fortunately, too, the Germans became fatally occupied with defence.

Throughout the Second War our inventory lacked a long-range day fighter which would have extended the range of our air superiority across France and into Germany, and would have helped Bomber Command in its epic struggle. We had built some of the best short-range fighters in the world, but we were prejudiced by our very experiences and thought that it was technically impossible to build a fighter with the range of a bomber. It is true that we used our fighters over France, but once the Luftwaffe moved its bases farther away Fighter Command could not be used in a true offensive role, and a great many Spitfires and Hurricanes remained idle in Britain while there was urgent work to be done elsewhere.

The Americans, however, came to our aid with an excellent long-range fighter and, after their Fortresses and Liberators had suffered some appalling losses, their lively Mustangs began to roam far and wide over Germany. Unlike ourselves during the Battle of Britain, where the radar warning was short, the Germans had ample warning about the approach of raids across the North Sea and were able to reinforce the threatened district and organise a strong and concentrated air defence. The American fighter pilots had to overcome this strong defence, which included jets, and the air battles were the greatest of the Second War. Thanks to good aeroplanes and aggressive leaders, such as Don Blakeslee and Hub Zemke, the Americans won a great victory which exposed all Germany to day and night bombing.

Fighter tactics depended upon an aeroplane's performance and the weapons it carried. During the Second War land-based aeroplanes were, as a rule, superior to those operating from aircraft carriers. Thus I have had little to say about fighting from aircraft carriers, for although they were invaluable in extending the range of fighters and strike aeroplanes, they had little influence on fighter tactics. The exception to the rule was the Japanese Zeke, a naval fighter commonly known as the 'Zero', which, for the first year of the Pacific War, was superior to all American fighters, whether flying from airfields or carriers.

Equally, I have not said very much about air fighting in the Far East, for the air war over Europe far exceeded, in numbers and tempo, that fought over the Pacific. There were many valuable lessons to be learned from some of the battles in the Pacific War. These included the total defeat of the United States Pacific Fleet by Japanese aeroplanes from six aircraft carriers—the end of the battleship's long reign; and the fact that big air–sea battles could take place in which the surface vessels, separated by two or three hundred miles, did not exchange a single shot. But these lessons were not connected with fighter tactics. It was the war fought over Europe which saw the great developments and improvements in aeroplanes and weapons—jet fighters, rocket fighters, pilotless aeroplanes, missiles, and rockets. Thus, the Japanese suicide missions apart, air fighting over Europe advanced fighter tactics far more than did the fighting over the Pacific.

During big air battles many pilots often found themselves badly wounded in their damaged aeroplanes. Under these conditions some pilots chose, while they still had control, to die either by ramming an enemy aeroplane or by diving into a ground target. During the Battle of Britain at least two enemy bombers were rammed by Polish fighter pilots, and several German fighter pilots rammed American daylight bombers; these attacks were not strictly suicide attacks, since these fighter pilots stood little chance of survival before they rammed.

The Japanese Kamikaze ('Divine Wind') attacks were an entirely different matter; for a pilot, or the entire crew of a bomber, stood not the faintest chance of survival if the pilot attacked properly and dived his aeroplane, laden with high explosive, into an American or British aircraft carrier. The Kamikazes destroyed many American ships, but even to the Japanese, who feared capture more than death, the Kamikaze tactic was a desperate measure which took the lives of thousands of their airmen.

The principles of air support for the ground forces were hammered out in the Kaiser's War and remained constant during Hitler's War, but our lack of trained ground-attack squadrons created a gulf between airman and soldier that was not bridged until the Eighth Army and the Desert Air Force got together. Confidence, once regained, was not lost again, and the air support of Allied Armies from Normandy to the Baltic was superb. In the East the Soviet Air Force was almost paralysed by the Luftwaffe. When the Russians recovered they devoted their air power almost exclusively to the support of ground operations. Their ground-attack arm did not compare in operational efficiency with those of the Western Allies; the main difference being that we always tried to extend our air superiority well beyond the ground fighting, whereas the Russians confined the activities of their ground-attack units to the front line and slightly beyond. Our methods for supporting ground forces were proved again in Korea, where the fighter-bombers saved the day at Pusan.

At the end of the Korean War the single-seat jet fighter was used for six purposes—for offensive and defensive day fighting, for visual and photographic reconnaissance, and for bombing and strafing. The jet fighter-bomber proved its worth in Korea and showed that it has a big future, and even if it is called a reconnaissance strike fighter, or something of the sort, it is merely the modern version of Trenchard's bomb-loaded scout.

Bigger piston engines and, later, jet engines meant that speeds and heights were always increasing, that turning arcs were becoming wider and, despite radio telephones, leaders found it more and more difficult to control big formations, especially at the ceiling of any fighter, where its stalling speed approaches its cruising speed. Leaders wanted to fly as high as possible, to jump their opponents and control the air battle, and when, in 1941, we began to fight at 30,000 feet it was not possible to control a Balbo of four or five squadrons, and Balbos were not seen again after the Battle of Britain. For offensive fighting over France the fighter wing consisted of two or three squadrons, but the introduction of jet fighters in 1944 saw the fighting unit reduced to a squadron of about a dozen aeroplanes.

Fighter Command could cope with the German flying bombs, but the ballistic rockets could be countered only by offensive action. The ballistic rocket struck the death knell of the fighter-interceptor.

In Korea near-sonic speeds made it impossible for a leader to hold a squadron together, and so sections of four jets flew separately to the combat area and, controlled by the wing leader, supported each other. Once fighting began, sections were soon split into the basic fighting unit introduced by Boelcke—the pair. Later, over the Formosa Strait, air fighting became more impersonal when Chinese Nationalist pilots, flying F.86Hs, fought Mig-17s flown by Chinese Communist pilots. Each Sabre carried two 'Sidewinder' homing missiles, and these were sometimes fired from ranges of about three miles. Even so, these missiles were so accurate that fourteen 'Sidewinder' rounds accounted for eleven Migs.

Today our supersonic fighter-interceptors train in pairs because it is safer than flying alone, but in combat they would operate singly, for vital seconds would be lost forming them into pairs. Within the last half-century the top speed of fighters has increased from less than 100 m.p.h. to more than twice the speed of sound, and ceilings have increased from a few thousand feet to the fringes of space. Within the last half-century the story of air fighting has gone full circle.

Unlike the fighter-bomber, the fighter-interceptor's days are numbered. Today's fighter pilot will soon become a sort of monitor or scope pilot, for the interception will be automatic, from 'chocks-away' to auto-landing, and the aeroplane will become a guided missile with a human brain which, it is said, will give the aeroplane that flexibility a missile can never possess.

Throughout the story of air fighting runs the quest for height, for the fighter on top had control of the air battle. The race for height continues, for the first nation to control space will also control, for good or evil, movement in the earth's atmosphere and on its surface, just as in the past 'elbow room', or air superiority, allowed us to move freely on the land and the seas beneath.

Although the qualities of leadership required of air fighters were similar in both conflicts against Germany, it is not possible to compare their achievements, because the conditions under which they fought were so different. In the earlier conflict our scouts patrolled beyond the front lines to a maximum distance of about twenty-five miles and had many opportunities to fight, because both friendly and hostile aeroplanes were concentrated in a small area. We saw how it was possible for Manfred von Richthofen to shoot down twenty-one machines during 'Bloody April' and how his brother, Lothar, got forty victories in less than three months—the opportunities were there. During the Normandy battles of 1944 my Canadian Spitfire wing was the first to be based in France. We were just behind our front lines, which stretched a few miles between Caen and Bayeux. The Luftwaffe were deployed on the other side of the front lines, and were usually to be found over the relatively small battle area. The tactical situation in the air was not unlike that at Arras in 1917. We knew where to find the enemy. Consequently during this period of heavy air fighting some of my most experienced leaders scored at a higher rate than did Richthofen three decades earlier. On the other hand, for months preceding the Normandy invasion it was possible to fly daily over France and Belgium and even to cross the German border without seeing an enemy aeroplane. Indeed, I have known fighter pilots complete a tour of operations without seeing the enemy in the air.

In the Second War radar and good communications helped the defensive air fighters, but when the Americans fought over Germany radar did not have the range to assist them. Except for the advantage of being able to talk to each other, they fought like the earlier scout pilots, but sometimes four hundred miles from their airfields. Don Blakeslee, still serving with the United States Air Force, was, I think, the greatest offensive air fighter of the Second War.

Neither is it possible to compare the scores of Allied and German air fighters during the Second War, for German methods of claiming victories not only differed from ours but also varied from year to year; for example, German kills at night were acknowledged as double those of day fighters, and the destruction of a four-engined bomber was considered equal to the destruction of two fighters. Little is known about the number of victories of leading Russian fighter pilots.

Some German fighter pilots served their apprenticeship in the early, bitter struggles against the R.A.F., and then fought for four years on the Eastern Front, where initially the Luftwaffe enjoyed such technical and tactical superiority over the Soviet Air Force that, it has been estimated, the Russians lost 20,000 aeroplanes in the first few months of the campaign; even in the later phases, when the Soviet Air Force became stronger and had better aeroplanes, the Germans still had the advantage in individual combat. So successful were some fighter pilots that the German top scorer in the East, Erich Hartmann, claimed three hundred and thirty-six victories. Several others claimed more than two hundred; it is impossible to say to what extent these claims were justified.

As in the First War, the fiercest air fighting was to be found

in the West, where it has been possible from our records to con-
firm most of the one hundred and one victories claimed by the
top scorer in Europe, 'Pips' Priller, who fought against us for
four and a half years. Likewise, Galland's ninety-four victories
in the first two years of the war, before he was taken off operational flying, and Mölder's victories, are, for the most part,
verified by records. Personal scores, however, were less important than teamwork, and Germany's greatest air fighter of
the Second War was undoubtedly Adolf Galland, an outstanding fighter pilot, superb leader, and sound tactician.
Galland had a profound effect on fighter operations and finished
the war as he began—fighting.

In my Service, modest John Cunningham, twenty victories
and now chief test pilot of de Havillands, and Bob Braham,
twenty-nine victories and now serving in the Royal Canadian
Air Force, were the outstanding night fighters. Their styles of
fighting were different, for John fought defensively over
Britain, while Bob, one of the most aggressive men ever to strap
an aeroplane on his back, specialised in night intruder
operations.

As for day fighting, I was the Allied top scorer in Europe,
with thirty-eight victories, which may be compared with
Priller's one hundred and one, for we both fought over the same
territory for about the same time, but he saw many more
hostile aeroplanes than I did, which, looking back, was perhaps
a good thing! Sailor Malan shot down thirty-two enemy aeroplanes before I opened my account, and our fighting days bear
little comparison, for Sailor, like Manfred von Richthofen,
fought defensively when the odds were heavy against him, while
I, like Mick Mannock, nearly always fought over Europe with
a squadron or wing behind me.

After our disastrous start to the Second War Sailor and
Douglas did more than anyone else to get our tactics right, and
we owe much to them. Douglas, twenty-two victories, was
brought down after two years of flying, and Sailor was taken
off operations at about the same time when he was completely
exhausted. During the Battle no one fought harder or led his
men better than the lion-hearted South African, and his combat claims were always very modest. For the remainder of the

war Sailor continued flying and teaching. He embarked on what amounted to a private crusade to spread the word about his ten basic rules of air fighting—soon called 'the ten commandments'. He did much to improve our gunnery training, returning home when it was all over. The R.A.F.'s greatest fighter pilot and leader died in 1963, after a long and painful illness.

My story about fighter tactics is written round fighter pilots and the aeroplanes they flew. The men were more important than the aeroplanes. Their prestige stood high, for they were the defenders of the people and sometimes they, and they alone, stood between victory and defeat. They lived a strange life, which alternated between short periods of intense excitement in the air, when they did not have enough time, and long spells on the ground, when they had too much. Once in the air they had the gift of becoming part of their fighters. Their morale was very high. In adversity they were bigger than their normal selves. Their devotion was well hidden beneath an outward flippancy.

INDEX

ATCHERLEY, Air Marshal Sir Richard, 100, 101

Bader, Group Captain Douglas, 99, 101, 120, 152, 158–160, 162, 168, 170–172, 174, 236, 278, 279, 285
Balbo, Marshal Italo, 169–174
Ball, Captain Albert, 21–24, 30–32, 39, 53–57, 62–65, 70, 75, 78, 99, 274, 275
Baring, Maurice, 26
Beauvicourt, Comte, 14
Berry, Squadron Leader, 253
Beurling, Flight Lieutenant 'Screwball', 197
Biggin Hill airfield, 79, 139, 142, 145–148, 150, 151, 153, 155, 167, 175, 228
Bishop, Captain 'Billy', 85, 274, 275
Böhme, Erwin, 40, 41, 45, 50, 51
Blakeslee, Colonel Don, 228, 233–235, 238, 239, 280, 284
Blériot, Louis, 1, 2
Boelcke, Oswald, 11–14, 16–20, 23, 32–34, 36–41, 43–52, 55, 58, 69, 95, 168, 270, 273, 276, 282
Boelcke, Wilhelm, 11, 38, 40
Boothman, Air Marshal Sir John, 102
Boyle, Marshal of the R.A.F. Sir Dermot, 100
Braham, Wing Commander Bob, 221, 222, 285
Brize Norton airfield, 139
Broadhurst, Air Chief Marshal Sir Harry, 100, 130, 152, 211–214, 250, 255, 259
Brown, Captain A. R., 82, 83

Buchanan, Wing Commander 'Buck', 208, 209

Camm, Sir Sydney, 103
Churchill, Rt. Hon. Sir Winston, 130, 180, 182, 238
Cobham, Sir Alan, 261
Colerne airfield, 139
Cross, Air Marshal Sir Kenneth, 114
Crowe, Captain 'Billy', 65
Croydon airfield, 69, 139, 147, 153
Cruikshank, Captain G. L., 47–48
Cunningham, Group Captain John, 102, 104, 205

Darwin, Wing Commander Jackie, 209, 210
Debden airfield, 145, 147, 153, 170, 237, 239
Dempsey, General Sir Miles, 250
Desert Air Force, 202, 205–207, 210, 211, 214
Detling airfield, 139, 145, 147
Donaldson, Squadron Leader 'Baldy', 113, 114
Donaldson, Air Commodore Teddy, 100, 117, 118, 130
Douai airfield, 16, 18, 34, 36, 37, 60, 64, 252
Douglas, Marshal of the R.A.F. Lord, 8, 169, 172, 173
Dowding, Air Chief Marshal Lord, 104, 105, 113, 119, 121, 127, 128, 132–133, 135, 159, 160, 165, 169, 171–174, 176, 251
Driffield airfield, 139
du Peuty, Commandant, 25
Duxford airfield, 170

Eagle, 191, 196
Eastchurch airfield, 139, 145, 147

287

Fighter Groups (U.S.A.A.F.):
  (4th), 227–228
  (56th), 239
Fokker, Anthony, 15, 16, 37, 43, 273
Fonck, René, 38, 276
Ford airfield, 139
Franco, General, 90, 97
Furious, 114

Galland, Lieutenant-General Adolf,
  89–94, 117, 123, 124, 164, 165,
  174, 220, 229, 230, 236, 254,
  258–260, 285
Garros, Roland, 15
Gentile, Captain Don S., 237,
  238
Gibson, Wing Commander Guy,
  181
Glorious, 113, 114
Gneisenau, 114
Godfrey, Captain John T., 238
Goldsmith, Flight Lieutenant, 197
Goose airfield, 262
Göring, Reichsmarschall Hermann,
  83, 88–92, 126, 132–135, 138,
  141, 142, 144, 145, 147, 158,
  164, 165, 174, 175, 179, 215,
  226, 234, 238, 254, 255, 258–
  260, 277, 278
Gosport airfield, 139
Gravesend airfield, 147, 166, 167
Green, Lieutenant George, 237
Groups:
  (10), 152, 153, 174
  (11), 127, 132, 149, 152–156, 159–
    161, 166, 168–171, 173, 175
  (12), 127, 132, 152, 153, 159, 161,
    174
Guynemer, Georges, 38, 39, 55, 63,
  274, 275

Haig, Field Marshal Earl, 80
Hal Far airfield, 195
Harris, Marshal of the R.A.F. Sir
  Arthur, 219, 222, 224–225
Hartmann, Erich, 284
Hawker, Major L. G., 58

Hawkinge airfield, 139, 140, 153
Hesselyn, Squadron Leader Ray,
  197
Hitler, Adolf, 90, 108, 158, 161, 165,
  174, 188, 216, 220, 232, 251,
  254, 255, 259, 260
Hornchurch airfield, 143–146, 153,
  160, 170, 172
Houston, Lady, 102

Immelmann, Max, 18, 20, 23, 34,
  36, 37, 45, 58

Jagdgeschwader Number One (*J.G.1*),
  68, 77, 83, 112
Jagdstaffel Boelcke, 52
Jagdstaffeln (German Air Service):
  (2), 40, 43, 48, 52
  (11), 58, 59, 64, 68

Kain, Flying Officer 'Cobber', 124
Kammhuber, General, 216, 217,
  220
Kenley airfield, 99, 139, 146, 147,
  151, 153, 155
Kent, Wing Commander Johnnie,
  107
Kepner, Major General, 238
Kesselring, Field Marshal, 138, 148,
  164
Kimpo airfield, 268, 270, 272
Krause, Johann, 223
Kum Sok No, Senior Lieutenant,
  272

Lagnicourt airfield, 41, 43, 44, 47,
  49, 50
La Marsa airfield, 208
Lanchester, F. W., 30
Larkhill airfield, 2
Lee-on-Solent airfield, 139
Leigh-Mallory, Air Chief Marshal
  Sir Trafford, 132, 152, 160, 169,
  170–173
Llewelyn, Flight Lieutenant, 204
Lloyd, Air Chief Marshal Sir Hugh,
  194, 200

INDEX

Lucas, Wing Commander 'Laddie', 196

Luqa airfield, 193, 195, 197

Luton airfield, 145

Lympne airfield, 139, 147

Malan, Group Captain 'Sailor', 107, 130, 131, 152, 279, 285, 286

Mannock, Captain 'Mick', 84–86, 99, 131, 152, 275–278, 285

Manston airfield, 139, 142–144, 153, 155, 164, 262

Martlesham airfield, 139

Mathy, Heinrich, 54

Maxwell, Wing Commander Gerald, 63, 70, 77

May, Lieutenant W. R., 82, 83

McArthur, General, 265

McConnell, Captain Joseph, 272

McCubbin, Lieutenant, 37

McCudden, Major James, 69–72, 74–78, 85, 86, 99, 275

McKennon, Major, 237

McNair, Group Captain 'Buck', 197

Skalski, Squadron Leader S., 213

Messerschmitt, Willi, 106

Meyer, Major, 246

Middle Wallop airfield, 139, 170

Mitchell, Reginald, 102, 103

Mölders, Werner, 94, 96, 97, 122–124, 137, 148, 165, 174, 285

Montgomery, Field Marshal the Viscount, 211, 213

Morice, Group Captain Tim, 60–62, 252

Mussolini, 201

Northolt airfield, 155

North Weald airfield, 143–145, 147, 153, 158, 160

Nowotny, Walter, 255

Park, Air Chief Marshal Sir Keith, 120, 121, 132, 149, 151, 152, 156, 158–162, 165–174, 178, 200, 278

Paulus, Field Marshal von, 215

Peltz, Major General Dietrich, 257, 258

Prenzlau airfield, 237

Priller, 'Pips', 285

Quesada, Lieutenant-General 'Pete', 262

Ramsbottom-Isherwood, Wing Commander, 242

Ramsgate airfield, 142

Rawnsley, Wing Commander J., 182, 184

Reimann, 45

Reinhard, Wilhelm, 83

Rhys-Davids, Lieutenant, 70, 73, 74, 77

Richthofen, Baron Manfred von, 39–41, 45, 47–50, 55, 57–61, 63 64, 66, 68 70, 73, 76, 77, 81–83, 85, 89, 90, 94, 134, 152, 252, 274, 276, 277, 283–285

Richthofen, Field Marshal Wolfram von, 89, 91, 92, 98, 108, 243, 244

Richthofen Jagdgeschwader, 83, 88, 90

Richthofen, Lothar von, 59, 63, 64, 89, 283

Rickenbacker, Captain Eddie, 276

Ritchie, Colonel Bill, 262

Robinson, Lieutenant Leefe W., 54, 60

Rochford airfield, 153

Rommel, Field Marshal, 199, 201, 210, 211, 251

Rudel, Colonel, 242

Rundstedt, Field Marshal von, 256–258

Scharnhorst, 114

Schilling, Colonel David C., 261, 262, 268

Schmidt, General, 220–222

Schnaufer, Heinz, 223, 224

Sealand airfield, 139

Sections (German Air Service):
(13), 11
(62), 12, 18

INDEX

Skalski, Squadron Leader S., 213
Smart, Flight Sub-Lieutenant B. A., 78
Smuts, Field Marshal, 189, 274
Sperrle, Field Marshal, 138, 148
Squadrons:
 (23), 99
 (46), 114
 (60), 86
 (73), 124
 (74), 84–86
 (77, R.A.A.F.), 266
 (85), 85, 86
 (133, Eagle), 228
 (209), 82
 (242), 152
 (263), 113, 114
 (501), 253
 (601), 190, 196, 198, 199, 202
 (602, City of Glasgow), 251
 (603), 190
 (604, County of Middlesex), 182
 (615, County of Warwick), 117
Squadrons, Royal Flying Corps:
 (11), 31
 (13), 21, 30
 (25), 37
 (56), 55, 60, 64, 66, 68–71, 74, 77
 (151), 79
 (209), 78
Stainforth, Wing Commander, 102
Streib, Werner, 223

Taegu airfield, 263
Takali airfield, 193, 195, 198
Tangmere airfield, 139, 170, 175, 176
Terry, Flight Lieutenant, 204
Thorney Island airfield, 139
Tizard, Sir Henry, 103
Trenchard, Marshal of the R.A.F. the Viscount, 25–27, 30, 35, 39, 50, 54, 60, 64, 67, 68, 112, 189, 205, 222, 273, 274

Trollope, Captain J. A., 80
Tuck, Wing Commander Bob, 107, 152

Uiju airfield, 271
Upavon airfield, 21

Vandenberg, General Hoyt S., 262, 264
Voss, Werner, 73, 74

Waghorn, Flight Lieutenant, 102
Warburton, Wing Commander Adrian, 207, 208
Warmwell airfield, 145
Wasp, 190–192
Watson-Watt, Sir Robert A., 103, 104
West Malling airfield, 139
Weyland, Lieutenant-General O. P., 264–265, 268, 272
Wilson, Captain Robert, 44, 45
Wings:
 Biggin Hill, 162
 Duxford, 158, 160, 162, 165, 166, 169–172
 Kenley, 162
 North Weald, 162
 (244), 209
Woodhall, Group Captain, 159, 160, 171, 195–196
Woodley airfield, 101
Wright, Orville, 1
Wright, Wilbur, 1
Wühlisch, Lieutenant von, 12–14, 16, 17
Wykeham, Air Vice-Marshal Peter, 266–267

Yarmouth, 78

Zemke, Colonel Hub, 239, 280